Annche,
I expect to read your
speeches in future volumes!

IRISH WOMEN'S SPEECHES
VOLUME II

No pressure.
Happy Xmas
xx
Joe

GW00658651

Irish Women's Speeches Vol II

A Rich Chorus of Voices

SONJA TIERNAN

UNIVERSITY COLLEGE DUBLIN PRESS
PREAS CHOLÁISTE OLLSCOILE BHAILE ÁTHA CLIATH
2022

First published 2022
by University College Dublin Press
UCD Humanities Institute, Room H103,
Belfield,
Dublin 4

www.ucdpress.ie

ISBN 978-1-910820-84-1 pb

CIP data available from the British Library

Typeset in Dublin by Gough Typesetting Limited, Dublin
Text design by Lyn Davies
Printed in England on acid-free paper by
CPI UK, Ltd, Croydon CR0 4YY

For Barry and Mary

Contents

List of Illustrations

1. Charlotte Stoker. Courtesy of the Bram Stoker Estate Collection, www.bramstokerestate.com

2. Maud Gonne, c. 1900. Inscribed in ink below image 'To Miss Crissie Doyle, with kindest regards from ([le?]anbha) Maud Gonne, le cathughadh is le dócasughadh'. Photographer, J. E. Purdy & Co. (Boston, Mass.). Courtesy of the National Library of Ireland.

3. Maud Gonne on Red Cross duty during the Irish Civil War, 4 July 1922. Courtesy of the National Library of Ireland.

4. Alice Stopford Green, c.1885. Photography by Henry Herschel Hay Cameron (The Cameron Studio). Public domain.

5. Alice Stopford Green addressing a crowd. Tierney/MacNeill Photographs Collection, Image LA30/PH/402, UCD Digital Archives. Reproduced by kind permission of UCD Archives.

6. Women's Social and Political Union poster showing a suffragette prisoner being force-fed, 1910. Artist Alfred Pearce nom de plume 'A Patriot'. Wikimedia Commons.

7. Sarah Purser by William Osbourne, Portrait of a Lady, 1887. Wikimedia Commons.

8. Stained-glass window depicting the Passion at St. Brendan's Cathedral, Loughrea, County Galway. Design by Sarah Purser and glass painting by Alfred Ernest Child, created in An Túr Gloine. Photographer Andreas F. Borchert. Creative Commons Attribution-Share Alike license.

9. Margaret Cousins, 2 July 1932. Image from cover of National Woman's Party journal *Equal Rights*, Vol. XVIII: No. 22, Washington, D.C. Wikimedia Commons.

10. Maureen O'Carroll, c. 1956. Courtesy of Eilish O'Carroll.

11. Máirín de Burca with the sculpture by artist Jesse Jones. Courtesy of Dublin City Council Culture Company and by kind permission of photographer Julien Behal.

12. Oscar winner Brenda Fricker at the 62nd Annual Academy Awards, 26 March 1990. Photograph by Alan Light. Creative Commons Attribution 2.0 Generic license.

13. Veronica Guerin Statue, gardens of Dublin Castle. Photographer Corse-calvi. GNU Free Documentation License.

14. Nuala O'Faolain, publicity photograph for *My Dream of You* published by Riverhead Books, 19 February 2001. Photograph by Perry Odgen. Courtesy of Mairead Brady.

15. Nuala Ní Dhomhnaill, i mBéal Feirste, 3 April 2009, Contributor Ériugena. Creative Commons Attribution-Share Alike 3.0 Unported license.

16. Salome Mbugua. Photograph courtesy of Salome Mbugua.

17. Maureen O'Hara and her mother from *Modern Screen* magazine, February 1948, Dell Publishing. Wikimedia Commons.

18. Maureen O'Hara and Barry Fitzgerald, lobby card for *The Quiet Man*, 1952. Republic Pictures. Wikimedia Commons.

19. Lydia Foy and David Norris at the launch of Dublin Pride, 9 June 2010. Photograph by Neil Ward. Creative Commons Attribution 2.0 Generic license.

20. Edna O'Brien, speaking at the Hay Festival, Hay-on-Wye, 30 May 2016. Photographer Andrew Lih. Creative Commons Attribution-Share Alike 3.0 Unported license.

21. Lian Bell. Photographer, Róise Goan. Waking The Feminists collection, courtesy of the National Library of Ireland.

22. The first Waking The Feminists public meeting at the Abbey Theatre, Nov. 2015. Photographer, Fiona Morgan. Waking The Feminists collection, courtesy of the National Library of Ireland.

Acknowledgements

Researching and writing about Irish Women's Speeches has been an enjoyable and rewarding journey. I owe a debt of gratitude to the many people who enthusiastically supported volume one, after publication. Through their willingness to contribute to public talks and to provide endorsements, their support encouraged me to write this second volume. I am most grateful to Olivia O'Leary for her thoughtful and astute foreword to the first volume and for engaging in public talks and media requests about this work. Thank you also to Catriona Crowe for chairing a launch of the first volume in her usual vibrant style and for creating such an engaging and thought provoking event. Many thanks to Ivana Bacik for taking time out of her busy schedule to take part in the launch. Also to Alison Gilliland who, in her position as Lord Mayor of Dublin, attended and gave a lovely address to mark the publication.

In my quest to get further information about women included in this volume I have been in contact with a host of wonderful people. While seeking copyright permission to reproduce texts and images, I have corresponded with many inspirational women and men. I am indebted to those who granted me permission to reproduce extracts from their speeches or from the speeches of their relations. Thank you to Máirín de Burca for permission to include an extract from her speech. Also to artist Jesse Jones for supplying information regarding her sculpture in honour of de Burca and to photographer Julien Behal for kindly granting permission to reproduce the wonderful image of de Burca with the sculpture.

Brenda Fricker generously granted permission to include her speech, thank you for this and for taking the time to hear about this project. Many thanks to Jimmy Guerin, for providing permission to include his sister's, Veronica Guerin, speech. Also thank you to Alan English, editor of the *Sunday Independent*, for taking the time to arrange contact with Jimmy. My thanks to Mairead Brady for permission to include an extract from Nuala O'Faolain's speech and for taking the time to source images of her aunt. To Simon O'Connor, director of the Museum of Modern Literature (MoLI), for enabling contact with Mairead. Thank you to Nuala Ní Dhomhnaill for permission to reproduce an extract from her speech and to Noelle Moran for helping establish contact with Nuala. My thanks to Salome Mbugua for her kind permission to include her words in this volume.

Many thanks to Elga Liliana FitzSimons for granting permission to include the speech by Maureen O'Hara and to Margaret O'Shaughnessy at Foynes Flying Boat Museum for facilitating contact with Elga. My thanks to Lydia Foy for permission to include her speech and to Sara Phillips, former chair of Transgender Equality Network Ireland, for arranging contact. I am indebted to Edna O'Brien for her kind permission to include her speech and for taking the time to engage on this. Also, many thanks to Declan Heeney of Gill Hess Ltd for facilitating contact with Kate Burton at Faber, Edna O'Brien's publisher, who was so helpful throughout the process. Thank you also to Lian Bell for permission to use her speech and for sourcing images from the National Library of Ireland for inclusion. Many thanks also to Jenne Stoker for taking the time to arrange permission for the inclusion of Charlotte Stoker's photograph. This generosity by you all is much appreciated.

This book owes much to the works of other historians, academics and activists acknowledged in reference notes and especially to those who read and advised on various aspects. Thank you to Denise Charlton and to Hilkka Becker for taking the time to read a draft and advise on the area of immigration legislation in Ireland. Any errors or misinterpretations remain my own. My thanks to Diane Urquhart for her thoughtful comments on the manuscript. Thank you also to Denise Casey who helped me to source essential material, your support is always appreciated.

Publication of this book would not be possible without the dedication and hard work of others. Many thanks to Lisa Marr for proof reading and for compiling the bibliography and index. To Noelle Moran, the most supportive and efficient editor I have worked with. It has been a pleasure to work with all of the team at UCD Press including Conor Graham, Deirdre Roberts, Nigel Carré and Órla Carr.

I am forever grateful for the encouragement of friends when I am researching and writing. Without repeating those friends mentioned in the first volume I am also especially thankful to Siobhán Ní Mhaolagáin. I remain grateful for the support of my 'partner in crime' Liam McIlvanney. Also, to Val McDermid and Jo Sharp for their inspiration and friendship.

My final thanks are to my family for their endless support, and encouragement. Especially my parents, Chris and Marie. My nieces and nephews; Marc, Conor, Lorcan, Eva and Molly. Finally, as always I am ever grateful to my wife, Charlotte, for always being ready to proof read, offer insights and for just making everything worthwhile.

Foreword

It is fitting that this second volume of *Irish Women's Speeches*, focused on the arts, culture and heritage, opens with a reference to the feminist rising in 2015 in response to the Abbey Theatre's commemorative programme 'Waking the Nation'. Appalled that only one play by a woman was included in the list of ten plays, a more general sense of frustration with the continued silencing of women's creative voices was crystalised and burst onto the public sphere with the hashtag 'Waking the Feminists'. The power of women's testimonies of discrimination that poured forth on social media and on the air waves resulted in numerous creative outputs, but also in the Abbey Theatre publishing principles on equality. Other creative institutions and organisations, who had not already done so, followed suit. 'Waking the Feminists' resonated across the creative global sparking similar conversations elsewhere, reminding all of us of the power of women's voices and the endurance of gender-based discrimination even (or maybe most particularly) in the creative arena.

Sonja Tiernan was spoiled for choice with the speeches and words of women to choose from and her selection is both judicious and enriching, reflecting in many senses the creative process itself. Thus, this volume charts the history of women's creative role and impact on the arts and creative arena, from the mid-nineteenth century to the present day. What is particularly satisfying for the reader is the broad definition Tiernan lends to the creative process including the political activist, the human rights campaigner, the politician, the feminist, the historian, the journalist, the playwright and the artist.

This book both reminds us of women's role as cultural producers and as shapers of the creative sphere. It also underscores, particularly for the nineteenth century, the importance of newspapers in reprinting speeches and performances, thus massively increasing the audiences for women's words during a period when it was exceptionally difficult for them to be heard. The *Freeman's Journal's* reproduction of Alice Stopford Green's speech, for example, at the launch of her 1908 history book, meant her view of how history had been used to efface a people's identity reached many more people than attended her launch.

It is also more than appropriate that the life and work of women such as Margaret (Gretta) Cousins should be brought to a wider contemporary audience through the inclusion of her 1932 speech, from the dock in an India courtroom, in this collection. Cousins' life and work were quite extraordinary, but relatively unknown in Ireland. She was involved in many of the key movements of her time, including nationalism, suffragism, the literary revival, theosophy and vegetarianism. In 1915, she moved with her husband to India, where she became involved in reform campaigns related, in particular, to labour and gender issues. In 1932, she was arrested for addressing a meeting in response to Mahatma Gandhi's call for a civil disobedience movement and would spend one year in prison (not for the first time). Her speech on that occasion was both a careful attempt to put her work on the record *and* to assert that the only people who fear freedom of speech are those with something to hide.

Indeed, several of these speeches highlight the bravery required in speaking out, such as Maureen O'Carroll's speech in 1956, in Dáil Éireann, regarding the adoption of Irish children in America. O'Carroll, the inspiration for Agnes Brown of the acclaimed sitcom *Mrs Brown's Boys*, had an impressive political career as a Labour TD. In her 1956 speech she quite simply pointed out that the removal of Irish children from the State for adoption in America was illegal. By including her, Tiernan reminds us of the diverse ways in which women can feed into the creative process and how long some must wait for due recognition.

The speeches in this book are performances of women's influence and reach in literary, symbolic, and physical ways. From Maud Gonne's graveside oration in Co. Roscommon in 1901 to Brenda Fricker's 1990 Oscar award acceptance speech in the United States. These women were both chroniclers, reformers, campaigners and witnesses. Historian, Alice Stopford Green lamented in her 1908 study, *The Making of Ireland and Its Undoing, 1200–1600*, that 'the history of the Irish people has been left unrecorded', it is, therefore, important that her words are among the many in this volume which ensure that women's history does not suffer the same fate. As Eavan Boland's 1994 poem 'Anna Liffey', in which she reimagined James Joyce's river-woman and mother, ALP, as a woman and poet, reminds us: 'In the end/ Everything that burdened and distinguished me/ Will be lost in this: I was a voice.'[1]

Lindsey Earner-Byrne
Professor of Irish Gender History, UCC
November 2022

Introduction

A feminist rising took place on the stage of the national theatre of Ireland on 12 November 2015. Led by Lian Bell, women and men took the stage of the Abbey Theatre to deliver speeches. In their many addresses, people demanded gender equality in the performing arts and for the work of female artists to be championed. Since it was established in 1904, the Abbey has been a site of many protests and riots. Historically, developments in Irish arts and culture have often aligned with contemporary political and social movements. Many creative practitioners in Ireland continue to be outspoken commentators and vibrant speech makers.

Irish Women's Speeches Volume 2: A Rich Chorus of Voices showcases 17 speeches broadly related to arts, culture and heritage. The speeches that follow are a compilation of Irish women's voices, including those of authors, journalists, actors, artists and women who have influenced arts and culture more generally. The speeches are ordered chronologically. The earliest speech was given in 1863 by Charlotte Stoker, whose writings inspired her son Bram to write the celebrated gothic novel *Dracula*. The most recent speech is by Lian Bell at the launch of the Waking The Feminists archive in the National Library of Ireland in 2021. The deposit of these papers in the national library signifies the importance of this grassroots movement that brought about substantial change for gender equality and economic parity in the Irish theatre industry and beyond.

The time period from 1863 to 2021 covers a century and a half, during which the social, political and cultural standing of women in Ireland changed radically; this is particularly evident from their speeches. Women were often confined to the margins of cultural production in the nineteenth century. Such was the case with Charlotte Stoker: although her writing had a major influence on her son's work, her speeches were not directly related to creative practices. Stoker campaigned to improve social conditions in Ireland. Her speech relates to the lack of state provision of education for people with disabilities in Ireland.

In the last quarter of the nineteenth century, there was a resurgence of Irish culture that thrived into the 1920s. The Irish cultural revival promoted

Irish language and sports and re-told Irish legends through literature, theatre and music. Organisations were founded that supported the revival, including the Gaelic Athletic Association (GAA), established in 1884; the Gaelic League, founded in 1893; and the Irish National Theatre Society, established in 1903. Some organisations, such as the Celtic Literary Society, established in 1893, initially refused to admit female members, so women established their own societies. In 1900, Maud Gonne established Inghinidhe na hÉireann (Daughters of Ireland), and one of Inghinidhe's main objectives was 'to encourage the study of Gaelic, of Irish literature, History, Music and Art'.[1] The cultural revival had a deep connection with the Irish nationalist movement, through which the re-establishment of a national consciousness drove the fight for independence from Britain. The erasure of Irish language and culture was seen as a consequence of colonisation and British rule. This connection is clear in Gonne's speech given in 1901 at the unveiling of a memorial to John Lavin, who had been a leader of the Irish Republican Brotherhood in Roscommon.

Throughout this volume we can chart the progression of women and their involvement in arts and culture in twentieth-century Ireland. Gonne played a key role in the Irish cultural revival, and the year after her speech at Roscommon, she played the lead role in *Kathleen Ni Houlihan*, written by W. B. Yeats and Lady Augusta Gregory. Gonne helped establish the Irish National Theatre Society. Historian Alice Stopford Green was the first person to effectively challenge what she described as the 'Englishman's history' by rewriting the history of Ireland. In her speech, she described her objectives for writing *The Making of Ireland and Its Undoing*, which was published in 1908. This book was the first in a series of three by Stopford Green that underpinned a re-imagined national consciousness that supported Irish cultural revival.

The artist Sarah Purser's speech focuses on the establishment and progress of An Túr Gloine (The Tower of Glass). The Dublin-based stained-glass studio and workshop produced unique Irish stained-glass windows, which now adorn notable buildings across Ireland, including the Abbey Theatre, and can be found at many sites across the globe. Her speech in 1928 shows how the prominence of women as cultural producers in Ireland rose considerably through the twentieth century.

The subtitle for this volume is taken from Nuala O'Faolain's introduction to her ground-breaking memoir, *Are You Somebody?* First published in 1996, O'Faolain's book caused a sensation in Ireland due to the forthright account of her life. Her memoir includes a heartfelt description of her difficult childhood and she writes openly about exploring her sexuality. O'Faolain was born in 1940, and she was raised during a time when women's sexuality was contained and shamed, often through church-controlled institutions aided by the Irish state. The last Magdalene Laundry in Ireland only closed in 1996, the same year that O'Faolain's memoir was published.[2] Mother and Baby Homes continued to operate in Ireland until 1998.[3] In a revised edition of *Are You Somebody?* O'Faolain describes how she feared that her book would receive a hostile reception. However, her publication was timely. During the 1990s, numerous religious abuse scandals were exposed, and many Irish people began to question the control established by the Catholic Church. *Are You Somebody?* received remarkably positive responses from readers and reviewers alike and became a global bestseller. O'Faolain recounted how her 'small voice was answered by a rich chorus of voices!'[4] O'Faolain's speech in this volume was given at the launch of *Are You Somebody* in America.

Other speeches in this volume focus directly on the creative practice of Irish women in the twentieth century. Speeches by actors Brenda Fricker and Maureen O'Hara relate to their awards from the film industry. In 2022, Fricker remains the only Irish woman to have received an Oscar for acting. O'Hara received, among other high honours, a Lifetime Achievement award from the Irish Film and Television Academy. These speeches reveal the range of Irish women's involvement in arts and culture.

The speeches in this volume also include talks given by women who influenced arts and culture. Often in these cases, their speeches are not directly related to a creative practice. Such is the case with Maureen O'Carroll, the first female Irish Labour TD, who had a surprising influence on Irish popular culture and entertainment: the character Agnes Brown in *Mrs Brown's Boys* is based on Maureen. O'Carroll's speech, delivered in 1956 on the floor of Dáil Éireann, challenged the culture of silence surrounding the adoption of Irish children in America.

The speeches in this volume were given to a range of audiences and from widely different platforms, ranging from a public address in a graveyard to an acceptance speech at the Oscars. Six of the speeches were delivered outside the island of Ireland. Amongst the speeches delivered abroad, Margaret (Gretta) Cousins gave a speech from the dock in a courtroom in India before she was sentenced to prison. Cousins, a poet, a musician and a champion of the Irish literary revival, was a vibrant social reform activist and a supporter of Gandhi's philosophy of non-cooperation with the British authorities. Journalist Veronica Guerin spoke at a venue in New York upon receiving the International Press Freedom award just months before her brutal murder. These two speeches provide an insight into the fate of women who challenged the authorities.

Not only were many of the speeches given abroad, but a number of the Irish women in this volume lived outside of the island of Ireland. In some cases women emigrated to further their careers; Maureen O'Hara is an example of this. O'Hara went to America in 1939 to film *The Hunchback of Notre Dame*. She stayed in America, barring a period from 2005 to 2012 when she lived in Glengarriff, county Cork. It is fair to assert that O'Hara would not have become the most successful Irish woman in the Hollywood film industry if she had remained in Ireland. As an emigrant, O'Hara was extremely proud of her Irish identity throughout her life; this is particularly evident in her speech upon receipt of the award from the Irish Film and Television Academy.

Unlike O'Hara, Edna O'Brien did not move abroad to further her career. However, her move to London in 1958 kickstarted her long and successful literary career. Experiencing a sense of alienation while living abroad, O'Brien began to write a novel centred on two young women in Ireland. It became the first book in the trilogy *The Country Girls*. Her novels shocked Irish society because she wrote frankly about women's sexuality; her trilogy was initially banned in Ireland. O'Brien remains living in England, though most of her literary endeavours have an Irish theme and she returns to Ireland regularly. Undoubtedly, O'Brien's path to literary success would have been made considerably more difficult had she stayed in Ireland in those early years. O'Brien's speech is her response to *The Country Girls* being chosen as the Dublin One City One Book in 2019. The organisers of this prestigious award aptly declared O'Brien's trilogy 'a twentieth-century literary masterpiece'.

Records of speeches related to arts and culture are not easy to discover. Many of the orators featured in this volume are artists, actors and writers who transmit their opinions through their art rather than through speeches. Such is the case with Sarah Purser. As well as producing noteworthy paintings and sketches, Purser had significant influence in the promotion, production and dissemination of Irish art. She established the Friends of the National Collections of Ireland, which continues to preserve Ireland's artistic heritage and donate works of art to national museums, art galleries and libraries across the island of Ireland. She was a force behind the establishment of the Dublin Municipal Gallery of Modern Art, now known as the Hugh Lane Gallery. Purser also established An Túr Gloine. She dedicated her time to the pursuit of artistic endeavours and was not given to publicly speaking. However, after discovering that she gave a speech on the twenty-fifth anniversary of An Túr Gloine, a copy of Purser's speech was secured after a trawl through archival sources.

In some situations, it was possible to track speeches through radical journals that printed significant speeches in their entirety. Such is the case with Norah Dacre Fox, a journalist and writer from Dublin. Dacre Fox became a key member of the militant suffragette organisation the Women's Social and Political Union in England and played a significant role writing and editing their newspaper, *The Suffragette*. She was imprisoned on a number of occasions for her activities and went on hunger strike while imprisoned in Holloway. After her release from prison in July 1914, Norah addressed a large audience at Knightsbridge Hall in London, describing her time in prison. The speech was later reproduced in *The Suffragette*, and her words are included in this volume.

Copyright permission for reproducing an extract of a given speech remains complex. While some of the speeches are now out of copyright or are available through re-use of public sector information, relevant individuals and organisations were contacted to secure permission in other instances. It was not always possible to make contact with relatives of speakers who are now deceased. In other cases, organisations have no system in place to grant copyright permission. It was particularly disappointing that speeches by some women could not be included for these reasons.

Most of the women in this volume are artists, actors and authors; however, in other cases, speeches have been included that are more broadly related to culture. In recent years Ireland has benefited from becoming a multi-cultural country, yet this led to a resistance to or misunderstanding of certain cultures in Ireland. In Leinster House in 2003, Salome Mbugua addressed the Joint Committee on Justice, Equality, Defence and Women's Rights. Her speech is a pertinent reminder of how negative cultural stereotyping feeds into dangerous racist beliefs and stagnates cultural growth in Ireland. Similarly, Lydia Foy's speech detailing her campaign to gain basic human rights is a timely reminder of how transgender rights have become a bitterly contested issue in the culture wars, to the personal detriment of many individuals.

The speeches that follow have not been altered from their originals, although many have been reduced because the original speeches are lengthy. Such is the case with Irish language author Nuala Ní Dhomhnaill, whose speech at Queen's University Belfast on the Irish literary landscape was extensive and detailed. Similarly, author Nuala O'Faolain, who was known for her exuberant and engaging discussion, spoke for over half an hour at a book event in New York. It was not practical to include such lengthy speeches in their entirety, but references are included for the original sources. Many of the speeches can be read in full at these sources, and some may be viewed online, where possible this is cited in related sections.

Irish Women's Speeches: Voices That Rocked the System presented 33 speeches by Irish women, spanning 140 years. Those speeches were delivered to a range of audiences on a myriad of topics; although mainly political in focus, they addressed themes such as suffrage and labour rights, Irish independence and the partition of the country. The two volumes of *Irish Women's Speeches* combined now highlight 50 inspiring speeches from the nineteenth century to the present time. While these speeches are significant and can be read on their own, each speech is preceded by a detailed introduction that illuminates the context in which the speech was made and provides background on each orator. *Irish Women's Speeches Volume 2* showcases Irish women who, in Nuala O'Faolain's words, provide 'a rich chorus of voices' and continue to shape contemporary Irish arts and heritage as well as impacting on culture more broadly.

ONE

Charlotte Stoker

1818–1901

Speech on state provision of education for people with
disabilities
Statistical and Social Inquiry Society,
35 Molesworth Street, Dublin

13 MAY 1863

'To meet the educational wants of this mass of human misery.'

Charlotte Stoker lived an exceptional life. Her writings, her storytelling
and her speeches have left an indelible mark on Irish culture, yet her name
is not widely known. She is credited with being the influence behind the
celebrated gothic novel *Dracula*, although the depth of her influence is
disputed by some literary scholars. Published in 1897, *Dracula* became
the most popular novel based on vampire legends and that publication
influenced a genre of literature and film which still prevails.

Charlotte Matilda Blake Thornley was born into a financially secure,
though not wealthy, Protestant family on 23 June 1818. The Thornley
family lived near Old Market Street in Sligo town. Charlotte experienced
severe trauma and was surrounded by death from an early age. Before
she reached her fourth birthday, a famine swept across nine counties in
Ireland, including Sligo, and many people in the area died of hunger or
of typhus. Ten years later, when Charlotte was just 14 years old, a cholera
epidemic struck Sligo town.

Cholera morbus first broke out in India in 1826 and spread slowly but
steadily across Europe over the following six years, reaching Ireland in May
1832. On 11 August 1832, Sligo town held a market day that attracted

people from neighbouring counties. The influx of people into the town also brought cholera. The *Leitrim Observer* newspaper reported that 'the fever raged throughout the month of August and during that time at least 1,500 people and possibly more perished.'[1] After witnessing many of their neighbours die horribly, the Thornley family fled Sligo and sought refuge with relatives in Ballyshannon in county Donegal until the fever had passed. Thousands of people fled Sligo at this time. Prior to the epidemic the town had an estimated population of 15,000 people. Historian Fióna Gallagher has shown that 'Only an estimated 4,000 people remained, with the rest escaping into the adjacent countryside, camping under hedges and in ditches, where makeshift shelters dotted the landscape.'[2]

1. Charlotte Stoker. Courtesy of the Bram Stoker Estate Collection.

In 1844, Charlotte married Abraham Coates Stoker from Coleraine, a senior civil servant in Dublin Castle, then the seat of British administration in Ireland. Within months of their marriage, the subsistence crisis became the great famine which swept across much of Ireland with devastating consequences. Charlotte and Abraham had seven children: their third child, named after his father, Bram, is now recognised as a significant literary figure. The Stokers initially lived at 15 Marino Crescent in Clontarf on the northside of Dublin. Bram was a sickly child and was bedridden for most of his early years; during this time, he became particularly close to his mother, who recounted to him dark stories from her childhood in Sligo.

Charlotte's children excelled in education and became highly successful in their later lives. As well as Bram, Charlotte had four other sons: Thornley, a surgeon who became president of the Royal College of Surgeons Ireland and was knighted by Queen Victoria in 1895; Thomas, who became a chief secretary in the Indian civil service; Richard and George, who both became army surgeons. Charlotte's two daughters, Matilda and Margaret, later moved with their parents to continental Europe where they finished their education. Records from Charlotte's children portray their mother 'as the family's driving force and suggest a sense of awe at her energy, intellect, and will'.[3]

In 1858, Charlotte and her husband moved to 17 Upper Buckingham Street in the Mountjoy area of Dublin city, and Charlotte became directly involved in social and political matters. The late 1850s and early 1860s witnessed some reforms for women in terms of greater access to education and employment. The National Association for the Promotion of Social Science was founded by Lord Brougham in 1857 'to coordinate the efforts of the experts and the politicians' to bring about reform in areas such as public health, female education and employment.[4] In 1861, the association held its Social Science Congress in Dublin which attracted a host of prominent speakers; Abraham and Charlotte attended. Among the many esteemed speakers, the feminist reformer Frances Power Cobbe addressed the topic of protecting girls and young women in cities.[5]

The following year, another society opened its ranks to women and Charlotte Stoker became instantly committed. Historian Mary E. Daly describes how the Statistical Society broke its links with the Royal Dublin Society (RDS), two voluntary organisations tasked with improving social and economic conditions in Ireland. The Statistical Society 'changed its name to the Statistical and Social Inquiry Society of Ireland (SSISI), and drafted a new constitution. One of the clauses in this constitution provided that ladies should be admitted as associate members.'[6] Abraham became a member and Charlotte became an associate member. In May 1863, Charlotte gave the first address by any female associate member to the society; it is detailed in this section. Her speech powerfully advocated the establishment of state-run education for people unable to speak or hear.

Stoker's speech displays the impressive research that she engaged in as an advocate for the disenfranchised. She made full use of the most recent census, taken in 1851. In the wake of the great famine, that census enumerated for the first time the status of disease and, 'in addition to treating of the number of people suffering from sickness, dealt with the deaf and dumb, the blind, the lunatic and idiotic, and the lame and decrepit'.[7] These were terms of categorisation deemed appropriate in the mid-nineteenth century although now outdated and offensive. Stoker confirmed through census records that there were at least 3,000 people categorised as 'deaf and dumb' who were of age and circumstance to require education, yet only 400 of these people were attending educational facilities.

In her speech, Stoker is scathing of the government's lack of concern for people who could not hear or speak, highlighting the lack of any state-run schools to educate and train these children and young people. During the nineteenth century, only small organisations that operated in a voluntary capacity educated children with these needs. The Claremont Institute for the Deaf and Dumb in Glasnevin was established by Dr Charles Orpen in 1816. It would take thirty years before a second facility would open. 'In 1846', writes historian Fiona Fitzsimons, 'the Catholic Institution for the Deaf and Dumb opened St Mary's, a residential school for girls in Cabra, Dublin, which was managed by Dominican nuns.'[8] According to Fitzsimons, this action was taken by the Catholic order because Orpen's institute was 'under the patronage of the Church of Ireland', which caused the hierarchy of the Catholic church in Ireland concern. The following year a residential school for deaf boys, St Joseph's, opened in Cabra; it was managed by the Christian Brothers.

Stoker's speech highlights the fact that while the state funded education and training for criminals, there was no provision for children who could not hear or speak. Her speech was supported in the highest quarters: immediately following her address, a discussion was led by William Wilde, then the census commissioner for Ireland. Wilde was an esteemed surgeon and had been appointed 'surgeon oculist in ordinary to the queen in Ireland in 1853'.[9] Wilde was impressed with Stoker's use of the census figures to animate her argument. He noted that 'the subject was one of such importance that it had engaged the attention of himself and his colleagues in the Census Commission of 1851, when they brought the subject of educating deaf mutes prominently under the notice of the executive.'[10] Wilde further praised Stoker for her contribution, stressing that 'The importance of the subject brought under the notice of the Society should be admitted by all.'[11] Following this talk, Stoker formed a friendship with William Wilde and his wife, Jane. Jane was a poet and a prolific feminist who wrote under the pen name Speranza, and she built an impressive literary circle in Dublin. No doubt this literary circle greatly influenced their son, Oscar Wilde, who became a significant author in his own right. The Wilde family later provided valuable support to Bram Stoker during his years at Trinity College Dublin and in his early literary endeavours.

Charlotte wrote another powerful speech for the SSISI the following year on 'Female emigration from workhouses'; her paper was read by the secretary, Mr Gibson.[12] Stoker was a workhouse visitor, and through her experiences visiting inmates she concluded that the only way to truly help these women was through a system of government-assisted emigration. She focussed once again on education as a central concern. Stoker maintained that because workhouses did not provide any educational route for inmates they could not become self-supporting. Stoker questioned 'why should the door of hope be closed on those poor women, and why refuse them the means of attaining that independence in other countries which they are debarred from in this?'[13] However, as literary theorist Michael Wainwright observes, 'Charlotte's selective relocation according to gender did not attract political attention. Hence despite her prominence at the SSISI, Charlotte had to print her thesis . . . privately.'[14] She published her paper as a pamphlet through the esteemed Dublin printer Alexander Thom, who would later be appointed as the Queen's Printer for Ireland. According to Harry Ludlam, a biographer of Bram Stoker, Charlotte 'was so many years ahead of her time that she shocked her own sex as much as she surprised male society'.[15] Stoker continued researching and writing papers for the society and in 1867 delivered a speech on 'Widows and children of civil officers'.[16]

Charlotte's husband, Abraham, retired in 1865, and when his health deteriorated the couple moved to the continent in 1872. While Charlotte was living in Caen, northern France, Bram asked her to record her memories of the cholera epidemic in Sligo. The resulting account, 'Experience of the cholera in Ireland 1832', written on 5 June 1873 is thought to have heavily influenced her son's most famous novel, *Dracula*.[17] From the opening section of Charlotte's account, it is clear to see why many scholars credit this writing with influencing her son's gothic horror fiction. Charlotte begins:

> In the days of my early youth so long ago that I forgot the date, our world was shaken with the dread of the new and terrible plague which was desolating all lands as it passed through them. And so regular was its march that men could tell where next it would appear and almost the day when it might be expected. It was the *Cholera*, which for the first time appeared in Western Europe. And its utter strangeness and man's want of experience or knowledge of its nature, or how best to resist its attack, added if anything could to its horror.[18]

This deadly and mysterious plague echoes in the early chapters of *Dracula*. Charlotte's account continues with her description of the horror that crept across Sligo town, including reports of people being buried alive. When one traveller was taken ill with cholera symptoms on the roadside outside the town, a group of people 'dug a pit and with long poles pushed him living into it and covered him up *alive*'.[19] Others who were buried alive, such as a Sergeant Cullen, rose out of their coffins, resembling Bram Stoker's undead. Charlotte describes Sligo as a 'City of the Dead'; she could 'see a heavy sulphurous looking cloud hang low over the town, and we heard that the birds were found dead on the shores of Lough Gill'.[20]

Leading Bram Stoker scholars, including Barbara Belford and Peter Treymane, agree that Charlotte's stories and writings influenced her son in the writing of *Dracula*.[21] Charlotte's account was republished in *The Green Book: Writings on Irish Gothic, Supernatural and Fantastic Literature* in 2017. The editor of the journal, Brian J. Showers, is 'dubious' about the influence of Charlotte's account on Bram's writing. However, Showers notes that 'Charlotte's eloquent text stands entirely on its own, and serves as a reminder that the roots of Irish literary horror were often nourished by real blood.'[22]

Abraham died in Italy in 1876, and a few years later Charlotte returned to live in Dublin where she continued her interest in social reform. She died on 15 March 1901 at the age of 82 in her home at 72 Rathgar Road on the southside of Dublin.[23] She is buried in Mount Jerome Cemetery in Harold's Cross, Dublin.[24] Her headstone carries an inscription in her memory and to that of her husband who is buried in Cava de Tirrini in Italy. Her son William and his wife, Emily, were later buried in the same plot as Charlotte.

No significant obituaries were published in honour of Charlotte Stoker: a simple death notice appeared in the *Evening Herald* and in the *Irish Independent*.[25] It was only in later years that Stoker and her writings gained public recognition but mainly in relation to her famous literary son. Many people in Sligo remain particularly proud of Charlotte's legacy. Sligo Walking Tours offers a Sligo Dracula tour, which 'focuses on Sligo's connections to the gothic author Bram Stoker and the Cholera Epidemic, that devastated the town in 1832'.[26] In 1973, the *Sligo Champion* reproduced Charlotte's recollection of the cholera epidemic under the title 'Dracula and the cholera plague in Sligo', recounting how:

> Throughout the English speaking world and far beyond there are few people who have not read or seen on screen or stage the story of Dracula.
> Strangely enough the opening scenes of this classic horror-thriller, it is said, were inspired by the dreadful epidemic which hit Sligo in the year 1832. If one were told that Charlotte Stoker, the mother of Bram Stoker, author of DRACULA, was born in Sligo and lived here throughout this epidemic, then one can reasonably accept the theory. This is strengthened by the account she wrote for her son in later years.[27]

The Stoker family papers, including writings by Charlotte, are held at

Trinity College Dublin.[28] The proceedings of the Statistical and Social Inquiry Society of Ireland are recorded in its annual journal, which is available online from Trinity's Access to Research Archive (TARA), including Charlotte Stoker's speeches and discussions arising from her research.[29] Charlotte is honoured on a blue plaque mounted on a building on Old Market Street in Sligo where the Thornley family lived. The plaque is inscribed: 'Charlotte Matilda Blake Thornley 1818–1901 mother of author Bram Stoker lived on this street. Her experiences in 1832 of the Great Cholera Epidemic in Sligo provided the inspiration for Stoker's great Gothic novel "Dracula".'

'The condition of the uneducated mute is worse than that of the heathen; the most barbarous and savage nations have some notion (however faint) of a Supreme Being, but a deaf mute has no idea of a God. The mind is a perfect blank; he recognises no will but his own natural impulses; he is alone in the midst of his fellow-men; an outcast from society and its pleasures; a man in outward appearance, in reality reduced to the level of the brute creation.

That the capacity for receiving education exists in most cases cannot for a moment be questioned, from the numerous instances in the present day of highly educated and even accomplished mutes. Seven years is the period thought necessary by experienced teachers to complete the education of a deaf and dumb person; and mutes are found to be most easily instructed between the ages of eight and eighteen; but within the last year an experiment has been made at Claremont of establishing an infant school, which is found to answer well.

The average of those born deaf and dumb to the entire population of Ireland is about 1 to 1,380, which is very nearly the average all over Europe.

According to the census of 1851, there were in Ireland 5,180 deaf and dumb; of these, 3,000 were of an age and capacity to receive instruction, the remaining 2,180 were either too old or too young to be educated, or were idiots as well as mutes.

To meet the educational wants of this mass of human misery and ignorance we have a few private institutions, supported wholly by individual charity, in which about 400 are educated, leaving the remaining 2,600 to utter ignorance.

True, in the amended Irish Poor Law Act, in the year 1843, . . . Poor Law Guardians are empowered to pay out of the poor rates for the education and maintenance of deaf and dumb children under eighteen years old, at any institution where such instruction is given. But it is to be observed, that among the poor, who are so utterly destitute as to become inmates of the workhouse, there are comparatively few deaf and dumb; only 82 are at present provided for under this Act. . . .

It is among the mass of the people such as those for whom national education is provided, who, although not belonging to the class of paupers, are nevertheless unable to pay the sum necessary (or indeed, in most instances, any sum at all), that a state provision for the education of the deaf and dumb is required.

It is a startling fact, that while state provision is made in France, in Prussia, in America, and other countries, nothing of the sort has been done in Great Britain. . . .

In New York, where the population is more than three times as great as in Dublin, and the number of mutes less—as in 1856 they had only 125, while in Dublin there were 163—there is not only a State institution for deaf and dumb, but a *church* in which the sign language is used, and they were then about establishing a reading-room and library for the benefit of this class. Seeing that America and other countries have provided so amply and liberally for the education of their deaf and dumb, should we be so far behind in such a cause? . . .

This subject is one of such national importance as would seem to call for the interference of the representatives of the people, who, by a zealous and united appeal to the Legislature, could scarcely fail to obtain a grant to meet so imperative a necessity as a National Institution for the Education of the Deaf and Dumb.

While ample provision is made for lunatic asylums and reformatories; while criminals are taught and provided for at a vast expense, and in the most careful and efficient manner; surely, if brought properly under their notice, the Government of this country could not refuse so reasonable a demand as the maintenance of an institution for instructing in morality and religion, as well as for fitting for some useful occupation, those who would otherwise remain burdens on themselves and on society. Let us hope that the time is not far distant, when, for the instruction of Ireland's 3,000 mutes, proper means will be adopted to bridge the gulf that divides them from their fellow-men.'[30]

Two

Maud Gonne

1866–1953

Speech at the unveiling of the John Lavin memorial
St Joseph's Cemetery, Castlerea, Roscommon

8 September 1901

'Never rest until we have a free and independent Nation.'

Maud Gonne is often recalled in relation to the men in her life: as mistress
to French journalist and politician Lucien Millevoye; as muse to Irish
author W. B. Yeats; as wife to nationalist leader John MacBride; and as
mother to Irish politician and Nobel Peace Prize winner Seán MacBride.
Undoubtedly, Gonne was surrounded by prominent male characters, and
this has, to some degree, placed her in their shadows. However, Gonne
was a forceful and capable woman who garnered much public recognition
during her lifetime for her own accomplishments including for her writing,
her contribution to Irish cultural movements and as a central force in the
Irish Literary Revival.

Gonne was born on 21 December 1866 at Tongham Manor, near
Farnham, Surrey, in England. She was born into a wealthy family but had
a troubled childhood. During the 1860s, the fenian movement, seeking
independence for Ireland, spread across the Irish emigrant population and
nationalist leaders exiled abroad. A fenian rebellion in March 1867 led
to what is now termed a fenian panic in Britain and across its colonies.
In response, British military operations intensified in Ireland in order to
control Irish nationalist activities. In April 1868, Maud's father, Thomas
Gonne, a captain of the 17th Lancers, was appointed brigade major of the
cavalry in Ireland and stationed at the Curragh military camp in county

Kildare. Maud and her parents moved to Ireland and her younger sister, Kathleen, was born later that year.

When Maud was just four years of age, her mother, Edith Frith Cook, died of tuberculosis shortly after giving birth to another daughter; baby Margaretta died months later. As historians Margaret O'Callaghan and Caoimhe Nic Dháibhéid note, 'Tuberculosis was to shadow Maud and her sister Kathleen for most of their lives.'[1] The Gonne sisters lived with their father and a nurse initially at the Curragh but later moved to Howth in north county Dublin. When Maud reached six years of age, her father sent her and her sister to live with their maternal aunt, Augusta Tarlton, in London and later with Augusta's brother, Francis Cook, at Doughty House in Richmond Park.[2] Gonne describes how they hated spending time in London 'after our free Irish life where we were allowed to play with the children of the many mud cabins which existed then everywhere'.[3] The family later lived for a time in France but Maud had an affinity with Ireland. She claimed that the Gonne family was from county Mayo and that her great-grandfather moved abroad after he was disinherited.[4]

During Gonne's early years in Ireland, the land war (1879-1882) was intense. This was a time of economic depression in Ireland and only three percent of Irish farmers owned their land. Tenant farmers unable to pay their rents faced eviction, destitution, and possible starvation.[5] The National Land League and the Ladies Land League campaigned aggressively for rent reductions and tenant protection. Gonne became particularly affected by evictions, sympathising with the plight of Irish independence. She claimed that her father also sympathised with Irish nationalism, and during a conversation in 1886 he told her that 'the Land War had made him realise that as an Irishman he felt he must resign from the English Army and that he intended standing as a Home Rule candidate at the next elections'.[6] He died of typhoid fever in November 1886 and could not pursue this path.

Maud and her 18-year-old sister were left in the guardianship of their paternal uncle, William Gonne, in London. It was during this time that Maud decided to become an actor, but her attempts were soon thwarted when she contracted tuberculosis, this illness had repercussions for her health throughout her life. Her great-aunt Mary took Maud to Royat in the Auvergne to recuperate, while there Maud met Lucien Millevoye and they began a long-term relationship. The couple agreed to dedicate themselves to overthrowing their common enemy, Britain.

When Gonne reached 21 years of age in 1887, she inherited trust funds left from her mother's estate, making her financially independent. She returned to Dublin in 1888 where she stayed initially with the whiskey distilling family the Jamesons at Airfield House in Donnybrook. Ida Jameson introduced Gonne to Charles Hubert Oldham, through him she met the fenian leader John O'Leary. Following his prison sentence and enforced exile for a sentence of treason, O'Leary had returned to Ireland where he and his sister, the poet Ellen O'Leary, became central figures in Irish cultural and nationalist movements.

Gonne later took an apartment over Morrow's bookshop on the corner of South Frederick Street and Nassau Street where she entertained her new circle of literary and nationalist friends. In January 1889, Maud first met W. B. Yeats in London. Yeats' letters at this time express how he was instantly enamoured with her. He 'loved her with an unrequited passion thereafter'.[7] Yeats would later write that this encounter was when 'the troubling of my life began'.[8] Much of Yeats' literary work is inspired by his passion for Gonne, and many of his poems are written explicitly about her.

Gonne gave birth to a son, Georges Sylvère, in January 1890 in Paris, the son of Millevoye. Georges died from meningitis on 31 August 1891. Gonne gave birth to a daughter, Iseult, in Paris on 6 August 1894, also fathered by Millevoye. That year Gonne's sexual relationship with Millevoye ended, although they remained political conspirators. By this time the Gaelic League (Conradh na Gaeilge), formed in 1893, was actively encouraging the speaking of Irish, and the promotion of modern literature in the Irish language. The cultural movement was linked with political nationalism which also drove the Irish Literary Revival. Gonne became firmly immersed in encouraging Irish cultural revival and proved herself to be a motivating and inspirational orator on the cause of Irish independence.

In May 1897, she launched a radical pro-independence journal, *L'Irlande Libre*, the organ of the Irish colony in Paris, disseminating ideas of Irish nationalism to continental Europe. She built up a remarkable circle including James Connolly, who wrote an article for the journal on 'Socialism and Irish nationalism' later that year.[9] In her study of women and journalism during the Irish revival, Karen Steele describes Gonne's 'two favourite modes as a journalist, [as] lyrical allegory and fact-finding reportage' a style which Steele attests was 'also evident in her speech-making style, where she routinely juxtaposed lantern slides that documented evictions . . . with heated rebukes against the injustice of evictions'.[10]

In 1897, Gonne embarked on a fundraising tour of America, raising money to establish a memorial to Wolfe Tone for the centenary celebrations of the 1798 United Irish rebellion. Gonne was a central member of the 1798 committee. As historian Senia Pašeta aptly observes, the commemoration of the centenary of 1798 'presented a remarkable propaganda opportunity to Irish nationalists of every hue, and . . . attracted both established nationalists whose political careers were in dire need of resuscitation, and young, advanced nationalists eager to make their mark on the Irish political scene'.[11] Gonne was assuredly in the ranks of the advanced new nationalists who retaliated against the constitutional campaign for achieving Irish independence. The committee organised a series of centenary events, including the erection of a plaque at Wolfe Tone's birthplace, 44 Stafford Street in Dublin city, now Wolfe Tone Street, and the laying of a foundation stone for the Wolfe Tone Memorial at St Stephen's Green. However, not enough money was raised to erect the planned statue. The original foundation stone is now housed at the Croppies' Acre Memorial Park on Wolfe Tone Quay in Dublin, thought to be a mass grave site of 1798 rebels.[12]

2. Maud Gonne, c. 1900. Courtesy of the National Library of Ireland.

Along with newspaper editor and later founder of Sinn Féin, Arthur Griffith, Gonne established the Transvaal committee in October 1899 that supported the Boer republics in their war against Britain (1899–1902). The two promoted the Irish brigade, led by John MacBride, which fought alongside the Boers to help overthrow the British. In January 1900, Gonne set sail for America on another fundraising tour, this time seeking money to support Griffith's paper the *United Irishman*. Griffith had established the nationalist paper along with William Rooney in the wake of the centenary fever of 1898. Steele describes how 'one of the remarkable features of the *United Irishman* was the extent to which women's writings and women's concerns were featured in its pages.'[13] Gonne played a role in its publication by contributing financially and writing articles for the paper. Many significant female activists wrote articles for it, including Constance Markievicz, Kathleen Clarke, Alice Milligan, Hanna Sheehy Skeffington and Delia Larkin.

Gonne's most famous articles 'Famine Queen' and 'Her subjects' launched scathing attacks on Queen Victoria. Steele describes how these articles suggest 'the extent to which Gonne's speech-making successes were due to her rhetorical skills rather than her statuesque beauty'.[14] During the royal visit of Queen Victoria, Gonne wrote:

> For Victoria, in the decrepitude of her eighty-one years, to have decided after an absence of half-a-century to revisit the country she hates and whose inhabitants are the victims of the criminal policy of her reign, the survivors of sixty years of organised famine, the political necessity must have been terribly strong; for after all she is a woman, and however vile and selfish and pitiless her soul may be, she must sometimes tremble as death approaches when she thinks of the countless Irish mothers who, shelterless under the cloudy Irish sky, watching their starving little ones, have cursed her before they died.[15]

Victoria arrived into Dun Laoghaire port, then Kingstown, on 4 April 1900 and stayed in Dublin until 26 April. Gonne had staged a protest the day before Victoria disembarked. Once copies of the *United Irishman* began to circulate, the Dublin Metropolitan Police were quick to seize and destroy remaining copies. Undeterred, Gonne responded with her article 'Her subjects', focusing on the subjects whom Victoria reigned over, 'more starving millions of human creatures than any other queen in history' has ever ruled.[16]

Without doubt, Gonne's most notable contribution to the Irish nationalist movement was the establishment of Inghinidhe na hÉireann (Daughters of Ireland). In 1900, Gonne established this organisation exclusively for women with a focus on politics, socialism, feminism and cultural revival. This was the first female-centred organisation in Ireland since the Ladies' Land League, established by Anna and Fanny Parnell, was forced to disband in 1882. Hanna Sheehy Skeffington credited Gonne with forming Inghinidhe because she 'found that all the male groups, even the cultural ones, of the early Irish Renaissance movement were automatically closed to women'.[17] Indeed, Gonne had been refused entry to many organisations, including the Celtic Literary Society, purely because of her sex. Later the Celtic Literary Society lent Inghinidhe na hÉireann their rooms for meetings and events until they found their own premises. The inaugural meeting of Inghinidhe na hÉireann took place in October 1900. Gonne was elected president along with vice presidents Jenny Wyse Power, Annie Egan, Anna Johnston and Alice Furlong. Dora Hackett, Elizabeth Morgan and Maire Quinn took roles as secretaries. The women adopted St Brigid, a national saint of Ireland, as their patron saint.

Inghinidhe na hÉireann laid out clear goals for their organisation. Historian Margaret Ward fittingly notes, 'unlike many other groups, the women were completely open in detailing what they hoped to achieve.'[18] Their list included:

> The re-establishment of the complete independence of Ireland.
>
> To encourage the study of Gaelic, of Irish literature, History, Music and Art .... .
>
> To support and popularise Irish manufacture.
>
> To discourage the reading and circulation of low English literature, the singing of English songs, the attending of vulgar English entertainments at the theatres and music halls, and to combat in every way English influence, which is doing so much injury to the artistic taste and refinement of Irish people.[19]

In her speech in this section, Gonne pursues these goals, encouraging her audience to fight for an independent Ireland and to revive the Irish language, identifying how she connected nationalist politics and the revival of Irish culture. She also encouraged her audience to buy only Irish goods and actively discourage the recruitment of Irish men into the British army. Gonne ensured that members of Inghinidhe na hÉireann actively discouraged this latter practice. Members engaged in publicly humiliating Irish girls seen, as they described it, 'walking through the streets with men wearing the uniform of Ireland's oppressor'.[20] Gonne organised teams of women to distribute leaflets along the main thoroughfare of Dublin city, in public houses, on trains and on the streets. Leaflets implored 'Irish girls [to] make a vow, not only that you will yourselves refuse to associate with any man who wears an English uniform, but that you will also try and induce your girl companions to do the same'.[21] Such anti-recruitment work was dangerous: soldiers often retaliated by lashing out with their belts, and the women had to frequent disreputable areas where soldiers could be found, including the vicinity of the General Post Office, which was on the side of the road considered out of bounds for decent people.

In the winter of 1900, Gonne met John MacBride and the two toured America the following year. When she returned to Ireland in 1901, Gonne's popularity was at its highest. She was invited to unveil a number of monuments and memorials to fenian leaders around the country. Gonne's presence at such events gained national attention. The evening before the unveiling ceremony in Roscommon, on 7 September 1901, Gonne attended an Irish concert in the National Schoolroom, Roscommon. She was presented with an address on behalf of the Gaelic League who commended her for all her efforts in Ireland's cause. Gonne took the opportunity to deliver a speech in which she lambasted nationalist MPs for 'failing to obtain any real reform for Ireland after thirty years constitutional legislation, thereby showing that they were powerless to do so'.[22] Gonne advised those present not to financially support the Parliamentary Fund which aided Irish Parliamentary Party (IPP) MPs. The IPP had returned 77 seats at Westminster in the 1900 general election. The main objective of the IPP was to secure home rule, seeking self-government for Ireland within the British Empire. Gonne sought complete independence from British rule and her tone set the scene for her speech the following day.

On 8 September, Gonne unveiled a memorial to John Lavin at St Joseph's Cemetery in Castlerea. Lavin was a noteworthy businessman and served as leader of the Irish Republican Brotherhood (IRB) in Roscommon and as a member of the Fenian Supreme Council until his death. Lavin died on 8 March 1899 from complications related to pneumonia. His death was announced in the *Freeman's Journal* under the heading 'Death of a prominent Roscommon man'; the article noted that 'his loss, from a Nationalist standpoint, is a sad one for the Midlands.'[23] The people of Castlerea went into mourning, and the local newspaper described how 'the town wore a most solemn appearance, all the houses being closely shuttered and the blinds drawn.'[24] A meeting was held to discuss how to memorialise John Lavin as 'the services of Mr Lavin to the national cause were such as deserve an enduring perpetration of his memory amongst the people of Castlerea.'[25] A memorial was agreed and supported with financial donations from local people.

The monument was designed by Edward O'Shea of Kilkenny Marble Works, and it was modelled on the Monasterboice High Cross, standing 14 feet high and four feet wide over Lavin's grave. The unveiling ceremony was a high-profile event with a special train operating from Dublin to transport people for the occasion. Several renowned nationalists attended, including John O'Leary, Arthur Griffith and the Mayor of Limerick, John Daly.[26] There were several speeches at the unveiling ceremony, but it was undoubtedly Gonne's that received the most enthusiastic response from those gathered. The cheers from the crowd were noted by the reporter for the *Westmeath Independent* under a heading, 'enthusiastic reception for Miss Maud Gonne'.[27]

In April 1902, Gonne fulfilled her dream of acting in an Irish play, one that incredibly influenced the Irish theatre movement and inspired a new wave of revolutionary republicanism. She played the lead role in *Kathleen Ni Houlihan* written by Yeats and Lady Augusta Gregory, performed at St Teresa's Temperance Hall in Clarendon Street. The play was staged for three nights from 2 April along with George Russell's *Deirdre*. The plays were produced by the newly formed Irish National Dramatic Company. Irish literary scholar P. J. Mathews identifies these performances 'as a moment when ideas of romantic nationalism radicalised a generation of rebels who would end up in the GPO in 1916'.[28] Mathews summarises the obvious political message of the drama as 'the old woman, Cathleen (an allegorical figure who represents Mother Ireland), has lost her four green fields and appeals to a young man to help her get them back.'[29]

In February 1903, Gonne became a vice president of the newly established Irish National Theatre Society, converted to Catholicism and married John MacBride. Yeats pleaded with her not to marry MacBride as did Arthur Griffith. After the marriage, Gonne spent much of her time in Ireland while MacBride remained in France, fearing he would be arrested if he returned to Ireland. Later that year Gonne staged a protest against the next British royal visit to Dublin. Edward VII arrived during the summer of 1903, and Gonne oversaw protests by Inghinidhe that culminated in the battle of Coulson Avenue, where Gonne flew a black petticoat from her home during the festivities. She described how she got 'an old black petticoat . . . tore it in half, nailed one half to the broomstick and hung it out of the sitting room window as a contemptuous though childish answer to the Union Jacks'.[30]

Gonne returned to Paris in 1903 and her final child, Seán MacBride, was born there in January 1904. Her marriage had by then broken down and she filed for divorce. Gonne asserted that MacBride was a drunkard and a sexual predator who had assaulted members of her family. There followed a high-profile scandal, which became more public when John MacBride sued the *Irish Independent* for libel. The scandal damaged Gonne's reputation in nationalist and literary circles in Ireland. John MacBride was executed by firing squad on 5 May 1916 at Kilmainham Gaol for his part in the Easter Rising. By the time of the civil war, Gonne was again leading high-profile demonstrations, this time against the Irish Free State government. In 1922, Gonne and her son Seán moved into

Roebuck House on Clonskeagh Road, Dublin, which they inherited from MacBride. Gonne lived there for the remainder of her life.

3. Maud Gonne on Red Cross duty during the Irish Civil War, 4 July 1922. Courtesy of the National Library of Ireland.

Gonne wrote her memoirs, *A Servant of the Queen*, in 1938, recalling her early years up to her marriage in 1903. She intended to write a second volume of her memoirs, but this never materialised. Gonne gave a detailed witness account of her nationalist activities from 1903 to 1922 that is now held in the Bureau of Military History, the military archives of the Irish Defence Forces.[31] She died on 27 April 1953. Obituaries of her appeared in all major national and most local newspapers, testifying to Gonne's great devotion to Ireland and her work on behalf of the Irish people. Her funeral mass was held at the Church of the Sacred Heart in Donnybrook in Dublin. The church could not accommodate all of the mourners and people overflowed into the grounds. After the funeral mass, a mile long cortege walked behind her coffin from Donnybrook towards Glasnevin cemetery; when the procession reached Westmoreland Street in the city centre, it was joined by representatives of the Old IRA and Cumann na mBan. Gonne's coffin was draped with the tricolour and traffic was halted on the route through the city centre, while thousands of onlookers stood reverently silent as her coffin passed.

At the republican plot, The O'Rahilly (Richard 'Mac' O'Rahilly) gave the graveside oration. O'Rahilly was treasurer of Clann na Poblachta (Family of the Republic), a republican political party established by Gonne's son, Seán, then a serving TD.[32] O'Rahilly affirmed that 'many people had made sacrifices on behalf of causes in the past but few had had the courage, the love of justice and the persistence that Maud Gonne MacBride possessed.[33]

There are no statues honouring Gonne, but there are numerous noteworthy paintings and depictions of her. These works include an oil painting and a pastel drawing by Sarah Purser; a watercolour painting and a pencil drawing by Jack B. Yeats; a chalk and charcoal drawing by Seán O'Sullivan, all housed at the National Gallery of Ireland. A plaster bust of Gonne by Laurence Campbell is held by the Hugh Lane Gallery of Modern Art, in Dublin.[34] Maud Gonne's speeches and her writings remain as testimony to her fierce character and to the role she played in both Irish nationalism and the Irish Literary Revival.[35]

'The men and women of Ireland are coming to believe, as John Lavin believed, for they have seen the failure of thirty years constitutional agitation. Taxation is rising, rising, rising, always in Ireland, and our people are flying away. The last quarter saw 17,000 Irishmen and women emigrating from this country! You know very well, fellow countrymen, that if emigration continues at this rate, in thirty years more there will no longer be a Nationalist or a Catholic majority in Ireland (hear, hear).

Fellow countrymen, is not this situation serious, indeed, after thirty years constitutional agitation? (cheers). This is the fact which you have to face. Our members of Parliament must know, and they do know, the importance, the vital importance, of checking the advance—of stopping this over-taxation of the country which is ruining, ruining, the country (hear, hear), and the ruin of the country is translated by the emigration of the people—the flying away of the nation (cheers). They know the importance of this, and that they have not succeeded in checking emigration, or in stopping the over-taxation of the country, only proves that they are powerless to do so (cheers).

After thirty years wasted National time, after £20,000 of Irish National money subscribed by Irish men and women the world over, they are face to face with this fact, that they cannot reduce over-taxation, and cannot stop emigration, which is growing and growing, and draining a Nation's life blood away (hear, hear). Fellow countrymen, I do not want you to be harsh with those men for their failure (hear, hear). I think that they have done their best, they have tried to do their best, but it is the principle, it is the system that is wrong (loud cheers). What is the use of our appealing for justice to England? England is the last country in the whole world to which you should be looking and appealing (loud cheers). The freedom of Ireland will have to be wrought out by Irishmen, and in Ireland (cheers). Don't waste any more time, don't waste any more National money in sending men over to London, or in looking to London for help (hear, hear).

Help yourselves in this country by encouraging your own industries, by wearing Irish material, by refusing to buy anything that is manufactured in England (cheers). By taking Irish goods you will be doing more to check emigration, by giving employment to the people at home, tha[n] those eighty members of Parliament, though they spent their whole lives at Westminster (cheers). . . .

Then many people say, "there is no alternative for us, we may as well support the Constitutional movement." But I think there is an alternative (hear, hear). We, here in Ireland, may be too weak to rise against England, while England is at peace in the world. But an opportunity will be coming when you will have a chance of winning your freedom (loud cheers). Do you suppose that, if during the last thirty years, we had spent our time and the National money that had been subscribed in ORGANIZING REBELLION in Ireland, as in the times of the Fenians (great cheering), do you think that last year, when England, in her terror of Boer victories (cheers for De Wet, and the Boers), withdrew all her troops from Ireland, do you think we should have been powerless, as we were, to take advantage of that great opportunity? (cheers)[.] Another, and a greater opportunity may be coming, and may be coming very soon, when England will be engaged in a war with one or other of the great Powers of Europe (loud cheers). But if we are unprepared, as we were last year, what will be the good of it for Ireland? (cheers). . .

Fellow countrymen, this is what I tell you, and what I ask you to do— prepare! so that the next opportunity which is coming shall not be wasted (loud cheers), and while you are waiting for that opportunity, there is plenty of National work for you to do—there is your language to revive and support (hear, hear); then you have to encourage home manufactures; buy nothing English; buy goods made in Ireland; burn everything that is English (hear, hear). Build up your nation yourselves without assistance from England; refuse its protection to build up industries which she has ruined, and if the Irish people are determined, they can boycott English goods, and persevere in the revival of Irish manufactures (hear, hear). Thus, instead of sending eighty gentlemen over to Westminster, if we sent one, or two, or three intelligent Irishmen into the different centres of Europe to represent Ireland, to be ambassadors for Ireland, and to keep the name of Ireland before the world as in the time of the United Irishmen (cheers), that those gentlemen might act as consuls for Ireland, and find markets for Irish trade, and stop the tide of emigration (hear, hear). If we would but look away from England, and go out to her rivals, we should find plenty of friends able and willing to help Ireland (hear, hear). But what we want is more individual independence and initiative amongst us all. But you must remember that the freedom of Ireland you will never get unless you are ready to fight for it (hear, hear). Never rest until Ireland is free (cheers). There is one more thing that I want to speak to you about . . . because it is a question vitally important to Ireland, and that is to stop the enlistment of Irishmen in the English army or in the English navy (hear, hear). You don't know the terrible harm that it has done to the National cause. It has brought disgrace on the pure name of our countrymen (cheers), to see so many of them wearing the red uniform of shame, standing in the ranks of the oppressor of their motherland (groans), to fight against freedom in the Transvaal (cheers for the Boers). Fellow countrymen, you don't know the harm that those Irish soldiers in England's pay have done to the cause of Ireland. But thank God we have John MacBride in the Irish Regiment (great cheering). We have John MacBride in the Irish Brigade to save Ireland's honour (cheers), and but for that Irish Transvaal Brigade, I don't think we Irishmen should have the liberty to raise our heads, when we thought that all those Irish soldiers and cowards were fighting for England. I know it is starvation, often, very often, that makes young Irishmen enlist, but we must not do it. The people have not done their duty, they have not spoken out against this crying evil.

But thank God, now, through the efforts of the Cummann na n Gaedhael [sic], and our only National newspaper, "The United Irishman," which, by the way, I hope you all read . . . because it is the only National newspaper in Ireland to-day—it is the only newspaper that is supporting the principles of John Lavin (hear, hear). It is by the efforts of that newspaper and the Cummann na n Gaedhael [sic] recruiting has so much diminished (hear, hear). The other day an English officer said that although recruiting was going on well in England and in Scotland, there was very little going on in Ireland (cheers). But still there are 2,000 recruits got from Ireland after all this (shame). But while there are 4,000 Irishmen got from Ireland to join England's army last year, and although they are getting recruits for the English navy, recruiting is almost stopped in Ireland (hear, hear). That shows that there is something for you to do in stopping recruiting. The recruiting sergeant should be chased out of any town he dares raise his head in (hear, hear). Any foolish or drunken boy who might be tempted to join them should be reasoned with, and stopped. The recruiting sergeant should be chased out of every town (cheers). Fellow countrymen, it is indeed a pleasing and inspiring sight to see so many here to-day to honour the memory of John Lavin (cheers). But remember that the best way to honour the memory of that noble Irishman—yes[—]and the memories of those patriotic Irishmen who fought and died in the past for the cause of Ireland is to carry on their work, and never rest until we have a free and independent Nation (tremendous cheering).'[36]

THREE

Alice Stopford Green

1847–1929

Speech on *The Making of Ireland and Its Undoing*
Irish Club, Charing Cross Road, London

12 DECEMBER 1908

'When a saner and more dignified history is restored to Ireland.'

The Irish cultural revival expanded in the first decades of the twentieth century mainly through the endeavours of key societies. These societies included the Gaelic Athletic Association (GAA), established in 1884; the Gaelic League, founded in 1893; Inghinidhe na hÉireann, in operation since 1900; and the Irish National Theatre Society, established in 1903. The successful revival of Irish language and culture was undoubtedly dependent on a knowledge base of Irish history. Alice Stopford Green maintained that 'the history of the Irish people has been left unrecorded, as though it had never been; as though indeed, according to some, the history were one of dishonour and rebuke.'[1] Stopford Green was the first person to effectively challenge what she described as the 'Englishman's history' by rewriting the history of Ireland. Three of her publications – *The Making of Ireland and Its Undoing* (1908), *Irish Nationality* (1911) and *The Old Irish World* (1912) – underpinned a re-imagined national consciousness that helped pave the way for Irish independence. Her speech in this section was given at the launch of her first book in this series in 1908.

Alice Stopford was born on 30 May 1847 in Kells, county Meath. The year of her birth was the harshest year of the Great Famine in Ireland, now referred to as 'Black 47'. Alice was one of nine children of Edward Adderley Stopford, the Anglican archdeacon of Meath and rector of Kells, and Anne Stoker (née Duke) from Sligo. Alice was provided with a good education befitting a girl of her class; she was educated by a governess at home. She read voraciously; she learnt Greek, Latin, German and French and travelled the continent during her early years. When she reached 27 years of age, her father died, and she moved with her family to Chester in England in 1874. Shortly after her move to England, Alice met the social historian John Richard Green, who had recently published his much-admired book *A Short History of English People*.[2] The couple married in 1877, and they published *A Short Geography of the British Islands* together in 1879.[3] They lived in a mansion in Kensington Square in London. John died of consumption in March 1883, less than six years after they had married.[4]

Alice dedicated herself to honouring her husband's memory and completed publication of his book *The Conquest of England* and oversaw revised editions of his other works.[5] In 1884, she applied unsuccessfully for the position of mistress of the recently established college for women, Girton College, Cambridge. Among those who wrote references in support of her application was the social reformer and founder of modern nursing, Florence Nightingale.[6] Stopford continued to publish historical works on her own and was held in high esteem by distinguished historians and academics, including the Irish historians William Edward Hartpole Lecky and James Bryce. She was commissioned by John Morley, who served as Chief Secretary for Ireland, to write a book on Henry II, for a biographical series of twelve English statesmen.[7] Alice soon began to focus solely on social history, and in 1894 she produced two volumes on *Town Life in the Fifteenth Century*, which she dedicated to the memory of her husband.[8]

Stopford Green's books and articles were well received, and she gradually acquired prestigious positions reflecting her academic reputation. She became the first woman to sit on the London Library Committee in 1894; she was elected to the committee on five occasions from 1894 to 1916. In 1901, she was elected as a fellow of the Royal Historical Society in London, and she was on the committee for the Nobel Prize for Literature from 1902 to 1911.

Alice was not a mere presenter and writer of history; she keenly engaged with contemporary issues. In 1900, she visited the Atlantic island of St Helena, which was being used by British authorities to house prisoners of war during the Boer War (1899–1902). Alice collected evidence of mistreatment of Boer prisoners and published her account calling for improvements. She co-founded the Africa Society in 1901, becoming its first vice-president. In 1904, Stopford Green helped establish the Congo Reform Association, through which she met Roger Casement who had served as British consul to the Congo and had published his report on atrocities there. From 1901 to 1906, Stopford Green edited the journal of the African Society.

4. Alice Stopford Green, c.1885. The Cameron Studio. Public domain.

Historian Angus Mitchell has done stellar work in recovering the life and accomplishments of Stopford Green. Mitchell attests that through Alice's 'commitment to understanding Africa, she simultaneously nurtured a much deeper commitment to Ireland'.[9] Stopford Green dedicated the following years to researching and publishing on the history of Ireland, resulting in the publication of her three major works from 1908 to 1912. Mitchell is clear as to her objectives in writing these works: 'first and foremost, these histories were a critical intervention into the identity politics of the time. She consciously used history as a challenge to the way that Irish history was written and taught and described how a deliberate process of defacement and erasure had been imposed under colonial rule to destroy that more ancient identity.'[10]

The Making of Ireland and Its Undoing focused on the medieval period from 1200 to 1600. During the final stages of editing, Stopford Green consulted with Richard Irvine Best, the renowned Celtic scholar and later director of the National Library of Ireland, to ensure that her references to the Irish language were correct.[11] The book was published by Macmillan in June 1908 with an initial print of 2,500 copies. Due to demand the book was reprinted a number of times over the coming months – in July 1908 and again in September 1908 and in January 1909.

The prestigious engraver and printer Emery Walker was commissioned to design the front piece, a map of Ireland that divides Ireland into five provinces. The reference to a fifth province recalls the ancient legend that Ireland was divided geographically into four quarters – Leinster, Munster, Ulster, Connaught – while a fifth province was placed at the centre. The legend of the fifth province was reintroduced into popular discourse by Mary Robinson during her presidential inauguration speech in December 1990.[12] Robinson used the fifth province as a symbol of reconciliation and healing, stating, 'the Fifth Province is not anywhere here or there, north or south, east or west. It is a place within each one of us — that place that is open to the other, that swinging door which allows us to venture out and others to venture in.'[13]

Stopford Green was insistent that *The Making of Ireland and Its Undoing* would be available and accessible to members of the Gaelic League. She organised a deal with her publisher, Macmillan, that she would oversee distribution of copies for Irish sale; these copies were stamped with 'the Gaelic league' on the base of the spine.[14] Mitchell summarises the intention of this book as 'a radical reimagining of the trade, social life and intellectual culture of medieval Ireland, and one that opposed, in no uncertain terms, the prevailing narrative of backwardness, violence and fragmentation'.[15] Not surprisingly, the response to the book in Ireland was overwhelmingly positive, and Stopford Green was invited to give a number of talks.

On Saturday, 12 December 1908, the Irish Club on Charing Cross Road in London hosted a dinner with Stopford Green as their guest of honour. After the evening meal, Thomas Kettle introduced the speaker to the 'very large audience' gathered. Kettle was then a serving MP; he first stood for election in the July 1906 by-election in East Tyrone as an Irish Parliamentary Party (IPP) candidate. He was a professor of national economics at University College Dublin. In his opening address, Kettle described how the Irish Club at Charing Cross was 'a sort of Irish colony in London . . . a meeting place in which they could bring together and entertain men and women who had brought distinction upon Ireland'.[16] The proceedings and Stopford Green's entire speech were published in the *Freeman's Journal*, a popular newspaper, established in 1763, that had by the 1880s become a voice for constitutional nationalism through its support of the IPP. Kettle assured those gathered that this evening they entertained a distinguished guest, describing how Stopford Green had 'won world-wide distinction in the purely intellectual domain'.[17] He went further by describing in somewhat amusing terms how Stopford Green had brought 'a new spirit into the writing of history, and she had engaged in the monstrous novelty of writing real Irish history for the first time'.[18] However, he was clear that through her painstaking research on the Elizabethan period in Ireland Stopford Green had 'revolutionised Irish history'.[19]

Kettle quipped that Stopford Green's book was seen as controversial in some domains, noting particularly how the Royal Dublin Society (RDS) refused to allow her book into their library. The RDS, a voluntary organisation established in the eighteenth century to aid the development of Irish culture and economy, houses an exceptional library. Kettle raised this matter in the House of Commons just days later, on 17 December. Kettle questioned the Chief Secretary for Ireland, Augustine Birrell, on whether he was aware that *The Making of Ireland and Its Undoing*, which 'has been acclaimed in the world of culture as the most important contribution to Irish history . . . and was in circulation in the National Library in Dublin and in many other public libraries in Ireland and Great Britain', had been banned by the RDS.[20] Birrell denied all responsibility for books held in the library of the RDS, which as a privately funded society did not fall under the remit of the government. Kettle was undoubtedly aware that the RDS could not be ordered to explain their decision; however, he had raised the profile of Stopford Green's book and highlighted how the writing of Irish history could be controversial. Although the library committee refused to accept Stopford Green's book in 1908, the RDS library in 2022 carries a complete list of her works.

Stopford Green rose to address the audience after a toast in her honour. She was loudly applauded, and her speech was described in the *Freeman's Journal* as 'brilliant'.[21] She began by stressing the importance of history to national identity. *The Making of Ireland and Its Undoing* was published during a time of heightened debate surrounding Irish national identity. Mitchell defines 1908 as 'a moment of burgeoning public debates and disagreements in and about Ireland'.[22] Stopford Green's new history of Ireland would play an important role in the growth of the Irish cultural revival and as an intellectual foundation for the independence movement.

In her speech Stopford Green lays out the repercussions of having Irish history 'obliterated' from the record. She remarks on how a young boy standing on the shore of Lough Oughter in Cavan would not be familiar with two significant characters in Ulster history: Owen Roe O'Neill and Bishop Bedell. O'Neill (*c.* 1580–1649) was the commander of the Irish Confederate Ulster Army during a major Catholic revolt (1641–52) against British rule in Ireland.[23] His major accomplishment was the defeat of the Scottish covenanter Robert Munroe at Benburb in June 1646, which ended Scottish hopes of conquering Ireland. William Bedell (1571–1642) was provost of Trinity College Dublin and bishop of Kilmore and Ardagh. Unlike other Protestant bishops, Bedell encouraged and supported the use of the Irish language, orchestrating the translation of many religious texts into the Irish language. During the 1641 Catholic rising against English settlers, Bedell was imprisoned but not harmed. After he died in prison of natural causes, Irish rebel forces escorted his body to the Kilmore churchyard, where he was granted a burial under his religious rites and a volley was fired over his grave. Such was the respect that Bedell had gained from Irish people.

In her speech, Stopford Green explains that while history books obliterate great Irish heroes, they focus instead on how the Irish were slaughtered 'by hunger, prison, exile by the sword, the scourge, and the hangman', from the reign of Elizabeth I (1558–1603) to the reign of Victoria (1837–1901). Stopford Green sets forth her challenge to re-write the lost and overlooked history of the 'splendid tales of chivalry, of high honour, of victory won from gallant foes; of a heroic contest ending in the respect of brave soldiers'. Mitchell pertinently observes that her book was 'an uninhibited attack on the central sources underlying unionist history and a denunciation of an account written for the benefit of the colonisers. . . . Such a negative representation of Ireland was intrinsic to the colonial mission.'[24]

The book was received with high praise, including by the socialist and nationalist James Connolly, who was fulsome in his praise. In his review, printed on the front page of *The Harp*, the journal of the Irish Socialist Federation, Connolly wrote that *The Making of Ireland and Its Undoing* is a 'wonderfully complete and systematic piece of historical architecture' that disrupts all the 'conventionally established standards' while applying 'modern historical methods to the elucidation of Irish history'.[25] The writer George Russell (Æ), who edited the *Irish Homestead*, the organ of the co-operative movement, pointed to the significance of the work for the Irish cooperative movement.[26] Mary Hayden, the historian and Irish language activist, wrote a series of articles for *The Sphere* on the topic of 'Irish history as she is written.' Hayden, who was later appointed in 1911 as the first professor of modern Irish history at University College Dublin, quoted Stopford Green's publication throughout her articles.[27] In this way Hayden showcased Stopford Green's work as a reputable historical source in the pages of a weekly illustrated London newspaper.

The Making of Ireland and Its Undoing was the first book in a series by Stopford Green in her quest to re-write Irish history and rectify previous histories written by British historians. She published *Irish Nationality* in 1911, tracing the history of Ireland from the Gaels to the Union with England (1800–1900).[28] She dedicated the book 'In memory of the Irish dead'. Her concluding sentence reinforced the nationalist tone: 'The natural union approaches of the Irish Nation—the union of all her children that are born under the breadth of her skies, fed by the fatness of her fields, and nourished by the civilisation of her dead.'[29] The following year, in 1912, she published *The Old Irish World*, which was the culmination of her many lectures concerning Ireland, rewritten in what she described as a form 'more convenient for country readers'.[30] This publication was also dedicated 'In memory of the Irish dead' and written at the request of a number of her friends in Ireland. Her works received positive recognition, and she was awarded an honorary Doctor of Literature from the University of Liverpool in 1913.

Following the publication of these three volumes, Stopford Green became increasingly active in the fight for Irish independence. By 1914, Ireland was on the edge of a civil war. Unionists in the north of the country armed themselves to resist home rule. In the south of the country, the Irish Volunteers vowed to protect home rule, but they lacked ammunition. In her capacity as chair of the London Committee, Stopford Green coordinated a fund for the Irish Volunteers to which she personally contributed a large sum of money. The fund was used by Roger Casement to secure guns and ammunition, which were smuggled into Ireland through the port of Howth in July 1914. Although she supported the ideal of nationalism, Stopford Green remained, as historian William Murphy says, 'uncomfortable with the violent struggle for independence'.[31] Despite these concerns she supported Casement when he was arrested for his activities relating to the Easter Rising in 1916.

Casement had been arrested before the Easter Rising began. He was captured on Banna Strand, on the coast of county Kerry, where he had landed from a German U-boat. The submarine was meant to rendezvous with the *Aud*, a German ship that was captained by Karl Spindler and carrying guns to arm the Irish Volunteers. As a former and highly respected official of the British government, Casement's involvement with the Easter Rising caused a serious political scandal in England. Upon hearing of his arrest, Casement's cousin, Gertrude Bannister, visited Stopford Green to seek advice. Stopford Green was well connected and introduced Bannister to George Gavan Duffy, a London solicitor who agreed to represent Casement.[32] Casement was sentenced to death after a trial at the Old Bailey in London. The day before Casement's execution, Stopford Green, Eva Gore-Booth and Bannister went to Buckingham Palace to have an audience with King George V, whom they begged for a royal pardon. All appeals were denied.[33] Casement was executed on 3 August 1916 at Pentonville Prison in London.

Stopford Green returned to Ireland in 1918; she secured a house at 90 St Stephen's Green. She employed the writer and nationalist Maire Comerford as her secretary. The house at St Stephen's Green was regularly raided by the Dublin Metropolitan Police because of the many nationalist activities and meetings held there. Stopford Green continued to research and write Irish history. She published propagandist pamphlets, including *Ourselves Alone in Ulster* and *The Government of Ireland*, which included a foreword by George Russell.[34]

5. Alice Stopford Green addressing a crowd. Tierney/MacNeill Photographs Collection. Reproduced by kind permission of UCD Archives.

Stopford Green supported the Anglo-Irish Treaty, established in December 1921, and she joined Cumann na Saoirse (League of Freedom), a newly formed women's association. She became a member of the Free State senate, although she rarely contributed to debates. In 1924, she presented the Seanad with a jewelled casket designed by the metalwork artist Mia Cranwill. The casket held a vellum scroll containing the names of the first senators. Stopford Green was unwell the day the casket was presented to the Seanad on 26 November 1924, and she sent a message to be read at the session. Her message described how 'The artist has magnificently proved the power of that spiritual inheritance which has been bequeathed to us from an Old Ireland; and has shown that a really living art has no need to copy in slavish routine, and can to-day be as free and original and distinguished as in the times of ancient renown, supposed to have been lost.'[35] Stopford Green ended her message with her insistence that 'No real history of Ireland has yet been written. When the true story is finally worked out—one not wholly occupied with the many and insatiable plunderers—it will give us a noble and reconciling vision of Irish nationality. Silence and neglect will no longer hide the fame of honourable men.'[36] The casket is now in the possession of the Royal Irish Academy.

Stopford Green published *History of the Irish State to 1014* the following year, in 1925.[37] She suffered a heart attack that year, and her health deteriorated over the coming years. She died on 28 May 1929 at her home on St Stephen's Green. She was buried in Deansgrange Cemetery on the southside of Dublin on 1 June 1929. Her headstone aptly describes her as 'Historian of the Irish People'. Alice Stopford Green's papers are held in the National Library of Ireland.[38] A plaque to her memory was unveiled by the Minister of State, Helen McEntee, on 7 December 2019 at the Old Courthouse in Kells, county Meath. The plaque was commissioned by the Meath Archaeological and Historical Society and is inscribed in Irish and in English, 'Alice Stopford Green . . . Historian, Political Activist and Senator'. Her books and her speeches remain a significant contribution to our record of modern Irish history which continues to shape contemporary Irish culture.

'I think, perhaps, I had one qualification for writing the history of Ireland so far as I have done it. That was, I had no idea of what I was going to face in it, and, therefore, I may hope I was impartial. It was not written with a preconceived idea of what it was going to be (applause).

I have heard that anyone who attempted to spread a knowledge of Irish history was open [to] forms of criticism—one, that it was an act of folly, and the other tha[t] it was an act of malice. As to the folly of history, we might enter into long abstract discussions as to what use men could make of history, or why they should trouble about it. We need not be concerned ourselves with such disputations. For we are confronted by one big overwhelming fact. Ever since man got out of the ape stage every human community has made its history—aboriginal tribes of the tropical forests, wandering races that peopled Egypt, Greece, Rome; the later emigrants that made the United States, Canada, Africa, even town Corporations of the last century, Birmingham, Manchester, and the like—all those communities, as soon as they come to any kind of self-consciousness, express it by shaping to themselves a history. It is as if some compelling instinct forced them to drive their roots deep down into the soil where they live, lest, perchance, they might be like some tree with vast spreading branches and roots, diseased or severed, so that it became the mockery and sport of every gust of wind that swept across this troublesome world till it lay upturned and its miserable and shallow hold was revealed to all.

The people that has no history, that has ceased to hallow its allotted earth with great recollections and filial pieties, has sunk below the prerogative of man, that which distinguished him from the brute beasts, and has fallen to the plane of the unreasoning things who see with indifferent stupidity the passing generations swallowed up by silent death (applause). Such people are themselves doomed to the rapid oblivion they have meted out to their ancestors. Let us remember, too, that in Ireland we have had a fine, a magnificent experiment in proclaiming the folly of history. . . .

The success of obliteration in Ireland has been prodigious. It is as if the habitations of men had been ploughed and sown with salt. You may ask a boy in Cavan or on the shore of Lough Oughter who was Owen Roe O'Neill or Bishop Bedell; he will but gaze at you bewildered. In Ireland, therefore, the experiment of proclaiming the folly of history has been fully tried—and what is the result? Well, man being man, history is no sooner driven out of the door than it comes in through the window. But it is not the same history. Authentic history is gone; and what we may here call unauthorised programmes have taken its place. There are several of them in Ireland. Let us take two that represent the two races in the island (applause). There is the history of the Irish people; against a dim, pre-historic background there emerges the colossal figures of heroes, warriors, statesmen and prodigious conflicts, all exalted by a passionate poetry, with a thousand sites consecrated by the great deeds done there. Then come a thousand years or so of confusion, into which no one looks very closely, because that time is represented as a sort of cauldron of anarchy and ruin (applause). . . . Then follows the time from Elizabeth to Victoria, where across the centuries pass the endless procession of ghosts of slaughtered men slain by hunger, prison, exile by the sword, the scourge, the hangman, and luminous figures in the dock proclaiming the righteousness of their cause. There is plenty of truth in this history, and it is hopelessly incomplete. For the last 300 years, so far as I know, not a single word to justify the industry, the commerce, the learning, the civil policy of Irish Ireland throughout the Middle Ages after about 1000 A.D. (applause).

What effect can such history have, moral or intellectual? Morally we are a people torn between pride and abasement; pride of their antique glories and of their later fortitude in every form of martyrdom; abasement of a high-spirited people at the fact that they stand before Europe with a history of defeat, ruin, and rebuke; a race without the dignity of having ever had a true civilisation; a race condemned as incapable of development in the land they wasted, poor suppliants for the crumbs of industry falling from rich England's table. . . . Intellectually, too, we see too well its evil consequences. What can an Irishman see in such a history but a medley of catastrophes, a whirl of chance, the triumph of successful violence? What is there in such a record to steady his mind or train his judgment? The law of chance and violence, the spirit of helpless indignation or self-distrust, and despair—this is all that so imperfect a tale can teach him. Truly there have been false prophets in the land (applause).

Side by side with the Irish we have the Englishman's history. He has invented for himself a story compounded of his national conceit and his Puritan conscience. He pictured an island, inhabited by inveterate savages that nothing could cure—a people of which only the human form remained to show that they were men—for the honour of England and the glory of God (laughter), an island blessed by nature had to be redeemed from these children of the devil, predestined to bring forth naughty fruits. The Englishmen in this acted the emissaries of Providence, but they showed as much humanity as was possible under the circumstances. They used, in fact, no more force than was necessary to slay half the inhabitants, and they only took all the land and all the trade (laughter).

The attempt to develop the country into a good portion for their younger sons was much impeded by the remnant of the natives, whom, therefore, a righteous God from time to time, through Englishmen's hands, swept with the besom of destruction (applause), and this with no more difficulty than the virtuous man must expect in this naughty world. They continued to hope that by firm government they would repress the unruly and extend civilisation. It seems wonderful to have invented a story so dull. An intelligent people might have done better. What a lost opportunity.

Suppose they had thought of an epic to match the Irish; the clash of two fine civilisations, a Titanic conflict at the meeting of worlds new and old; splendid tales of chivalry, of high honour, of victory won from gallant foes; of a heroic contest ending in the respect of brave soldiers for each other (applause). This would seem more stirring than a record of ferocious man hunts and poison cups, and massacres at feasts and the legend of a wealthy, highly civilised, well-armed people, pursuing with their guns and their Bibles starving savages over bogs, and pounding naked beggars with their cannon. What credit is to be got out of such a tale? What writer can make a readable hash about it? Who has any curiosity to read such a tale? (Applause.) The intellectual effect of such a history must evidently be to stop all curiosity or inquiry. No one cares to investigate farther a history of no importance, and instead of study we have vague clamour. Hear common opinion as Tennyson puts it—"Kelts are all made furious fools . . . They live in a horrible island, and have no history of their own worth the least notice. Could not anyone blow up that horrible island with dynamite and carry it off in pieces—a long way off?" and so on.[39] Here we see the paralysing effect on the intelligence of attempting to live with no better substitute for history than this barbarian legend. It is a poison bed for the growth of folly and ignorance—what wisdom or statesmanship can spring out of it? (Applause). . . .

I am led to think that it will be no action of malice when a saner and more dignified history is restored to Ireland—and when both peoples, the English and the Irish, are given back the self-respect, and the respect for others, which that history must teach: when the tremendous character of the conflict shall be seen, and the part played by brave men, and when chivalrous men will have no more of slanders. There will be no danger in the true history, and in men who honour one another. All danger lies in the false and mutilated fictions. Surely in the work that lies before me, and the real University for Ireland, there can be no greater obligation, and no more beneficent accomplishment, than the restoration of a true Irish history (loud applause).'[40]

FOUR

Norah Dacre Fox

1878–1961

A prisoner's speech
Knightsbridge Hall, High Road, London

JULY 1914

'When they took my fingerprints I smashed every window in my cell.'

The women's suffrage movement engaged with art and culture in many forms, including literature, music, drama, painting and photography. Suffragists used cultural endeavours to express their views and generate publicity for the cause of votes for women. The sale of leaflets, newspapers, postcards and other paraphernalia raised much needed funds for the suffrage struggle. Such cultural engagements were particularly evident in England in the early twentieth century, especially through the endeavours of the militant suffragette organisation the Women's Social and Political Union (WSPU). In their assessment of 'women's suffrage and cultural representation,' Christopher Wiley and Lucy Ella Rose, note that 'the movement involved many professional and untrained artists, writers, musicians and performers.'[1] One such writer was Irish woman Norah Dacre Fox who became a significant campaigner for the WSPU and used her writing and her speeches to further the cause of women's suffrage.

Norah Doherty was born in Blackrock, south county Dublin, on 5 May 1878. Her family moved to London when she was ten years of age. Norah's father, John Doherty, was a supporter of home rule and a founding member of the Irish Protestant Home Rule Association.[2] Norah would later employ her suffrage campaigns to embarrass anti-home rule politicians in England. Little is known about Norah's educational background, but it can be assumed that she received a good education as in adulthood she was articulate, intellectually driven and a prolific writer. Norah married Charles Richard Dacre Fox in 1909 and thereafter went by the name Norah Dacre Fox, although it transpired that Dacre was in fact her husband's middle name. The marriage broke down within a few years, according to historian Patrick Maume, partly due to Norah's involvement with the militant suffragette movement in England.[3]

In 1912, Norah joined the WSPU, first established in 1903 by Emmeline Pankhurst with the support of her daughter Christabel. Mrs Pankhurst had become disillusioned with the incessant lobbying of MPs by suffragists seeking the introduction of a women's suffrage bill. A new wave of young, educated women joined the ranks of the WSPU. Members keenly followed the WSPU's motto 'deeds not words' and inaugurated a series of militant tactics from October 1905, demanding votes for women. The first imprisonments of WSPU members occurred that month when Christabel and Annie Kenney, a lead organiser, interrupted a Liberal Party meeting in the Free Trade Hall in Manchester. The women were charged with causing a public affray, and Pankhurst was also charged with 'spitting at a police superintendent and a police officer and hitting the latter in the mouth'.[4] Both women were fined and on refusing to pay the fines were sentenced to serve time in Strangeways prison. The WSPU gained media attention for their cause and their membership numbers grew.

The WSPU moved their headquarters to London, and by 1912, when Norah joined, militant feminist activities were a daily occurrence across the towns and cities of Britain. Members disrupted political meetings, held large-scale demonstrations, interrupted postal services by setting fire to post boxes and attacked public buildings, at times burning them to the ground. As militancy escalated so too did arrests and imprisonments of suffragettes. Women imprisoned for the cause of votes for women demanded political status, and from 1909 suffragettes adopted hunger striking in prison as a tactic to receive their demands. The authorities did not succumb to the women's demands and reacted by force-feeding those female prisoners on hunger strike. Force-feeding was conducted by prison guards physically restraining a woman while medical staff inserted a rubber tube into her nose or through her mouth. Liquidised food was then poured into the tube to pass into the woman's stomach. In this way suffragettes not only suffered emotional distress but also experienced physical trauma, including broken teeth, bleeding and choking if the food reached their lungs.

The WSPU retaliated by printing graphic illustrations of women being force-fed. One of the most widely distributed was drawn by artist Alfred Pearce, a member of the Men's League for Women's Suffrage, using the pseudonym of A. Patriot. The image was initially published in the WSPU newspaper, *The Suffragette*; depicting a woman strapped to a chair and restrained by five prison wardens, while a doctor poured fluid into the tube inserted through the woman's nose. The image was reproduced as a poster during the 1910 general election in Britain, warning, 'Electors! Put a stop to this Torture by voting against The Prime Minister'. Leaflets were distributed with accounts by recently released suffragettes, such as Mary Richardson, printed under the heading 'Tortured women. What forcible feeding means: A prisoner's testimony'.[5] The British public were generally outraged that women were being treated in such appalling ways in prisons across Britain.

6. Women's Social and Political Union poster showing a suffragette prisoner being force-fed, 1910. Artist Alfred Pearce. Wikimedia Commons.

Under public pressure, the government banned force-feeding in prisons and introduced the 1913 Prisoners (Temporary Discharge for Ill-Health) Act. The Act became known as the Cat and Mouse Act because under this law a suffragette prisoner on hunger strike would be released when she became ill and re-arrested when she was fit enough to return to prison. Once she returned to prison, her sentence would continue again. By this stage, Norah had risen through the ranks of the WSPU to the role of general secretary. Her granddaughter, Angela McPherson, records that Norah became 'a member of the inner Pankhurst circle'.[6] Grace Roe, the daughter of a prestigious Anglo-Irish family in London and a chief organiser of the WSPU, described how the Pankhursts valued Norah's public-speaking ability.[7] Norah became a leading WSPU spokeswoman, often sharing a stage with Emmeline Pankhurst at monster rallies including the Great Women's Demonstration on 7 December 1913.[8] Norah also played a significant role writing and editing *The Suffragette*, as well as submitting articles to the national press on behalf of the women's movement. Norah was summonsed, along with WSPU member Flora Drummond, to appear in court on 14 May 1914 to answer charges of 'openly and deliberately advocating acts of militancy and violence'.[9] The women did not appear in court, and instead Norah camped out at the home of Lord Lansdowne (Henry Petty-Fitzmaurice), the leader of the Unionist peers in the House of Lords. Lansdowne was vehemently opposed to home rule for Ireland. While Flora petitioned the leader of the Irish Unionist Party, Edward Carson, Norah brought a letter to give to Lansdowne explaining her reason for approaching him; the letter was later printed in *The Suffragette*:

> I have come to take refuge with you, as you yourself have delivered several speeches endorsing and inciting violent resistance to Home Rule, and yet the Government do not attack you. I have confidence, therefore, that under your roof I shall have the same immunity from arrest and imprisonment that you yourself enjoy. I am sure that you as a militant, will have every wish to protect another militant from the arrest and torture in prison with which I am threatened.
>
> Points in your speeches which have encouraged me to rely upon your help and protection in this matter are the following:
>
> At the Albert Hall on the first day of this month you spoke with sympathy on the gun-running in Ulster, described by the Prime Minister as 'a grave and unprecedented outrage,' and you praised what you called 'the extraordinary efficiency of the arrangements' carried out on that occasion.[10]

The episode gained huge media attention both for the cause of women's suffrage and for Irish home rule. The *New York Times* reported that Norah 'had been summoned to appear in the afternoon for making inciting speeches and as Lord Lansdowne had also been making inciting speeches, yet seemed to be perfectly safe from interference, she thought she had better be with him so that if they took her, they could take both'.[11]

Both Norah and Flora were arrested and imprisoned in Holloway, where Norah went on hunger strike. Under the terms of the Cat and Mouse Act, she was released when she became too weak to continue her sentence. Rather than recover her energies, Norah went to Westminster Abbey on 6 July and interrupted a sermon by the Bishop of London. She called on the bishop to 'stop the forceable feeding that is going on. I pray you stop it.'[12] When she left Westminster Abbey, she was re-arrested and brought back to Holloway Prison. On her next release Norah addressed a large audience at the public venue of Knightsbridge Hall on High Road in the city of London with the speech in this section, describing her prison sentence.

In her speech, Norah refers to Flora as General Drummond, a title by which she was affectionately known, because she led suffragette marches on horseback while wearing a military style uniform complete with cap and epaulettes. Norah mentions women attempting to present a petition to King George V. Shortly after delivering this speech, on 30 July, Norah was arrested again: this time at Buckingham Palace while attempting to present a letter from Emmeline Pankhurst to the king.

Britain declared war on Germany on 4 August 1914. Three days after war was officially announced, the Home Secretary, Reginald McKenna, declared that if suffragette prisoners agreed to refrain from militant anti-government activity they would be released from prison under an amnesty. The suffrage and suffragette movements broadly suspended their campaigns for women's enfranchisement during the period of World War One. Christabel Pankhurst announced her support of Britain in the war effort. During the autumn of 1915, Norah, along with Emmeline Pankhurst, Flora Drummond, Annie Kenney and Grace Roe, engaged in a public-speaking tour of South Wales, the Midlands and Scotland, encouraging trade unions to support war work.

Anti-German sentiment spread across Britain from the onset of the war, and Norah turned her public-speaking talents to speaking out against German people living and working in England. She joined the Anti-Alien Campaign (1914–20), and by the end of the war she had become particularly intense in her hatred of Germany and its people. *The Times* reported a section from a public speech she gave in August 1918, in which she demanded 'a clean sweep of all persons of German blood, without distinction of sex, birthplace, or nationality. . . . Any person in this country, no matter who he was or what his position, who was suspected of protecting German influence, should be tried as a traitor, and, if necessary, shot. There must be no compromise and no discrimination.'[13] She stood as an independent candidate on an anti-alien platform for the constituency of Richmond in Surrey in the 1918 General Election. She failed dismally but did secure 3,615 votes.

At the end of the war, Norah met Dudley Elam, a married man with two children. Norah and Dudley lived together and had one child, Aubrey, in 1922. Although not married, Norah adopted the last name Elam. Norah had a passionate love of animals throughout her life and claimed to be a founding member of the London and Provincial Anti-Vivisection Society.

During the inter-war years, her work in this area became more prominent and she published two anti-vivisection pamphlets, *The Vitamin Survey* in 1934 and *The Medical Research Council: What It Is and How It Works* in 1935.[14]

In 1934, Norah and Dudley joined the British Union of Fascists (BUF) led by Oswald Mosley. The BUF was known for 'distributing anti-Semitic propaganda, conducting hostile demonstrations in the Jewish sections of East London, and wearing Nazi-style uniforms and insignia'.[15] Historian Julie V. Gottlieb has written extensively about female fascists in Britain during this time period and notes that other former militant suffragette women joined the BUF, including Mary Richardson. Gottlieb aptly explains how these women imported 'with them the legacy of their militant feminist struggle in the pre-war period and their disillusionment with the post-war condition of the women's movement in the aftermath of female enfranchisement'.[16] Norah rose through the ranks of the BUF, she soon became the women's organiser for Sussex and went on to be a leading member of the organisation. Gottlieb asserts that although 'in principle, the movement was segregated by gender and women in positions of leadership were meant to have authority only over other women, Elam was quite evidently admitted to Mosley's inner circle'.[17]

From the time she joined the BUF, Norah published articles advocating that fascism was the best political course for women. In 1935, in her article 'Fascism, women and democracy', she rationalised that 'so far as British women are concerned, Communism makes little appeal. . . . Fascism seems to be the only solution. It has within it every principle peculiarly suitable and adaptable to the genius of the British character.'[18] Norah would again spend time in Holloway, this time for her involvement with the BUF, and, as Gottlieb highlights, she 'was the only ex-suffragette to be interned in Britain'.[19] On 23 May 1940, she was interned under Defence Regulation 18B: this recently introduced legislation gave the Home Secretary powers to detain, without trial, any person believed likely to threaten the safety of the realm. Other leaders of the BUF were also interned, including Mosley. The BUF was dissolved and all of their publications were banned on 30 May 1940. Norah remained interned until February 1942. She kept close ties with Mosely and later connected with even more radical fascists, including holocaust denier Arnold Leese. Norah and Dudley moved to Twickenham, and after Dudley died Norah spent her final years in what historian Patrick Maume describes as 'embittered proximity to her son and his family'.[20]

Norah died in Middlesex Hospital on 2 March 1961. She did not leave any archival papers behind. Norah's granddaughter, Angela McPherson, who lived with her grandmother for four years as a child, has researched and written about Norah. Along with her own daughter, Susan McPherson, Angela self-published a biography about the complex and challenging life history of Norah Elam.[21]

'It almost seemed to me as I lay in prison, and during this week when I lay in bed, after my release, that speeches, whether inciting or not, should now be done away with. I was so far in agreement with the Government who have imprisoned General Drummond and myself for making speeches, because it seemed to me that we required no more words, and that deeds are the jewels in our crown.

Now, I would say a word or two about incitement. You know that the charge upon which the General and I were tried was incitement. But it is not we who incite, it is the Government. It always has been the Government, and it always will be the Government. Look back upon the career of this Union. See the little deeds to which women were incited growing more and more, until to-day two thousand police are bidden out to stop a handful of women presenting a petition to the King. I speak in ironical terms when I say "handful." That is what some of the newspapers say. The whole point is the irony of the thing. If we are a handful, think of the power there is in that handful. I never remember such a scene outside the monarch's palace in this country. Most of us have lived in the reigns of three monarchs, and nothing of this kind has ever happened.

I heard an official at Scotland Yard, holding a high position there, speaking to a friend the other day, and comparing our movement to the Fenian movement. But I can tell him wherein it is more powerful than the Fenian movement. Those men never brought the law into disrepute. They would go into the courts and listen to the rubbish talked by the prejudiced judge; listen to the verdict given by the packed jury, and then serve their sentences.

I am not in the least disparaging these men. I only want to point out to the Government spies, who may be present this afternoon, that there has never been anything like this Movement, and that the Government cannot crush it. To those of you present in this hall to-day, who are the spies of the Government, I say to you, go tell your masters what you have heard.

I want also to couple my praises for my colleague, Miss Grace Roe, with those of the Chairman. I have been in close touch with her since the last raid, and I want to pay my tribute to her. If one is to be picked out of the galaxy of gems in this wonderful Union, I think, during the last year, the name of Grace Roe stands very prominent.

I could tell you things which perhaps none of you know, because I, being constantly with her, have seen it, how perhaps for some days she would have no food at all, working till two and three in the morning, and many times all night; going about her duties always with a light heart, always with her eyes fixed on the one thing, inspiring us who were fortunate enough to work under her. I wish I could convey to you what this great woman has been to us during that time.

I want to say that her trial and her fight is in keeping with all that she has shown us in the last year. I remember her saying to me, "I am not going to rely upon speaking when I go into the dock. I am no speaker, but I shall take other ways." And yet you see she was given a voice and words, eloquent words, to make her fight, and to bring that Court into disrepute and ridicule.

Now, I want to tell you a little of my prison experiences. They are amusing and were interesting to me. I adopted the course of refusing to undress, or wash, or eat, or drink, or do anything except that which I wished to do; and I lay upon my bed in my clothes from the moment I was taken there.

Then I had a visit from the chaplain. I had not seen him before. He said[,] "Good morning, Mrs Fox!" I said, "You hypocrite! and you torturer! You disgrace the Master you represent. Get out of my cell." I never saw him again. And then I saw two doctors, and every time they came in I told them the same thing, that they were torturers and ruffians, and if they did not get out of my cell I would get up and strike them.

When they took my fingerprints I smashed every window in my cell with that useful implement—the heel of my boot. Everything smashable was smashed. Then the Governor came in, and he said, "Norah Dacre Fox, you are reported for doing this, that, and the other, and you will now be sentenced to seven days' close confinement and bread and water diet." As I was already in close confinement and was eating nothing at all, this was preposterous. That was the last I saw of the Governor until I was going away. These were my tactics in prison, and you know that I was eventually released.

I had gone into prison for the first time, knowing nothing of it. I shall never forget the atmosphere of the place. For us Suffragettes, what does it matter! Wherever we are our surroundings touch us not at all; but it was the other women; the ordinary prisoners; it was the way those women are spoken to. It was the look in the eyes of the prisoner who came to wait in my cell— that frightened, hunted look!

Here in the 20th century men can still conceive that this is civilisation and they are prepared to go on with the present system, which no words can describe. Whoever gets into that prison, perhaps people not all bad, are likely to be turned out dangerous criminals.

So far as I am concerned, I remember the words of Ernest Jones the Chartist.[22] He said, "I went into prison a Chartist. I came out a revolutionary." I went into prison a Militant Suffragette. I came out fifty militants rolled into one.

I learnt a verse out of the Bible when I was in prison, which I am going to repeat to you this afternoon. St Paul says to the Romans: "I am persuaded that neither life nor death, neither angels nor powers, nor principalities, nor things present, nor things to come, nor height nor depth, nor any other creature, can separate us from that which we believe to be right."[23]

FIVE

Sarah Purser

1848–1943

Speech at the twenty-fifth anniversary of An Túr Gloine
Shelbourne Hotel, Dublin

19 JANUARY 1928

*'Ireland would undoubtedly now be the greatest
centre of religious art in the world.'*

The Celtic Revival, which emerged in the late nineteenth century, was most evident in Ireland through a restored interest in Celtic languages, mythology and history. The campaign to achieve Irish independence was accompanied with a search for national identity. This period witnessed the formation of the Gaelic Athletic Association; the establishment of the Gaelic League; and the emergence of the Irish Literary Revival. The focus on national identity was also evident in Irish art including stained-glass windows, created by Irish artists depicting Irish iconography. Sarah Purser was the driving force behind the successful production of unique Irish stained-glass windows which now adorn notable buildings across Ireland including the Abbey Theatre and St. Enda's School.[1] The production of Irish themed and produced stained glass can still be found much further afield in America, Canada and as far as New Zealand.

Sarah Purser was born on 22 March 1848 in the port town of Kingstown, now Dun Laoghaire, in south county Dublin. She was the third of eight children born to Benjamin and Anne Purser (née Mallet). Purser's family home was in Dungarvan, county Waterford, where she was raised. Her father was a prosperous brewer and flour miller. Sarah benefitted from a first-class education, although being female she was barred from attending Trinity College Dublin as her brothers did.[2] She was sent to a finishing school in Switzerland, the Institution Évangélique de Montmirail, from 1861 to 1863 where she first displayed a deep interest in and a fine talent for painting. Purser exhibited her first painting at the Royal Hibernian Academy (RHA) in 1872, and the following year she enrolled in the Metropolitan School of Art in Dublin where she studied for three years.

Just one year after Purser began her studies at the School of Art, her father's business failed. Benjamin Purser went bankrupt and he left Ireland in disgrace. Benjamin moved to America; Sarah never saw him again and he died in Carolina in 1899. Purser settled in Dublin with her mother, in what the esteemed author Elizabeth Coxhead described as very modest terms, 'letting it be known that she no longer expected any friends to call on them'.[3] During this time Purser won a Royal Dublin Society (RDS) landscape-painting prize. She initially depended on her brothers financially, but she resolved to become financially independent. She accepted a gift of £30 from her brothers that enabled her to further her studies in Paris for six months during 1878 and 1879. She attended the Académie Julian, a private art academy established in 1868 as an alternative to the official École des Beaux-Arts. The Académie Julian admitted women to a ladies' section, and Purser mixed with a progressive group of female artists from France, Greece, Russia and Scandinavia.

Purser returned to Dublin and rented a studio at 2 Leinster Street. In 1880, she secured a profitable commission to paint Miss Jane L'Estrange of Sligo. During a social occasion at the L'Estrange home, Lady Georgina Gore-Booth was introduced to Purser. Lady Georgina was so impressed with the painting that she commissioned Purser to paint a portrait of her two eldest daughters, Eva and Constance Gore-Booth. Within weeks Purser arranged to paint Eva, then ten years of age, and Constance (later Countess Markievicz), who was then twelve.[4] As a testament to the artistic merit of this painting, it was sold by Christie's for €240,000 at a public auction of the contents of Lissadell House in 2003. Currently, in 2022, the painting remains on public display at The Merrion Hotel on Upper Merrion Street in Dublin.

Purser had only recently taken up portraiture to earn a living. She maintained that painting the portrait of Eva and Constance was a defining moment in her artistic career. In a witty exchange, Purser described how after completing the Gore-Booth commission, demand for her paintings soared, and she 'went through the aristocracy like the measles. Then I attacked the English, and to this day you will find vestiges of the outbreak on the walls of the stately homes.'[5] Purser had a positive impact on the two Gore-Booth girls, who undoubtedly viewed this young independent woman as an exciting role model. Eva and Constance both established a friendship with Purser that was to last throughout their adult lives. Constance later studied art at the Académie Julian, no doubt encouraged to attend because Purser had studied there.

Coxhead describes how Purser was 'enormously industrious, she made money, and banished the ghost of the poverty-stricken years'.[6] As well as her artistic talent, Purser developed an accomplished business mind. In 1886, the Guinness brewing company became a joint stock company. The Purser family was connected with the establishment of the famous brewery. Benjamin Purser's great-grandfather, John Purser, came to Ireland in 1776 to brew porter. His son and grandson, both also named John, became brew masters at St James's Gate Brewery, where they introduced porter and stout and became partners.[7] Due to their family connections, the Pursers were offered the opportunity of investing in Guinness stock early. Purser invested all the savings she could muster, which was an astute and very profitable investment. She continued to invest money on the stock exchange throughout her life, and by the time of her death she had amassed a fortune. Coxhead observes that Purser had 'the largest fortune, it is fair to say, that any Irishwoman has ever amassed by her own unaided efforts'.[8]

7. Sarah Purser by William Osbourne, Portrait of a Lady, 1887.

Having become financially secure, Purser moved her studio to a premises at 11 Harcourt Terrace. Her biographer John O'Grady notes that 'she had a niche in Dublin social, cultural and patriotic circles. From 1881 her studio at 2 Leinster Street attracted callers as lively as her Parisian set, and on her move to 11 Harcourt Terrace in 1886 they followed.'[9] By then Purser was in high demand among the elite families of Ireland and Britain seeking portraits of family members. In the period from 1887 to 1890, she had more portraits exhibited in the prestigious halls of the RHA than any other artist, a significant accomplishment for any painter but all the more noteworthy for a woman in a then male-dominated environment. In recognition of her accomplishments, she was elected to honorary academician status of the RHA in 1890; women were then not granted full membership status.

Purser was by now highly esteemed both as an artist and as an art critic. She was appointed to the committee for an RHA exhibition of modern continental and British art in 1899. Through this appointment, she met Edward Martyn, who lent some of his collection for the exhibition. Martyn was a dramatist, a patron of the arts and a nationalist; he was also 'an extremely devout catholic'.[10] From the 1890s, Martyn had been writing and speaking about the poor standard of religious architecture and adornment in Ireland. When he attempted to order stained-glass windows for his parish church, he was appalled at the styles and quality on offer from factories in Birmingham and Munich. Purser was particularly aware that mass-produced stained glass was being imported for use in churches and many other major buildings across Ireland. She supported the idea of national self-sufficiency for the production of stained glass that would not only improve the standard of such art but also provide work for struggling Irish artists. It is 'estimated that at the turn of the 20th century there were probably 100 stained glass artists living and working in Ireland'.[11] Purser and Martyn collaborated with T. P. Gill, secretary of the Department of Agriculture and Technical Instruction, on a scheme for a Dublin-based stained glass workshop. Purser would finance and manage the workshop. The group planned to hire Alfred Child, a tutor in stained glass at the Metropolitan School of Art, to supervise the work on site.

Purser was extremely generous in giving time and energy to promote other artists. In 1901, she organised a special exhibition to promote the work of two artists: Nathaniel Hone and John B. Yeats. Purser believed that both artists were being neglected in Ireland and she was driven to showcase their work. Hone was a gifted seascape artist, and Purser believed that he 'was not receiving the recognition he deserved; indeed, he had become so discouraged by Ireland's persistent neglect that he had ceased to exhibit, and almost ceased to paint'.[12] John B. Yeats was a talented portrait artist, but he had failed to make a living from his work.[13] Yeats had returned to live in Dublin in 1900 after his wife, Susan (née Pollexfen), died. Purser rented a small exhibition space at the Royal Society of Antiquaries' rooms at 6 St Stephen's Green and organised for Hone and Yeats to submit 40 of their canvases for display.[14] The exhibition was displayed from 21 October to 3 November 1901. Purser funded the showing and compiled the catalogue herself.[15]

The exhibition was destined to chart a new course for Irish art. The young art dealer Hugh Lane, a nephew of Lady Augusta Gregory, attended. Although only 26 years of age, Lane had already amassed a fortune from his art dealership in London.[16] Lane was an expert in the Old Masters and had not, until his attendance at Purser's exhibition, showed interest in contemporary Irish art. He was so impressed by the work of Hone and Yeats that he instantly purchased a number of their paintings. Coxhead declares that 'from this show, too, arose his [Lane's] dream of forming a personal collection of modern painting, and then presenting it to Ireland, which would build a fitting gallery to receive it'.[17] Purser became Lane's 'principal collaborator in trying to realise [this dream] during the next fourteen years'.[18] In 1902, Lane organised an exhibition in the RHA, and the following year he was appointed to the board of the National Gallery of Ireland.[19]

In 1903, Purser's vision for a Dublin-based stained glass studio and workshop was to be realised. An Túr Gloine (The Tower of Glass) cooperative opened on New Year's Day, a fitting day to designate a new beginning for Irish stained glass production. The site chosen was 24 Upper Pembroke Street. The speech in this section is Purser's first ever public address, which she gave on the 25th anniversary of An Túr Gloine. Her speech was later published in a celebratory anniversary pamphlet, a copy of which is held in the National Library of Ireland.[20] The pamphlet includes a range of testimonials from members of the religious hierarchy praising the quality and beauty of the cooperative's stained-glass windows installed in cathedrals and churches in Ireland and abroad. Amongst these testimonials are ones given by Cardinal O'Donnell, Archbishop of Armagh; the Most Rev. C. F. D'Arcy, Archbishop of Armagh, Primate of All Ireland; the Most Rev. Dr White, Bishop of Limerick; and Rev. T. H. Brewin, rector of St Bartholomew's, Ottawa, Canada.

Other testimonials provide evidence of the wide reach that windows designed by An Túr Gloine artists had. William Ferguson from New Zealand noted, 'the designs I consider excellent, and both in design and execution your artists and workpeople are to be congratulated.'[21] Ferguson was an engineer and secretary-treasurer of the Wellington Harbour Board; he was also one of the earliest proponents of crematoriums. Ferguson had studied at Trinity College Dublin, and he commissioned windows from

Purser in memory of his mother-in-law, Jane Ann Moorhouse, and his daughter, Louisa Sefton Ferguson, who had died in 1910 as a child of only eight years old. The windows were installed at the Karori Crematorium and Chapel in Wellington, New Zealand. The building is now listed as a category one heritage site and remains adorned with windows from the An Túr Gloine cooperative: two windows are by the artist Wilhelmina Geddes and three by Michael Healy.[22]

8. Stained-glass window depicting the Passion at St. Brendan's Cathedral, Loughrea, County Galway. Design by Sarah Purser and glass painting by Alfred Ernest Child, created in An Túr Gloine. Photographer Andreas F. Borchert.

In 1909, Purser and her brother John Mallet Purser, the Regius Professor of Medicine at Trinity College Dublin, took a lease on an eighteenth-century mansion, Mespil House. This was to be her home until her death. The house was situated in five acres of secluded grounds with a stream and a duck pond, surrounded by lavish trees. Mespil House was located in an urban district of Ballsbridge, not far from the canal. It was perfectly positioned for Purser to host salons on the second Tuesday of every month, where large numbers of artists, authors and the cultural elite would gather to discuss and debate contemporary issues. Purser's salons were at the centre of cultural activity in Dublin, and she continued to host the gatherings for over thirty years. In 1912, Purser was elected to the Mansion House committee, and she began to plan in earnest for a modern art gallery in Dublin. In 1914, she was appointed to the board of governors and guardians of the National Gallery of Ireland.

The following year Purser was shaken by the loss of a dear friend and collaborator. At 3.25 p.m. on 7 May 1915, a telegram arrived in Cunard's Liverpool office; it read, 'Lusitania torpedoed off Kinsale. Has sunk.'[23] The great liner was attacked by a German U-boat and sank just off the Irish coast. Nearly 1,200 people had lost their lives. Irish cultural circles were devastated when news came that Hugh Lane was on board. In 1912, Lane had donated a large collection of his paintings to Dublin on the understanding that a permanent gallery would be built to house them. The Municipal Gallery of Modern Art had opened in Dublin in 1908 at a temporary premises on Harcourt Street. Dublin Corporation did not believe the gallery was financially sustainable and therefore they would not agree to oversee management. A suitable gallery did not materialise, and in desperation Lane removed a number of his paintings from Dublin in 1913. He lent the collection, including works by Degas, Renoir, Monet and Manet, to the National Gallery in London. Later in 1913, he made a will bequeathing these works to the London gallery on his death.

Lane did not survive the German attack, and his body was never recovered. Shortly after his death, a codicil to his will was discovered in his desk at the National Gallery of Ireland. Lane had written the codicil in 1914, reversing his decision to grant any paintings to London and instead granting his entire collection to the city of Dublin. The codicil was signed by Lane, but because it was not witnessed it was deemed invalid under British law. The collection housed at the gallery in London remained there. A dispute over ownership of the collection would rage between the galleries in Dublin and London until 1959, when it was agreed that the Lane bequest would be shown in Dublin, on loan, every five years. In 1993, the agreement was updated and a decision was made that 31 of the 39 paintings in the Lane collection would remain in Ireland.[24] In 2013, four more paintings from the Lane collection were returned to Dublin.

The Lane controversy highlighted that there was little or no state funding for securing prestigious art work for public display in Ireland. In response, Purser established the Friends of the National Collections of Ireland (FNCI) in 1924. The FNCI was formed as a voluntary organisation with the aim of preserving Ireland's artistic heritage. The organisation raises funds to buy works of art and objects of artistic importance to donate to national museums, art galleries and libraries across the 32 counties of Ireland. The FNCI remains active to this day, describing themselves as

'Ireland's oldest arts charity', having donated over 800 works of art to public galleries and museums across the country.[25] Also in 1924, Purser became a full member of the RHA, the first woman to achieve this honour.

In 1928, Purser discovered that Charlemont House on Parnell Square was being vacated by a government department. She contacted the Taoiseach, W. T. Cosgrave, advising him that the building would make an excellent public gallery. Cosgrave agreed and the building was formally presented to Dublin Corporation for the purpose. The following year work began on renovating the gardens and extending the house to accommodate a gallery. In 1933, Charlemont House first opened as the Dublin Municipal Gallery of Modern Art. It is now officially called the Hugh Lane Gallery and houses an impressive collection, including a number of works by Purser and stained glass examples. Purser retired from An Túr Gloine in 1940, by then she was in her nineties. Artist Catherine O'Brien took over directorship until the workshop was destroyed by fire in the 1950s. The stained glass cooperative had produced thousands of windows with most remaining in public and religious buildings across Ireland and numerous other countries to this day. An Túr Gloine saw the best Irish artists through its doors, including Evie Hone, Beatrice Elvery, Wilhelmina Geddes, Michael Healy and Harry Clarke.

Sarah Purser died of a stroke on 7 August 1943 at the age of 95. She died at her home in Mespil House, supposedly 'following an argument with President Douglas Hyde about the quality of a portrait of him that had appeared on a stamp'.[26] She was interred at Mount Jerome Cemetery in Harold's Cross, Dublin. Her headstone is engraved with the most fitting epitaph: *Fortis et Strenua* (Strong and Vigorous). It was only when funeral arrangements had been completed that a friend realised that Purser's funeral would take place on the second Tuesday of the month, the scheduled day of her monthly salon. As Coxhead observed, Purser 'entertained her circle to the last'.[27] Mespil House was demolished in 1951. Three rococo ceilings and wall ornaments were removed from the house and placed in the president's residence at Áras an Uachtaráin. A plaque in honour of Purser is now attached to the wall of her previous studio at 11 Harcourt Terrace.

On 30 October 1975, an episode of *Irish Men and Irish Women* focussed on Sarah Purser. It was presented by Ronnie Drew, and Purser was portrayed by Geraldine Plunkett.[28] The series aired on RTÉ television from 1975 until 1977 and examined notable Irish people in history who were, as producer Joe O'Donnell described, 'mainly unsung heroes . . . not unknown, but outside the orthodoxy of our national pantheon'.[29] In 2020, An Post launched a series of postage stamps celebrating five pioneering Irish women in the areas of Fashion, Film, Aviation, Athletics and Art.

Sarah Purser featured as did Carmel Snow, Editor-in-Chief of *Harper's Bazaar* magazine; Maureen O'Hara, renowned Hollywood actor; Lillian Bland, the first woman to design, build and fly an aeroplane; and Maeve Kyle, the first woman to represent Ireland at the Olympics and Ireland's first triple Olympian. Purser would not have disputed the art used to depict her on the stamp: they were her own self-portraits.

Sarah Purser is not a household name. However, it is almost certain that every day, somewhere in the world, a person looks in admiration at a stained-glass window produced through her efforts. Purser's speech in this section is a vivid reminder of just one of her many accomplishments for the sake of Irish art and culture.

'I . . . not only am unaccustomed to public speaking, but this is my very first attempt in that line, and I hope you will allow me courage, if not discretion, or consideration for you.

But it seems too good an occasion to miss, for explaining one or two matters, so with your leave I go on:

First it may be asked in what way the work done in Pembroke Street differs from that done in the ordinary stained glass manufactory . . . Well in these shops the window is standardized, it is divided up among a number of nameless employees who each draw or paint a certain part to sample as it were. This method led to a sometimes skilful but always tiresome and dead uniformity, devoid of all personality, just *safe* at its best in style and colour. At its worst we know it too well.

Now *we* hold each window should be in all its artistic parts the work of one individual artist, the glass chosen and painted by the same mind and hand that made the design and drew the cartoon, in fact a bit of stained glass should be a work of free art as much as any other painting or picture. Thus with us, each person gets a window or mosaic panel to do, and does it alone all through according to his own ideas. The Co-operation goes no further than supplying the craft means to do this; for stained glass which Mr. Chesterton calls "the thing that is more intoxicating than all the wines of the world" is unluckily the least handy of the fine arts to make.[30]

You cannot do it in a romantic studio with silk cushions, but must work in a grubby work shop, and must have kilns, and a large stock of glass and lead, etc., and someone to cut and glaze, etc., for you. All this is troublesome and expensive, and it is obvious no young artist uncertain of his orders could embark on it. Hence the "Co-operative"—for though only legally established this last year, our system has always been the same. . . .

Our grief is that we are not 125 years old instead of 25. Think of the chance Ireland had then. *All* the Catholic Churches and great ecclesiastical establishments to be built through Ireland—almost all the Protestant Churches either to be built or remodelled, and all the glass, altars, furnishings of all sorts to be got.

A people full of genuine piety, ready out of their poverty to give unstintingly, and gifted in the most remarkable way for decorative and manipulative art. Well, we know the result—if only the architects and Schools of Art and the clergy had joined hands and worked up to this enormous demand Ireland would undoubtedly now be the greatest centre of religious art in the world. No other Nation was quite in the same fortunate position. It seems a simple idea to grasp, but the usual Great Enchantment fell on us, and the chance was lost, and in the matter of glass the current was set so firmly towards Birmingham and Munich that most of our energy has to go persuading people against bringing in a poorer art than they could get here.

It has been a bit disappointing that the Churches have not been more generally enthusiastic in realising we were doing their work, that we should have to look abroad for orders, and to our sorrow to discourage many obviously talented young artists from joining us. . . . Still we have held on, and have a lot of work to our account, our last order is numbered (637) in our books. We have glass in a Museum at Detroit, in Canada, New Zealand, in India, in Smyrna—(think of glazing the "Seven Churches of Asia Minor!") in the States, in England and Scotland, besides the large secular work in glass and Mosaic in Singapore. Our work is in every county in Ireland, in all sorts of remote little spots. We purpose now, since motors and busses can easily bring folk to all of these, to get a list of them for the Tourist, and so hope to spread the light.

I myself, though I hope I am some judge of glass, am not a stained glass worker in the sense *we* give to the word, as I explained it before. My only output is a tiny window in the porch at Loughrea, something in the nature of a curiosity. I designed . . . some of our early windows, but though the real glass artists obligingly painted them, we never found it satisfactory. Now I would not have troubled you with these personal matters only that it is greatly on my mind to correct a misapprehension I very often come upon, and which annoys me very much—that the artists in 24 Pembroke Street are in some way my pupils and under my directions. This, of course, is entirely not so. They are each born with their own imagination and sense of colour, and learned to draw before specialising in stained glass, and have each developed their technique on lines of their own for handling the material, and are not interfered with by anybody, and, as far as is possible, in this rather confusing business they get the credit or blame personally for their work. . . .

Our relations with our patrons have been most happy. The "Bishops and curates, and congregations committed to their charge," have been kind and satisfied. I have drawers full of testimonials and expressions of their approval.
. .

On that 1st January, 25 years ago, we had our first tea party. . . The shop was quite new, and, oh, so cold! We gathered round the kiln and drank champagne out of tea cups—it didn't taste very well, and we betook ourselves to the teapot. Now the much grander and snugger tea you are giving us must be getting cold, so we can all only ask you to believe us sincerely grateful and very much touched and heartened by this expression of your liking for us, and this testimony of your appreciation of the work we have done, and which we will go on the more courageously doing for the memory of this evening.'[31]

SIX

Margaret (Gretta) Cousins

1878–1954

Speech from the dock
Madras Court, India

10 December 1932

'A challenge to every believer in free speech.'

On 7 November 1878, Margaret (Gretta) Gillespie was born in Boyle, a small town at the foot of the Curlew Mountains in county Roscommon. She was named after her mother, Margaret, but she was known by the name Gretta. She was the eldest of 15 children in a Protestant family. Gretta had a most unremarkable start to life. Yet in 1932 she gave an impassioned speech from a courtroom dock in India. She had been arrested for addressing a public meeting in response to Mahatma Gandhi's call for a civil disobedience movement. Gretta was subsequently sentenced to one year in Vellore Jail for women. She was no stranger to prisons: by that point in her life, Gretta had already spent periods incarcerated in prisons in Ireland and in England. Historian Jyoti Atwal has done insightful research that has drawn attention to the social and political reforms led by Gretta in India. Atwal notes that Gretta 'was more than an Irish suffragette or a humanitarian worker or an anti-colonial activist in India,' and she was 'shaped in part by the Celtic revival in Dublin'.[1]

Gretta excelled at school. She describes getting 'a good sound elementary education in a co-educational National School'.[2] She won a competitive scholarship to attend Victoria High School for Girls in Derry. Gretta boarded at the school for four years and passed her matriculation there. The school, founded in 1877, educated only Protestant girls. While

61

religious segregation in education was common across Ireland, such segregation in Ulster 'had the effect of reinforcing already deep divisions in society'.[3] The Gillespie family held strong unionist beliefs, and Gretta's schooling should have fortified ideals of Irish unity with Britain. However, Gretta supported the plight of Irish nationalism from a young age and showed concern for those who suffered at the hands of British Imperialism.

On completing her secondary education in 1898, Gretta moved to Dublin, where she attended the Royal Irish Academy of Music, graduating with a Bachelor of Music in 1902. She was an avid reader all of her life and wrote poetry from a young age. Her poetry was first published in the pages of the *Daily Express*, shortly after she moved to Dublin. A friend introduced her to the writer and journalist George Russell (Æ). Gretta became a regular visitor to Russell's house first in Coulson Avenue and later when he moved to Rathgar Avenue. She mixed with an eclectic group of intellectuals from that point.

Gretta and Russell shared similar interests, including in theosophy, a New Age esoteric religion which combines science, eastern religions and spirituality. The Theosophical Society attracted members of the Celtic Revival, including W. B. Yeats and Eva Gore-Booth. Annie Besant, whom Gretta mentions in her speech, became president of the Theosophical Society in 1907. Besant was initiated into the society through her concern for gaining Irish Independence. Like many other theosophists, Gretta experimented with seances and astrology as well as automatic writing. In 1899, Gretta met James Cousins, a young writer from Belfast, at the Annual Conference of the Wesleyan Methodist Church in Ireland. In their joint memoir published in 1950, the couple described how they formed an instant bond. They married in 1903, shortly after Gretta graduated. Gretta was intent on remaining financially independent and she worked part-time as a music teacher.

James worked as a clerk in Dublin, but his real passion was writing. He immersed himself in the Irish literary revival movement in Dublin. He befriended leading authors of a vibrant literary circle in Dublin, including Russell, W. B. Yeats and Edward Martyn. In 1901, James gave Russell's play *Deirdre* to the Fay brothers, William and Frank.[4] The Fay brothers established the Ormonde Dramatic Company in 1891 and later the Irish National Dramatic Company. The brothers planned to stage *Deirdre* at St Teresa's Temperance Hall in Clarendon Street in 1902 with their new company. Historian Diarmaid Ferriter describes this as 'a turning point' in William Fay's career.[5] Indeed, the plan caught the attention of Maud Gonne, who approached the Fays to stage a performance of Yeats' and Lady Gregory's *Kathleen Ni Houlihan*.[6] The two plays were staged each night from 2 to 5 April 1902. The respected theatrical producer and playwright, Tomás Mac Anna, noted that it was this 'humble production in St Teresa's Temperance Hall which led to the founding of the Abbey', Ireland's national theatre.[7] In this way James Cousins 'made a significant contribution to the formation of the Irish National Theatre Society, and on its foundation in 1903 he became a committee member'.[8] The theatre society staged *The Sword of Dermot* in 1903, a play written by James with the music composed by Gretta.[9]

Gretta and James were vegetarians; Gretta was appointed honorary secretary of the Irish Vegetarian Society upon its establishment in 1905. She was invited to speak at a vegetarian conference in Manchester in late 1906. While there, she first encountered the National Council of Women, who were holding a conference in the city. Gretta describes this event as life-altering, saying, 'it made me aware of the injustices and grievances which were taken for granted as the natural fate of my sex. Here I found a large organisation already challenging the continuance of inequality of opportunity between man and woman.'[10] Gretta returned to Dublin intent on becoming involved in the suffrage movement there. She met with Anna and Thomas Haslam who had established the Dublin Women's Suffrage Association, which later became the Irish Women's Suffrage and Local Government Association (IWSLGA). These organisations are best described as suffragist, pursuing votes for women through constitutional and non-violent means. Members lobbied government for women's suffrage through petitions, sought support from individual politicians, held suffrage parades and raised awareness for women's rights through public meetings and speeches. Gretta joined the IWSLGA, but she quickly became despondent by the lack of results achieved by the organisation.

In July 1907, Gretta and James met and befriended Annie Besant when they attended a convention of the Theosophical Society in London. This friendship would have life-changing implications for the couple.[11] By this time suffragette militancy had begun to take hold in Britain. Members of the Women's Social and Political Union (WSPU), founded by Emmeline Pankhurst with her daughter Christabel, began staging somewhat extreme protests in their campaign to achieve votes for women. Militant action included smashing the windows of public buildings and placing incendiary devices at key sites. Gretta and political activist Hanna Sheehy Skeffington took action and formed the first Irish suffragette organisation, the Irish Women's Franchise League (IWFL) in 1908.[12] Historian Frances Clarke observes that 'as one of its most influential and high-profile members she [Gretta] regularly spoke at its open-air meetings in Dublin and on suffrage tours of the country, irrespective of the occasional hostility which at times greeted her addresses.'[13]

The activities of the IWFL began with a low-key approach, but they stepped up their militancy when the campaign for Irish home rule intensified. In the 1910 British general elections of January and December, the Irish Parliamentary Party (IPP) held the balance of power and formed a government with the Liberal Party under Prime Minister Henry Asquith. The main objective of the Irish Party was to achieve home rule. Gretta and Hanna demanded that female suffrage be included in the terms of any home rule bill sought. The leader of the IPP, John Redmond, made it clear that he would not support the enfranchisement of women, either in the House of Commons or in Irish self-government, in the event that Ireland received home rule. Redmond's colleague John Dillon MP was even more forthright. Dillon asserted that 'women's suffrage will . . . be the ruin of our Western civilisation. It will destroy the home, challenging the headship of man, laid down by God.'[14] Members of the IWFL became even more committed in their campaign.

Gretta and Hanna maintained close links with the WSPU. In November 1910, Gretta was one of six Irish women who attended a parliament of women protest in London. The WSPU organised a number of such protests to coincide with parliamentary debates on women's suffrage at Westminster. After the gathering Gretta was arrested for smashing windows at the prime minister's residence on Downing Street. She served her first prison sentence of one month in Holloway Prison that November. She returned to Dublin, where she engaged in more intense militancy. Gretta was jailed again for one month in January 1913 for breaking windows at Dublin Castle. During her incarceration in Tullamore Gaol she went on hunger strike, seeking status as a political prisoner. Hanna and Gretta were fully supported by their husbands, Francis Sheehy Skeffington and James Cousins, who jointly established the *Irish Citizen* as the official journal of the Irish suffrage movement and not just the voice of the IWFL.[15]

In June 1913, Gretta and James Cousins were forced to leave Ireland for financial reasons. The couple moved to Liverpool where Gretta continued to support the suffrage movement, joining local groups, and contributing articles to the *Irish Citizen*. She also represented the IWFL in England when required. Gretta and James became immersed in the work of the Theosophical Society in Liverpool and were encouraged to move to India, the spiritual home of theosophy, with the society's headquarters based in Adyar. In October 1915, the couple set sail for India, where they were met by Annie Besant, then president of the Theosophical Society. Besant had been a key player in the women's trade union movement in England. She had exposed the dangerous working conditions and meagre pay of women employed in the match company Bryant and May's and is credited with inspiring women to strike in what is infamously known as the match-girl strike of 1888. It is apparent from the membership records of the Theosophical Society that after Besant became president the English section of the society became dominated by women.[16]

The couple immediately immersed themselves in social reform movements in India. Gretta began teaching in a school at Madanapalle and James took up a post as literary sub-editor of *New India* before he became principal of the Theosophical College.[17] Atwal observes that Gretta 'had a long political career in India where she provided leadership to the Indian women's political rights movement by carving out their role in the freedom struggle'.[18]

In 1916, Gretta was appointed as the first non-Indian member of the Indian Women's University at Poona, the first women's university in India. In 1917, she co-founded, with Annie Besant and the support of Indian women, the Women's Indian Association, a non-sectarian feminist movement. Gretta acted as honorary secretary of the association and editor of their monthly journal *Stri Dharma* for a number of years. In 1919, while working at Madanapalle, Gretta met Rabindranath Tagore, the writer, social reformer and close friend of Gandhi. Tagore was awarded the Nobel Prize in Literature in 1913. He was knighted in 1915, 'but within a few years he resigned the honour as a protest against British policies in India.'[19] While at Madanapalle, Tagore translated his Bengali song 'Jana Gana Mana' into English, 'Morning Song'. He asked Gretta to compose the musical accompaniment. The song would later become the national anthem of the Republic of India. Atwal highlights how 'this song was a moment of integration for the Cousins – they felt that they were "some kinds [sic] of agents in the Karma of India".'[20]

That same year, on 13 April 1919, the Jallianwala Bagh massacre occurred when British troops fired on a crowd of approximately 10,000 unarmed Indian people without warning. At the end of World War One, the British government extended repressive controls across India through legislation known as the Rowlatt Acts. The legislation included the right for political cases to be tried without a jury and for people suspected of political agitation to be interned without trial.[21] Not surprisingly, people across India, especially in the Punjab region, resented such draconian legislation. Many people in India, like those in Ireland, expected that by supporting Britain in their war effort, they would be granted some form of self-government or home rule after the war had ended. In reality, people in India were being placed under greater control by British authorities.

In response to the Rowlatt Acts, Gandhi initiated a non-violent protest that included calling for a general one-day strike across India. A series of riots and violence followed in Punjab and Delhi. Brig. Gen. Reginald Dyer was tasked with restoring order, and many new measures were introduced, including a ban on public gatherings. The 13 April was the Sikh New Year's Day, and people gathered to mark the event at Jallianwala Bagh in Amritsar, a large enclosed public area with one narrow exit. It seems most likely that those gathered were not aware of the new public order measures. Dyer mobilised 90 soldiers and two armoured cars to disperse the crowd. The troops, under Dyer's orders, opened fire on the crowd without any warning, releasing at least 1,650 rounds of ammunition over a ten-minute period, during which they reloaded a second round. A total of 379 people were killed and 1,500 people were wounded. Martial law was declared, which was backdated to 30 March, ensuring that anyone arrested after that date could be tried by military court.[22] The massacre incited many more people to join the nationalist movement in India.

From this point, Cousins became a supporter of Gandhi's philosophy of non-cooperation with the British. She was headmistress of the National Girls School in Mangalore from 1919 to 1920. Her book *The Awakening of Asian Womanhood* was published by a press in Madras in 1922. The large volume was a compilation of many articles she had published in newspapers and journals over her years in India, during which she engaged in, in her publisher's words, 'the campaign in India for the bringing of the direct power of women into all departments of public life'.[23] In the volume, Gretta makes a plea to allow women's full participation across all aspects of politics and society in India, arguing that:

> No movement for national, moral, or social progress can attain its true and maximum success if it studies the well-being and works through the agency of one sex only or primarily . . . a little thought enables one to trace many of the problems needing solution back to the failure to recognise the vital importance to India of the service which can be rendered to her only by her women.[24]

In 1923, Gretta was invited to take up the role as an Honorary District Magistrate of Saidapet Court of Madras, overseeing mainly civil cases for a year. In 1926, along with Besant, she organised the first All-India Women's Conference, which took place in Poona in 1927. Atwal notes that this conference and the Women's Indian Association 'continue to offer extraordinary service to women in modern day India'.[25]

By the time of her arrest in 1932, for violating the regulations against public speaking and public gatherings, Gretta was a well-respected educator and women's activist. As testimony to her commitment to free speech, Gretta insisted on giving a speech from the dock during her trial. In her speech she is scathing of the British control over India which she describes as sinking to the depths of 'oppression and suppression'. It is noteworthy that she does not plea for mercy from the court and instead recounts her many years dedicated to supporting home rule both for India and for Ireland. This is a carefully prepared speech; it was written by Gretta in advance and the text was later included in her joint memoir. There are no accounts of the reaction to her speech in the court, but she was sentenced to one year in prison, no doubt to punish her for her actions but also for her lack of contrition. The fact that she was sentenced to one year ensured that she would be incarcerated at Vellore Jail for women; women from across the Southern States sentenced to any period over three months served their time at Vellore. Other female political leaders were imprisoned at the jail around this time including Rukmini Lakshmipathi who was also jailed for one year for participating in the Salt Satyagraha, a protest against a salt tax imposed by the British authorities in India.

9. Margaret Cousins, cover image on National Woman's Party journal *Equal Rights*, 2 July 1932.

Gretta noted in her speech, that the authorities intended that her incarceration would strike her dumb. While this may initially have had the intended effect, once she was released, she became even more vocal. She gained further national respect after serving her prison sentence for the cause of Indian freedom. Her speech had proved that she was proud to serve her time for this cause. Gretta was elected president of the All-India Women's Conference in 1936, and in her presidential address on 23 December, she expressed her appreciation at being an Irish woman accepted as 'truly one of yourselves'.[26] When India finally gained independence in 1947, her contribution to achieving freedom was officially recognised by the Indian State through a national award. Gretta was unable to celebrate her own achievements or to fully appreciate the new independent state: her health had by then deteriorated. She suffered a series of strokes from the early 1940s that paralysed her until her death ten years later. Gretta died on 1 March 1954 in Adyar. She was out of public life during her final years and cared for at home by James. She was then dependent on financial contributions that she received from the Indian government in appreciation for her many years of service to the country. James died on 20 February 1956 in the Mission Hospital in Madanapalle.

A plaque in honour of Gretta Cousins was placed on her childhood home in Boyle. It states: 'Born in this house 1878 / Died in India 1954 / Irish suffragette / Wife of Irish poet Dr James Cousins / Founder, in 1921, of the All-India Women's Conference/First woman magistrate in India (Madras 1923).' As historian Margaret Ward pointedly notes, 'this was not, however, installed by an Irish body. It was unveiled by the President of the All-India Women's Conference on September 16, 1994, as a means of paying tribute to [Cousins'] work as an activist in India.'[27]

Gretta Cousins published numerous articles and four books during her life, including *The Music of Orient and Occident: Essays Towards Mutual Understandings*, a compilation of her lectures and press articles on music.[28] In 1941, an Indian publisher, Kitabistan, set about publishing a series of books 'relating to problems besetting the path of India's national progress as they have arisen in new complexity and proportions in the throes of the political, cultural and spiritual renaissance'.[29] Gretta was asked to write a book on the women's movement in India, and her volume on *Indian Womanhood Today* was published in 1941. The book was well received, and a revised and enlarged edition was published in 1947.

Her joint autobiography, *We Two Together*, written with her husband was published in 1950, recounting their many political, cultural and personal activities during their lives in Ireland, England and India. The final paragraph concludes:

> And so it happens that, as the signal goes down some distance from [the] terminus, short or long as the distance may be, we realise – one at 77, the other at 72 – that the values of life have a way of arranging themselves in an order that alters, sometimes reverses, the too easily accepted categories of daily life, and one comes face to face with ultimate realities.[30]

Gretta leaves an extraordinary legacy behind, of which her speech in this section is testimony.

'The fact that I am on trial in this court today is no accident. It is the result of seventeen years of intimate living and working with my Indian sisters and brothers. In moving freely with them in attempting to do constructive work, I and my husband learned how exploitation and injustice through foreign rule is crushing them down.

I was a co-worker for Home Rule for years with Annie Besant, and took part in the agitation connected with her internment in this cause. I also shared in formulating the Commonwealth of India Bill. Government repression of organised Congress opinion, the largest representative opinion in India, has become ever more severe since then. I watched it in 1930–31. I reported what I had seen, in New York and Geneva during my visits there in the past eighteen months. In those centres of international opinion I laid bare the dual game Britain is playing; its pretence of making a Constitution to give India freedom, but its determination to hold tight to everything essential to India's self-government. I showed that its demands for unity and social reforms as necessary to swaraj were conditions such as no country had ever complied with. I proved that, instead of freedom, government by Ordinances was designed to break, if possible, the spirit, ruin the health and cripple the resources of all the people of India who are determined to win the political freedom they want.

Representative associations of eighteen countries have deputed me to tell the people here that they "sympathise with them, and that they denounce the rule of violence now imposed on India," as the New York protest meeting expressed it. Now that I return I find that the Ordinances have been turned into law for three years. This is a challenge to every believer in free speech, free political assembly, free press, free picketting [sic], free peaceful self-expression. I adhere to everything I said in public. I reiterate that the Ordinance Bill and Ordinance Law should be made inoperative by everyone ignoring them by nonviolent defiance.

Evidently the Government think me a valuable ally of the Congress when they priced my freedom by bail at thirty thousand rupees. If it is their intention to strike me dumb for a year, are we to deduce that their new Constitution is going to be so unsatisfactory that I must be locked up for all that time to prevent my criticism of it? If this is British justice and democracy, then I am proud to stand here in support of free speech and Indian national freedom, and I am ashamed that English idealism has fallen to the present depths of oppression and suppression.'[31]

SEVEN

Maureen O'Carroll

1913–84

Speech on the transfer of Irish children to the USA for
adoption
Dáil Éireann, Leinster House, Dublin

18 JULY 1956

'Something illegal took place.'

Maureen O'Carroll led an incredible life. A graduate of Galway University,
she trained for the convent and later earned the title of the Irish Labour
Party's first female TD. O'Carroll challenged the political culture of 1950s
Ireland, which was established, in the main, by male politicians. While not
directly involved in culture and arts, O'Carroll would also have the most
surprising influence on Irish popular culture and entertainment. Writer
Mary J. Murphy aptly describes how O'Carroll was 'sometimes called
"Little Mo" in jest, usually by political detractors in Dublin [; however],
the only "little" thing about the mighty powerhouse that was Maureen
McHugh O'Carroll was her stature'.[1]

Maureen was born on Manor Street, on the north side of Dublin city,
on 29 March 1913. She was the eldest of four children born to Michael
and Elizabeth (née O'Dowd) McHugh. Maureen's father played an active
role in the fight for Irish independence and fought during the Easter Rising
in 1916. Journalist and author Ronan McGreevy writes that Maureen
'was one of the first beneficiaries of money raised in the United States
by women during the War of Independence, [1919-21]'.[2] The money
raised established the Irish White Cross fund in February 1921 'to aid
Irish families who were impoverished by the war'.[3] Through this funding,

Maureen attended the Jesus and Mary Convent, Gortnor Abbey in county Mayo, as a boarding student. She excelled in her studies and attended Galway University where she obtained a BA degree in English in 1935. Originally drawn to a religious life through her contact with the convent at Gortnor Abbey, Maureen returned there as a novice nun; however, she later decided this was not the path for her. After graduating from Galway University, she returned to Dublin and became a teacher.

In 1936, Maureen married Gerard O'Carroll, a carpenter, and, as a result of the marriage bar then in place, she was forced to resign from her teaching post. From there, Maureen contributed to Irish society through many other means. The state of emergency in Ireland during World War Two officially ended on 2 September 1946. Shortages of food and fuel continued, so rationing extended into the following decade. The Irish Housewives Association (IHA), established in 1941 under the leadership of Hilda Tweedy and Andreé Sheehy Skeffington, petitioned on a number of issues relating to pricing and distribution of goods and services. This activity caused many women, who were forced out of employment, to become politically active across Ireland. Maureen O'Carroll was one of those women. She co-founded the Lower Prices Council (LPC), which actively lobbied against excessive and unjust prices in the post-war period. The council had two representatives from the IHA, and O'Carroll took on the role of honorary secretary.

After the state of emergency ceased in Ireland, O'Carroll bombarded the Taoiseach's office about the control of prices, earnings and the cost of living generally. On 3 November 1947, after being refused a meeting with the Taoiseach, Éamon de Valera, O'Carroll wrote to him:

> Your letter to Senator L. J. Duffy, intimating that no useful purpose would be served by receiving a Deputation from the above Council, was forwarded to me. The Womens' [sic] National Council of Action has instructed me to write to you urging once again that you receive a Deputation. We feel that since the matters which we wish to discuss with you are of a domestic rather than an academic nature, that a memorandum would not achieve the same purpose.[4]

Her request was again denied.[5] O'Carroll was persistent, and numerous letters from her to the Taoiseach's office remain on record.

O'Carroll proved to be an active campaigner as secretary of the Lower Prices Council, and her no-nonsense interventions were often reported in newspapers. At a sitting of the Prices Advisory Board in 1951, to consider an application from Dublin coal merchants for an increase in coal prices, the IHA and the LPC strongly objected to the application. The reason coal prices should not increase, O'Carroll maintained, was because 'the poor were being sold coal which was practically all slack.'[6] In January 1953, milk suppliers demanded an increase in the price they received for milk. The Taoiseach, de Valera, refused their demands and a strike ensued. O'Carroll became a prominent voice during this time, calling for the army to deliver milk where required.[7] In response a number of milk suppliers offered free milk for children and the infirm. O'Carroll succeeded in getting milk supplied to those in the greatest need during this time.

Due to her now highly publicised actions, O'Carroll came to the attention of the Labour Party. Following the death of Fianna Fáil TD Thomas Brennan, a by-election was held on 18 June 1953 in Wicklow. O'Carroll acted as the director of elections for the Labour candidate. Although the seat was won by the Fine Gael candidate, O'Carroll had her first taste of party politics. The following month O'Carroll published her views on the next general election in the *Irish Independent* newspaper, declaring:

> When the General Election comes, as come it will, the women, who are the real sufferers under the present fantastic high cost of living, will give practical effect to that condemnation. Our vote is our power and we will terminate this continuous policy of placing national economic burdens on the shoulders of those least able to bear them.[8]

Two months later, the Labour Party announced O'Carroll as their candidate in the Dublin North-Central constituency at the next general election.[9]

O'Carroll was elected on 18 May 1954 in the general election for the fifteenth Dáil. Only five female TDs were returned out of a total of 147 seats. O'Carroll was one of only two female TDs in Dublin: the other was Celia Lynch, a Fianna Fáil candidate serving Dublin South-Central. O'Carroll became the first female Labour Party TD and the first female chief whip of any political party in the country. An Inter-Party Government formed through a coalition consisting of Fine Gael, the Labour Party and the farmer's party, Clann na Talmhan. The fifteenth Dáil first sat on 2 June 1954, when a debate regarding the nomination of the Taoiseach was the main order of business. Two names were put forward to a vote: Éamon de Valera and John A. Costello. O'Carroll voted in favour of Costello, who was subsequently elected as Taoiseach.

Historian Niamh Puirséil states that O'Carroll 'was regarded as a bit of a maverick'.[10] Indeed, she was a veracious voice in the Dáil, a true voice of the people. She questioned cabinet ministers on any issues that she felt affected everyday life during a punitive economic time, and she retained her position as secretary of the LPC. However, her contributions were in no way limited to economic affairs. In 1955, she moved a motion in the Dáil to have women admitted as members of An Garda Síochána.[11] Joan

Burton, a former Tánaiste and former Labour Party leader, describes this as a 'revolutionary idea'.[12] Indeed, it was seen as radical and this public call set a plan in motion. On 9 July 1959, the first group of 12 women joined the Irish police force.

In July 1956, O'Carroll gave notice to the Dáil that she would raise a subject relating to the transport of Irish children to the United States for adoption. She began her speech by reading the related subsections of the Adoption Act, which clearly laid out the conditions under which a child, who was a citizen of Ireland, could be removed from the State and be adopted abroad. She had travelled to Limerick to personally investigate the case of two children: Anthony Barron and Mary Clancy. The children had been removed from Croom hospital and sent to America for adoption.

Until the Adoption Act was introduced into Ireland in 1952, there was no legal system through which children could be adopted in the country. Prior to this time, illegal adoptions occurred with some regularity, and O'Carroll exposed how this unregulated system of adoption continued even after legislation was introduced. O'Carroll highlighted a hidden and disturbing aspect of the Irish state's treatment of children and women, especially unmarried mothers. She shattered a culture of silence surrounding illegal adoption of Irish children abroad by speaking on the topic in the Dáil chamber. In 1997, journalist Mike Milotte documented a detailed account of what he described as 'Ireland's baby export business' during the 1950s and 1960s.[13] This dark aspect of Ireland's history was brought further into the public domain in February 2021 when RTÉ Investigates aired *Ireland's Illegal Adoptions*, an investigative documentary exposing the story of thousands of children who were illegally adopted. The illegal adoption scandal has been linked to de Valera's son, Professor Éamon de Valera junior (1913–86), a consultant gynaecologist.[14]

The Department of Foreign Affairs (DFA) files show that from January 1950 up until October 1952, 330 passports were issued to Irish children to enable them to travel to the United States for adoption.[15] The exact number of such adoptions is unknown. A report commissioned by the Adoption Authority of Ireland, completed in 2018, clarified that there was 'a de-facto un-regulated domestic adoption system in Ireland prior to 1952, children were being sent to the USA for the purpose of adoption'.[16] In 1996, Catriona Crowe, then an archivist at the National Archives of Ireland, made a shocking discovery. While routinely checking a batch of documents submitted for archiving by the DFA, Crowe identified files from the Irish Embassy in Washington relating to 1,500 Irish children sent to the United States for adoption between 1949 and 1957.[17] This time period includes the date on which O'Carroll delivered her speech.

The Croom hospital at the centre of O'Carroll's case was originally a workhouse built during the famine period in the 1840s and adapted in 1924 as a general hospital serving county Limerick.[18] From its earliest existence, Croom hospital appears to be a centre for what were then considered *unwanted* pregnancies. The hospital features in the recent Mother and Baby Homes Commission of Investigation report, which notes that in 1926 'the resident medical supervisor of the Limerick County Hospital at Croom complained that unmarried mothers in Limerick city and county were sent to give birth at Croom. He claimed that "both parties are a stigma to the institution."'[19]

O'Carroll notes in her speech that the issue of unregulated adoptions from Croom hospital had been raised by Donogh O'Malley, a Fianna Fáil TD for Limerick East, the previous year. After O'Carroll's speech, and while acknowledging that this issue needed to be raised, O'Malley appeared concerned about keeping this issue out of the public eye by stating:

> There are too many outside bodies waiting to have a crack at this country, without mentioning any names, and they lose no opportunity of vilifying us. What has been stated in all sincerity by Deputy Mrs. Maureen O'Carroll will be splashed across many a paper, not only in Britain but in other countries, to the detriment of this nation.[20]

O'Malley did, however, support the basis of O'Carroll's position, and he added yet more concerning detail about the adoption of Irish children to America. He claimed that 'money is passing to the very close relatives of these children, in certain cases to the unfortunate mother of the type of child to whom Deputy Mrs. O'Carroll referred. It is a temptation to such a mother if she is offered £100 or £150 in order to get her consent.'[21]

The debate ended with the response from the Minister for External Affairs, Liam Cosgrave. Cosgrave maintained that the adoptions of Anthony Barron and Mary Clancy had taken place 'in accordance' with the Adoption Act and that 'very careful study [is] conducted by charitable organisations in the United States as to the circumstances, the background, the suitability and so forth of the adopting parents.'[22] He concluded, 'I deprecate the type of publicity which this debate will attract.' Again, the minister's concern was not for the children or mothers in question but for the reputation of Ireland abroad. He declared that 'It is significant that the only comments on this have appeared in what we here call the yellow English Sunday newspapers, who avail of every, and any, opportunity to smear the name of this country.'[23]

O'Carroll's speech did attract media attention and was duly reported in the pages of the national newspapers the *Irish Independent*, *Irish Examiner* and the *Irish Press* the following day. The *Belfast Newsletter* carried the headline 'Eire children sent to U.S. by "irregular methods"'.[24] That day O'Carroll's Labour Party colleague Daniel Desmond, TD for Cork Mid, raised a follow-on question for the Minister for Justice, James Everett, also a Labour Party politician. Desmond asked the Minister if he proposed to take any action or to make a statement regarding 'the transfer of babies from Croom Hospital to the United States of America'.[25] Everett stated that he was 'satisfied that there was nothing irregular or unlawful about this'.[26] O'Carroll again pushed to have the Minister clarify the facts of the case, but her request was denied and the debate concluded. While no immediate action was taken, O'Carroll had single-handedly raised a vitally important issue on the floor of the lower house of Irish government. Raising public awareness undoubtedly caused many in government and in institutions involved in unregulated foreign adoption to at least reduce the number and frequency of such adoptions. Historian Moira J. Maguire has documented how 'from the early 1940s to the mid-1960s thousands of Irish children were sent abroad under an informal (and probably illegal and unconstitutional) adoption scheme.'[27] This was, as Maguire aptly describes, a method through which the Irish State disposed of *unwanted* children.

O'Carroll continued to raise pertinent questions regarding the government's management of the country throughout her time as a TD. Her parliamentary contributions were frequently reported in national and local newspapers. In 1956, she gained the attention of Brian O'Nolan, the civil servant who wrote a satirical column in the *Irish Times*, 'Cruiskeen Lawn,' under the pseudonym Myles na Gopaleen.[28] On 30 October his column was devoted to an issue raised by O'Carroll noting:

> I regard Mrs. Maureen O'Carroll TD as the most valuable member of the Dáil of Erin. In a fug of drool and blather she looks for facts. She asks questions concerning the day-to-day outrage on my own constituents, the Plain People of Ireland. Last week she asked questions about Dublin bus fares. She was told by the Minister concerned that fares were a matter for C.I.E. Transportation by bus involves vicious taxation and Mr. Norton says the matter is one for C.I.E.[29]

O'Carroll stood unsuccessfully for election in the 1957 general election. Labour lost seven seats in that election. O'Carroll remained politically active.

O'Carroll's numerous contributions to the Dáil are all the more impressive considering that she served as a TD for only three years. Added to this, O'Carroll had 11 children, including one child she adopted from a reform school. Her youngest child, Brendan O'Carroll, the Irish actor and comedian, was born on 17 September 1955 while she was in office.

Maureen's husband, Gerard, died from cancer in the early 1960s, and she raised her children on her own in a council house in Finglas. Maureen suffered from a heart condition in later life and died on 9 May 1984 at her home in Ashbourne, county Meath, at the age of 71.[30] The *Sunday Press* noted how O'Carroll was 'the first woman since revolutionary times to win a Dáil seat while not being related to a former male Deputy'.[31]

10. Maureen O'Carroll, c. 1956. Courtesy of Eilish O'Carroll.

In 2018, Caroline Dalton produced a radio documentary *The Real Mrs. Brown* that includes interviews with Maureen's children; Brendan O'Carroll and his sister the actor Eilish, along with their siblings Martha, Michael and Finbar, about the life of their mother. Joan Burton features with her analysis of O'Carroll's impressive legacy, while historian Niamh Puirséil examines O'Carroll's many achievements. The name of the documentary refers to the character Agnes Browne in the globally successful television sitcom *Mrs. Brown's Boys*.

In 1992, Brendan O'Carroll wrote and performed in a radio soap, *Mrs. Browne's Boys*, on RTÉ 2FM. The daily show was immensely popular and Brendan wrote a book *The Mammy* based on a central character of Agnes Browne.[32] The character of Agnes Browne is based on Brendan's mother, Maureen O'Carroll. Brendan credits his mother 'with providing the inspiration for his most famous comic character'.[33] In 1999, the book was transformed into a movie, *Agnes Browne*, the screen play was co-written by Brendan and starred Anjelica Huston in the lead role. After this success, Brendan wrote a series of plays featuring Agnes Browne and formed a family theatre company. In 2011, the plays were adapted into a television sitcom, *Mrs. Brown's Boys*, which shortened the name from Browne to Brown. Maureen O'Carroll's determined nature and drive to shatter the culture of silence in Ireland is best remembered through her political speeches.

'I asked the Minister [for Justice] if he would make a statement regarding the circumstances which led to the transfer to the United States of America, with a view to adoption of Anthony Barron and Mary Clancy of Camos, Bruff, County Limerick, and if he would state the date of each transfer and the place from which each transfer took place. The Minister in his reply stated:— "From the inquiries that have been made I am satisfied that there was nothing unlawful or irregular about the removal of these children out of the State. In the circumstances, I have no further function in the matter."

I submit that not only was there something irregular about the manner of the removal of those children but something definitely illegal. My attention was drawn to this matter by a responsible association in this country and I based my questions on information supplied by that organisation. I made it my business to go to Limerick last Sunday. I went to the house where these children had been and I saw the grandmother of the children. I happened to see also the aunt of one of them.

I am satisfied beyond all doubt that Mary Clancy was born in 1952 and that Anthony Barron was born in 1953. The Minister's reply to me to-day states that both children were removed from this State this year. The ages speak for themselves. I was also informed, in reply to a further question, that Anthony Barron was removed from the Croom Hospital by his grandmother. I have here a photostatic copy of the letter from Anthony Barron's grandmother to the Mrs. Barron who had charge of the child. This letter was written after the removal of the child from the Barron household. The letter states:— "Dear Mrs. Barron: I hope you are well, as this leaves me the same. Well, Mrs. I was surprised to hear that the child was gone. It is in Croom Hospital waiting to go to the U.S.A. Will you take it back if I get it for you? I will go down to see it on Sunday. If you can, will you write by return post? Yours truly, N. Barron."

I mention those two documents to substantiate that, on the basis of these two specific cases, something illegal took place. Two children over one year and under seven were removed from this State with a view to adoption.

Deputy O'Malley put a question to the Minister for Justice last April. . . . "Mr. O'Malley asked the Minister for Justice whether any children, who were temporary inmates of the County Hospital, Croom, County Limerick, were adopted by American citizens and, if so, if he will state the circumstances of such adoption."

The Minister replied:— "The answer to the first part of the question is that some such children have been taken out of the country with a view to adoption. I am satisfied that there was nothing irregular or unlawful about this."

In a further question, Deputy Desmond directed the attention of the Minister to some Sunday newspaper reports. I did not see the reports myself, but his question was based on some Sunday newspaper reports alleging that there was traffic in babies in this country. The Minister referred the Deputy to the reply given to Deputy O'Malley, and again reiterated he was satisfied there was nothing wrong in the whole matter and that it was merely cross-Channel misrepresentation.

I would ask the House to consider that, while these two isolated cases alone would have justified the fullest examination of the facts, in reply to a further question of mine to-day, I was given the information that in the last three years 523 such children have left this country with a view to adoption in the U.S.A. Five hundred and twenty-three is an appalling figure in view of the circumstances.

The present Adoption Act, which was passed after many years of agitation by interested societies and social workers, in its present form deals with the adoption of children in this country, and its application has proved to be most successful, most efficient and most beneficial to the applicants for adopted children and to the children adopted. I fail to see why we cannot take the same protective measures to ensure that those children who are leaving this country are guaranteed the same protection with regard to religious duties, and with regard to the type of home they are going to.

I know the Minister has stated, and sincerely meant, that investigations do take place on this side when these children go. Our Adoption Act is not effective in the U.S.A. How legally binding, therefore, are the undertakings given by the people willing to adopt? I think this is a very serious matter. I have no objection to the transfer of these children to America as such. It is quite probable that many of these children are getting an opportunity in life they could not and would not get here, that they can start a new life and that they will not have to go through life in this country with the stigma they normally have to bear. But I do not see why it should have to be done in an illegal manner. I again ask the Minister if he cannot put any interpretation on this section other than the one that is on it, to ensure that at an early date legislation will be brought in to ensure that these children are adopted in this country before they go?

Section 10 of the Act states that when parents in this country are adopting a baby in this country they must be resident in this country for at least five years before the baby is adopted. In my opinion that should also apply to a limited extent to parents from America who wish to adopt our babies. They should have a residential term in this country, so that their whole moral character and religious outlook and ideas could be examined. I think legislation should be introduced at once to amend this Act. If the Minister cannot assure me in this, then I would suggest that the Act should be made more specific. If the points I am making are not correct—and I am at a loss to see they are not, in view of my investigations—or if I am not right in my beliefs, I hope the Minister will amend the wording of the Act to make it more clear so that these children will be protected.'[34]

EIGHT

Máirín de Burca

b. 1938

Speech on a feminist analysis of the Midnight Court
Merriman Summer School, Ballyvaughan, Clare

29 AUGUST 1980

'I don't believe that men can write intelligently of women's oppression.'

The 1970s and 1980s were decades of intense feminist activity in Ireland, often characterised by the campaigns of the, short lived but high profile, Irish Women's Liberation Movement (IWLM). Máirín de Burca was a founder member of the IWLM. Many women, and some men, staged campaigns to secure equality for women through moves to introduce contraception, divorce, equality in work and education. De Burca later faced arrests and imprisonments in the interest of constitutional reform, most notably to overthrow the biased laws restricting women from serving on juries. De Burca was also prominently involved in the culture wars in Ireland which included a feminist awakening in literature and poetry.

Máirín de Burca was born in Dublin on 22 October 1938. Her father, a carpenter from county Galway, and her mother, from Newbridge in county Kildare, had both emigrated to Chicago. Her mother went back to Ireland for Máirín's birth and returned to Chicago with her new-born child. Máirín spent her first nine years living in Chicago until 1947, when she returned to live in Ireland with her mother and brother. The family lived in Newbridge, and her father joined the family there when he retired a few years later. De Burca attended Newbridge Convent School. She left school at the age of 13 in 1951 and began working in a local shop at the age of 14.

De Burca recalls first becoming interested in nationalist politics after reading a large volume, *The Young Irelanders*, that included biographical essays on members of the political and cultural movement who campaigned for an independent Ireland.[1] She was inspired to join Sinn Féin when she reached the required minimum age for membership at 16. De Burca later moved to Bray in county Wicklow, securing a job in a shop and transferring to the local Sinn Féin branch there. De Burca was deeply committed to the nationalist cause though she struggled with the violence associated with republican groups. In 1962, de Burca left Sinn Féin for a brief period.

By the mid-1960s, left-leaning members of Sinn Féin began focussing on issues relating to poverty. Housing conditions in Dublin were then in crisis: the economic depression of the 1950s and the increasing population of the 1960s led to overcrowding in unsuitable premises. This social reform focus drew de Burca back in to Sinn Féin. She became General Secretary of the party and in 1967 became a co-founder and member of the Dublin Housing Action Committee (DHAC). To highlight the number of vacant buildings that could be used for suitable housing, the DHAC promoted squatting. The organisation drew media and political attention through their advocacy of squatting and by organising rallies and protests. De Burca was supported in her aim by Father Michael Sweetman, who appealed to the public to accept that housing had reached an emergency state. She progressively immersed herself in supporting the anti-apartheid movement for South Africa and also joined the protest group, Irish Voice on Vietnam, which led many public demonstrations against the Vietnam War (1954–75).

In October 1970, Richard Nixon, then president of America, visited Dublin. His visit occurred at a time when the war in Vietnam was raging. De Burca and Sinn Féin member Martin O'Hagan staged a protest by throwing eggs at the president's motorcade. De Burca disguised herself as an American tourist and later described how she 'did an overarm lob and I got it [the egg] dead centre on the windscreen. I was so proud of myself. Then I was grabbed by the guard and hauled across the bridge.'[2] She was charged and appeared in the Dublin District Court on 17 November 1970 before Justice Ó hUadhaigh. De Burca recalls that the hearing was 'quite funny' because Ó hUadhaigh, who was not a supporter of Nixon, 'kept making sarcastic remarks when the case came up'.[3] The charges of resisting or obstructing a garda and using threatening words or behaviour were dismissed, and de Burca was fined £2, the lowest possible fine, for throwing the eggs.

However, de Burca would not escape so easily after another anti-Vietnam war protest she organised. She, along with three others, burned the US flag at the American Embassy and threw cow's blood at the steps of the embassy building. This was a peaceful protest, arranged to coincide with a large peace protest in America, but de Burca was gaoled for three months in Mountjoy for her actions. The feminist journalist June Levine commented on the injustice of this sentence in her *Sunday Independent* column, noting that 'One cannot help wondering whether the insult to the steps of the Embassy and the Flag were the fundamental issue or is a slight to the not-so-almighty-as-hither-to dollar still to be avoided at all costs?'[4]

Levine and de Burca had recently collaborated on the formation of the Irish Women's Liberation Movement (IWLM). The group included an impressive mix of feminist women, and many were fellow journalists including: Mary Kenny of the *Irish Press*; Mary McCutchan, *Irish Independent*; Mary Anderson, *Irish Independent*; Nell McCafferty, *Irish Times*; and Nuala Fennell, a freelance journalist who later became Fine Gael Minister of State for Women's Affairs.[5] Another member, Margaret Gaj, owned a restaurant on Baggot Street, where the IWLM held weekly meetings.[6] The IWLM fired up feminist campaigns in Ireland with their manifesto *Chains or Change?: The Civil Wrongs of Irish Women*.[7] Founding member, Rosita Sweetman, described how 'crucially Chains or Change was the first time since the founding of the State that women's lot had been examined on its own.'[8] The manifesto 'was the first attempt at documenting just what religiosity, coupled with patriarchy, had meant.'[9]

The IWLM manifesto initially included five demands: 'equal pay, equality before the law, equal education, contraception for all, justice for deserted wives, unmarried mothers and widows'.[10] When the government proposed the Forcible Entry and Occupation bill 1971, de Burca insisted that a sixth demand for 'one family, one house' was included in the manifesto. The Forcible Entry bill made it illegal to squat or for a group to encourage or advocate squatting; essentially, this bill was introduced to combat the activities of de Burca and the DHAC. Levine noted that 'the inclusion of this additional aim reflected the concerns of the socialists in the group. Máirín de Burca argued that since Irish society defined woman's place as being in the home, equality could mean little in overcrowded, insanitary and insecure conditions.'[11] The IWLM disbanded later in 1971, but their activities inspired a new wave of feminist activism in Ireland.

De Burca was arrested along with fellow journalist Mary Anderson during a housing demonstration in 1971. The women's solicitor advised the pair to opt for trial by jury. Juries in Ireland at that time were comprised of men who owned property. Under advice from Mary Robinson, de Burca challenged the constitutionality of the Juries Act, under the 1937 Irish Constitution. The Supreme Court confirmed that the gender provision of the 1927 Act, which was enforced ten years before the constitution, 'to be unconstitutional, holding that the model of jury trial contemplated by the present Constitution required that juries be drawn from panels that were broadly representative of society'.[12] De Burca and Anderson drew attention to the extreme gender bias of the Irish jury system. Over the previous ten years, only nine women had been eligible for jury service out of the 700,000 people who had served. The women were only entitled to serve after applying to have their names included on the jurors' register. The women won their case, which led to a Juries Act being passed in 1976 that included an obligation for all male and female citizens to serve on a jury if called. This was a mammoth progression, which ensured that women could sit on a jury but also that jury members would be called from the electoral register and did not need to be homeowners.

In 1980, de Burca gave the speech in this section to the Merriman Summer School, an annual distinguished gathering that had been held every August since 1968. The school is named in honour of Brian Merriman, the Irish language poet and author of the celebrated eighteenth-century Rabelaisian poem 'Cúirt an Mheán Oíche' (The Midnight Court). The summer school is bilingual and participants examine wider general Irish-related topics.[13] In 1980, the summer school included a special symposium entitled 'The status of women since Merriman'. The session was chaired by the eminent historian and activist Margaret MacCurtain (Sister Benevenuta OP). Alongside de Burca, there were two other prestigious panel members: Mary Cullen, then a lecturer in history at St Patrick's College Maynooth and the first female member of the academic staff there, and Marian Finucane, a feminist activist and award-winning presenter with RTÉ.

De Burca presented a feminist analysis of 'The Midnight Court', using the poem to stress the contradiction of free love as a goal of the women's liberation movement. Her speech was brave, thoughtful, and it ultimately provoked much reaction. Many members of the audience retaliated against what some considered an attack on a great poet, a position most evident in an *Irish Times* headline: 'Merriman poem sexist rubbish, says speaker'.[14] The article reported that many of those gathered 'reacted with some force, declaring that it was a poem well ahead of its time. Merriman was a poet aware of women's sexuality and willing to discuss Irish sexual problems in an unhibited [sic] way.'[15] Other speakers from the floor concluded 'that women today were playing the most important role in Ireland, educating the children and bringing them up'.

The success and popularity of 'The Midnight Court' was best described by Eoghan Ó hAnluain, a former chairman of Cumann Merriman. Ó hAnluain professed that:

> Its success and lasting popularity lies in the perennial interest of its subjects and Merriman's powerful literary treatment of them: the despair of young women in failing to find suitable husbands because of their own lack of

material means; the institution of marriage itself, particularly its relevance for such women; the sexual frustration of those who marry in desperation old well-off but impotent men; their impatience with the imposed celibacy of the catholic clergy, whose young priests the young women find particularly attractive; and his impassioned insistence on the dignity and worth of the illegitimate child.[16]

Not surprisingly, attendees at the Merriman Summer School appeared somewhat protective of the poet and of the highly regarded epic poem. However, de Burca's analysis was measured and accurate from a contemporary feminist standpoint. This was one of the first occasions that a feminist reading was publicly presented in mainstream Irish cultural circles. Her speech was printed in *Women's View*, a magazine published by the National Women's Committee of Sinn Féin in the early 1980s.

De Burca continued working as a journalist after leaving Sinn Féin. From the early 1970s, she adopted a pacifist position, and she continues to confront those who support violence to achieve political aims. In the 1990s, when she reached her early fifties, de Burca made the decision to retire early; she had been working fulltime from the age of 14. She volunteered to work with the Credit Union, and her connection continued for some years with the community-based co-operative financial organisation.

On 5 December 2017, an honorary Doctorate of Laws was conferred on de Burca by University College Dublin in recognition of her social reform campaigns. In July 2018, a documentary based on de Burca's life, directed by Cathal Black, premiered at the 30th Galway Film Fleadh, *Five Red Roses – One for Every Syllable of Your Name*.[17] In 2020, the acclaimed artist Jesse Jones received a Creative Residency partnership between Dublin City Council Culture Company and The Honorable Society of King's Inns. Jones was particularly inspired by de Burca's life and legacy, and she produced the most remarkable permanent art piece in her honour. The sculpture, entitled 'The Left Arm of Commerce', is now housed in King's Inn. It is a Portland stone statue of de Burca's arm and hand, which is holding her personal copy of Bunreacht na hÉireann, the Constitution of Ireland. Jones notes that:

> The final part of this work has been made from burnt wood, a plinth designed with Sarah Murphy[.] I used burnt wood to reference the histories of the witch trials and connection to women's continued struggle. Máirín de Burca's arm is placed on top of this plinth of burnt wood, echoing our resistance and regenerative movements with and against the law.[18]

11. Máirín de Burca with the sculpture by artist Jesse Jones. Courtesy of Dublin City Council Culture Company and by kind permission of photographer Julien Behal.

As part of the project, Lisa Godson, a historian of design and material culture, collected an oral history account of de Burca's through a series of interviews. The oral history archive is to be housed with de Burca's own archive at King's Inns.

It is most fitting that a sculpture honours Máirín de Burca at the Honorable Society of King's Inns, Ireland's Oldest School of Law, which was established in 1541. De Burca challenged biased laws under which she faced arrests, imprisonments, court injunctions and fines. Ultimately, de Burca ensured that gender or class would not prohibit people from serving on a jury, which is a basic privilege and an obligation of citizenship. Excluding women from such basic aspects of citizenship had, as Senator Jennie Wyse Power warned in 1927, 'arrest[ed] the civic spirit' of Irish women.[19] De Burca's speech in this section is a reminder of how Irish feminists offered a broader re-evaluation of Ireland's cultural heritage.

'I am not a Gaelic Scholar, in fact I am not a scholar at all. My schooldays were comparatively few and, because of that, devoted to the bare essentials.[20] The bare essentials did not include an appreciation of poetry and so when I read the Midnight Court years ago, for the first time in translation, it was because I had been told that it represented the acme of liberated, anti-clerical, bawdy Irish life before the dark night of the famine came down and the nasty Brits made narrow-minded bigots of us all. I don't remember that it made any impression on me at all. Last week I read it again — David Marcus' translation — from the standpoint of a committed feminist.

First of all let me admit to a prejudice. I don't believe that men can write intelligently of women's oppression. The best that can be said is that some of them mean well but — as with novels written by foreigners about Irish oppression — when well meaning men try to interpret the struggle of women for human rights I appreciate the thought but I cringe and wish they wouldn't. There is no evidence of course that most of them mean well at all.

What I found in the Midnight Court was a series of sentiments which would not be out of place in twentieth century Ireland and which, if expressed with a little more decorum, could be accepted by any ninety year old parish priest in the country. In the first section a young girl deplores the reluctance of men to get married and suggests that, reluctant to marry, they are also reluctant to go to bed with any woman. She resents the fact that women, older and uglier than she, find husbands, she boasts of her looks and her fashionable dress and her single-minded dedication to catching a man. She dreads dying a "miserable old maid" and finally decides to accomplish her one purpose in life by means of magic spells.

In the second part, what Merriman/Marcus describes as a "wizzened old josser" takes up the woman's challenge and launches an attack, not on the sentiments she expresses but on her looks. He decries her parentage, her lack of a dowry, her inability to do housework of a high enough standard and, that old standby of the male, he attacks her virtue. He th[e]n bemoans his own fate since he married, again claiming to have been taken in by a woman without virtue (the virtue invariably meaning as in 20th Century Ireland sexual purity), the baby arrived the day after the wedding[,] and ends by making a stirring plea for free love in order that the male offspring of such unions will grow up powerful and strong. . . .

The woman rejoins the battle and does an exposé on the man's marriage. He tricked his wife into marriage she claims, with promises of wealth and luxury. She attacks what is usually described as his "manhood", takes a side swipe at the celibate clergy while managing to insinuate that they aren't all that celibate.

The judgement, when it is handed down by the woman judge, is sympathetic to the woman's case and the sentence is flagellation to encourage men to procreate, whatever their financial circumstances.

I submit that there is nothing particularly revolutionary there. Oh, the language is earthy and it is not the first time that explicit descriptions of anatomical appendages and sexual gymnastics was mistaken for the polemics of liberation. . . . I am familiar with the human anatomy and with what are curiously described as the "facts of life". They are neither e[s]pecially amusing or especially interesting — just necessary for the propagation of the species. Many people actually enjoy the whole process of course and good luck to them. However, until comparatively recently women could not enjoy sex without fear.

Gearoid O Tuathaigh in his essay "The Role of women in Ireland under the new English Order" claims that the Midnight Court is "a plea for the rights of women to sexual satisfaction" but another interpretation and one equally as valid is that it was rather a plea for men to marry the surplus women when they were both young, and by definition beautiful. Procreation was an occupational hazard for the woman who could spend anything from 20 to 30 years of this idyllic life expecting a child, having a child, miscarrying a child or nursing a child. As there were three women to every man her husband meantime would be encouraged to put other women he came across in the same condition so that they wouldn't degenerate into miserable old maids. No doubt but that this is every male's idea of women's liberation, the one with which he is in most accord but that is a myth not too difficult to demolish.

The most that can be said for Merriman is that he was the first to articulate, and in poetic fashion to boot, the curiously male notion that Liberation for women coincides exactly with the principle of free love. I saw the effects of this brainwashing on some of the women who came into the Liberation Movement. Not naturally promiscuous, they were conned by male reactions to the movement into adopting a lifestyle completely alien to their inclinations and principles. It was the old "you are a liberated woman you must prove it and sleep with me" syndrome. This caused a great deal of unhappiness for the women but of course a deal of satisfaction for some men. . . .

It will be said of course that I am taking things too seriously, that Merriman was composing a humorous commentary on the sexual mores of the day, that his sympathy came down on the side of the woman complainant and as for the rest we can enjoy the explicitness of his language in contrast with the narrow joylessness of the literature which came after the horrific events of the next century. But Merriman is not generally treated lightly. His poem has been investigated and inspected from every angle. Why not from the angle of a feminist?

There is nothing particularly amusing in the glorification of a work which reinforces the most despicable male prejudices against women.

I am aware that there is an argument which goes something like this; poets are by nature extraordinary beings, we cannot therefore judge them as ordinary persons, they are not of our mundane world but a race apart. When poets do stupid and malicious things then supporters of this argument turn somersaults trying to excuse them. . . . Someone will no doubt claim that since Brian Merriman was a poet he was therefore incapable of sexism. The answer to that is simple — Brian Merriman was a man, he was by definition and without the exercise of any particular faculty, a member of the oppressing class. . . .

So let us by all means enjoy his poem, let us laugh at it or rail at it or do whatever is fashionable with it but let's not cod ourselves or have ourselves codded that it is a feminist tract because it isn't. Sexual licence is not what women's liberation is all about however much men would like to persuade us that it is. Freedom and human dignity for women will come only with total economic independence for every woman whatever her sexual status, and with total and safe control over her fertility. Without these rights women are as much men's slaves today as they were in 1750.'[21]

NINE

Brenda Fricker

b. 1945

Oscar award acceptance speech
Dorothy Chandler Pavilion, Los Angeles

26 MARCH 1990

'Anybody who gives birth twenty-two times deserves one of these.'

The Academy Awards, commonly referred to as the Oscars, are presented annually for acting and technical merit in the film industry. The Oscars are considered by many people to be the highest awards in the entertainment industry globally. As of 2022, only one Irish woman has received an Oscar for acting. Brenda Fricker received an Oscar in 1990 for 'best supporting actress' in the Irish-produced film *My Left Foot*. Fricker's award and the success of *My Left Foot* had significant repercussions for the Irish film industry, which received new-found international esteem.

Brenda Fricker was born in Dublin on 17 February 1945, and she grew up in the southside suburb of Dundrum. She attended a prestigious school for girls, Loreto on the Green. Her mother, Bina (née Murphy), originally from Kerry, was a teacher at Stratford College, a Jewish secondary school in Rathfarnham. Her father, Desmond Fricker, was a journalist with the *Irish Times*. He worked as a press officer for the Department of Agriculture during the 1960s and presented a radio programme, *Down the Country*, under the pseudonym Fred Desmond.

Fricker spent much of her childhood in hospital. When she was seven years old, she experienced kidney failure and was hospitalised for almost a year. Fricker recovered, but at the age of 14 she was involved in a serious road accident when she was knocked off her bicycle; she spent almost two years in hospital. Shortly after her discharge from hospital, Fricker developed TB and was once again hospitalised, this time for eight months.[1]

Despite Fricker's childhood illnesses, her mother ensured that she and her sister, Gráinne, engaged in a range of extracurricular activities, including music, drama and Irish dancing lessons. The sisters attended Ena Burke's Drama School on Kildare Street in Dublin city. This was a reputable school that had trained some of Ireland's most prestigious actors, including Maureen O'Hara and Milo O'Shea. Fricker did not initially pursue an acting career; she began working in the *Irish Times* after she left school. She later got involved in radio drama, which led to a television acting job. In 1964 Fricker accepted a small role in an Irish soap opera, *Tolka Row*. The series followed the lives of two working-class families living on a North Dublin housing estate. Fricker took the role of Joan Broderick, a girlfriend of one of the main characters, Sean Nolan, played by Jim Bartley.[2]

Fricker moved to London shortly after her appearances in *Tolka Row*. There she appeared on stage with the Royal Court, the National and the Royal Shakespearean Company. She returned to television acting when she took on the role of Nurse Megan Roach on the hit BBC One series *Casualty*. Fricker appeared in the first episode on 6 September 1986. She became a well-known figure through this role, featuring in *Casualty* until 7 December 1990, when she left the series.

Fricker returned to acting work in Dublin when she played the title role of Maggie in John B. Keane's play *Big Maggie*, in a production at the Abbey theatre in 1988. The play opened on 21 November and it was a triumph. *The Kerryman* newspaper reported that 'according to a spokesman for the Abbey, standing ovations are an unusual occurrence on an opening night in a theatre.'[3] Yet the audience gave an enthusiastic standing ovation after that first performance of *Big Maggie*. Public demand to see the production remained high for the next 60 performances; extra box office staff were hired by the Abbey to cope with the pressure. The *Irish Press* newspaper reported on Fricker's success under the headline 'Brenda passes big test', describing how she 'powerfully recreated' the character of Maggie.[4]

In 1989, Fricker starred in the film *My Left Foot* opposite Daniel Day-Lewis. Fricker played a key character as the mother of the gifted author and painter Christy Brown. Brown was born on 5 June 1932 in Dublin. He was one of 22 children born to his parents. Seventeen of those children survived birth and four died in infancy, leaving Brown as one of 13 children in the family. Brown was born completely paralysed and unable to speak. It was not until his teens that he was diagnosed with cerebral palsy, a disability that caused the limited muscular control he experienced, apart from the use of his left foot. His father, Patrick Brown, was a bricklayer, who had fought for Irish independence in 1916. His mother, Bridget (née Fagan), refusing to believe that her son should be institutionalised, raised Brown at home and taught him to read.[5] During his teens Brown started to paint, and he wrote his autobiography, *My Left Foot*, first published in 1954.[6] The book was translated into five languages within the first year, and he became an international literary sensation. Brown died at the age of 49 in 1981, but his book has since been republished many times.

Irish producer Noel Pearson read the book again when he was in New York and decided that he would make a film based on it. He planned to produce the film through Ferndale Films, an independent production company based in Ireland, established by him in 1987.[7] Pearson was introduced to scriptwriter Shane Connaughton, who agreed to work on the project with theatre director Jim Sheridan. While co-writing the film script, Sheridan, who had never before directed a film, approached Pearson about directing *My Left Foot*. The film was a thoroughly Irish production, receiving financial support from RTÉ. The film centred on an Irish theme and was filmed in Ireland. Filming took place over seven weeks at Ardmore Studios in Bray, county Wicklow, and on location in Dublin, showcasing places such as Mulligans pub on Poolbeg Street and concluding on Killiney Hill with spectacular views across Dublin Bay. Donald Clarke, chief film correspondent for the *Irish Times*, aptly noted that before *My Left Foot* was produced 'Irish films were as rare as Irish aircraft carriers.'[8]

The film premiered in Dublin in March 1989, and it went on general release on 7 April. There was an instant positive reaction from critics and audiences alike. The now convicted sex offender Harvey Weinstein instantly recognised the potential of *My Left Foot*. He took over the worldwide distribution of the film for Miramax, the entertainment company co-founded by him and his brother. Fricker recalled Weinstein with contempt, noting in a 2017 interview that 'there was something dangerous about him and I disliked him intensely.'[9] The film was a box office success abroad, and in due course it was nominated for five Academy Awards: Best Film, Best Adapted Screenplay, Best Director, Best Actor and Best Supporting Actress. The cast and the crew attended the academy awards with no expectation of winning any of these much-coveted awards. The film had strong competition, including Oliver Stone's *Born on the Fourth of July*, which was tipped to win numerous awards.

Fricker was nominated in the category for Best Supporting Actress. The other nominees in that category were Angelica Huston (*Enemies, A Love Story*), Lena Olin (*Enemies, A Love Story*), Julia Roberts (*Steel Magnolias*) and Dianne Wiest (*Parenthood*). Fricker made a short speech on accepting the award. Her emotional speech, in this section, may be succinct, but it is significant. This was the first time that any Irish woman won an Oscar, and, as of the most recent 94th Academy Awards in 2022, Fricker remains the only Irish woman to have received this prestigious accolade for acting.

12. Oscar winner Brenda Fricker at the 62nd Annual Academy Awards, 26 March 1990. Photograph by Alan Light.

Fricker began her speech by giving personal thanks to her parents and to Ena Burke. It was particularly poignant that Fricker dedicated the award to Bridget Brown, the hero of Christy Brown's life. Fricker succeeded in capturing the sheer determination and drive of this heroic woman in her film portrayal. As the writer and critic Ulick O'Connor observed, 'Bridget Brown came from that masterful breed of women who held the Irish poor together for generations when conditions in Irish cities were the worst in western Europe.'[10] Fricker was undoubtedly the ideal actor to have played the role of Bridget, a performance that helped *My Left Foot* become a global box office success. When asked about receiving the Oscar, Fricker responded in her usual measured but humble style. She said, 'I'm very proud of being the first Irish actress to win an Oscar. I'm very proud of the fact that it puts me into encyclopaedias and history books. It would have made my mother proud. Mind you, I'm probably prouder of the fact that my name is Dublin rhyming slang for knickers.'[11]

Daniel Day-Lewis won the Oscar that evening for Best Actor. Two Oscars for a small Irish film production was a mammoth triumph. In his assessment of what this achievement meant for Ireland as a nation, Donald Clarke noted how, 'a few months later, the Republic of Ireland soccer team had that breath-taking run at Italia '90. Riverdance followed soon after. Then came the boom. It now looks as if *My Left Foot*, the story of one stubborn Dubliner with cerebral palsy, helped launch (for good or ill) an unexpected period of national confidence.'[12]

Despite attention from Hollywood, Sheridan and Pearson remained in Ireland for their next film, an adaptation of *The Field*, by John B. Keane, in 1990. Not surprisingly, Fricker was cast as a main character. She starred alongside Richard Harris, who played 'Bull' McCabe, with Fricker as McCabe's wife, Maggie. Fricker resigned from *Casualty* shortly after winning the Oscar and accepted a lead role playing Sister Agnes in *Brides of Christ*, an Australian six-episode series that first screened in 1991. The series was shot on location in New South Wales; it won a number of awards and was broadcast in the UK by Channel 4. In 1992, Fricker featured in the blockbuster film *Home Alone 2: Lost in New York*, in which she played the unforgettable role of the Central Park Pigeon Lady. Fricker went on to star in many more films, including as Veronica Guerin's mother, Bernie, in the 2003 film *Veronica Guerin*.[13]

Fricker was presented with the inaugural Maureen O'Hara award at the Kerry Film Festival in Tralee in November 2008. In 2011, she starred in *Cloudburst*, alongside fellow Academy Award winner Olympia Dukakis. The film centred on a female couple who drive from Canada to Maine to get married. The Canadian American film opened the 10th annual Jameson International Film Festival with a gala screening at the Savoy Cinema in Dublin. Festival director Gráinne Humphreys described the film 'as beguiling as its lovely title suggests'.[14] Fricker asserted that 'of all the films I've made, only three do I remember where I felt I'd moved forward as an actress: *Cloudburst*, *My Left Foot* and *The Field*.'[15] In 2022, Fricker starred in the TV adaptation of *Holding*, a series based on Graham Norton's novel of the same name.

In March 2022, An Post released a set of four stamps celebrating the achievements of Irish Academy Award winners. Fricker featured on one stamp with Daniel Day-Lewis. The other three stamps honoured Neil Jordan, winner of Best Screenplay for *The Crying Game* in 1993; Martin McDonagh, winner of Best Live Action Short Film for *Six Shooter* in 2006; and Glen Hansard and Markéta Irglová for Best Original Song in *Once* in 2008.[16] This was the second time that Fricker had been chosen by An Post. In 1996, a four-stamp set featuring 12 Irish actors in Irish films was released to commemorate the centenary of Irish cinema. Fricker appeared on a stamp for her role in *My Left Foot.*

Fricker actively promotes young Irish women in the film industry, most evident in her support of Jessie Buckley from county Kerry. During an interview on *The Late Late Show* with Ryan Tubridy in January 2020, Fricker declared, 'I think Jessie Buckley is far and away the best talent I've seen coming up in Ireland for a long long time.'[17] Fricker has developed a close relationship with Buckley over the phone in recent years. Buckley was nominated for an Oscar as best supporting actress in *The Lost Daughter* in 2022. While Buckley did not win the Oscar, Fricker maintains that she will win in the future as Buckley is 'bursting with talent'.[18] Brenda Fricker's contribution to Irish film and theatre is immense, and her speech in this section is a vivid reminder of just one of her many accomplishments.

'I don't believe this. I'd like to make a private thank you to Bina and Des and Ena Burke. And I'd like to thank every single member of the crew who worked on *My Left Foot* who created an atmosphere of fun and love and hard work. I'd like to thank Christy Brown, just for being alive. I'd like to thank Mrs. Brown, his mother. Anybody who gives birth twenty-two times deserves one of these, I think. I'd like to thank Jim Sheridan and Shane Connaughton for the best script I've ever been involved in. I'd like to thank Noel Pearson for producing the film. And Jim Sheridan, for just being the most incredible director. And the members of the Academy, for giving me this, which I will take very proudly with me back to Ireland. Thank you.'[19]

Ten

Veronica Guerin

1958–96

International Press Freedom Award acceptance speech
Marriott Hotel, New York

6 December 1995

'It is very unusual to hear that an Irish reporter has been shot or intimidated.'

Veronica Guerin was a professional journalist for just four years, yet she became, and perhaps remains, one of the most prominent female investigative reporters in Ireland. Guerin's reporting was unsurpassed. Guerin's quick rise to prominence did cause some controversy as noted by historian Patrick Maume, her success 'provoked the hostility of some established journalists, who felt themselves eclipsed by her rising star'.[1] Much of Guerin's success came from her style of journalism: she favoured a direct tactic, approaching her subjects in person for interviews.

As Guerin's career progressed, she became more focussed on exposing the activities of Dublin crime gangs. Her reporting of criminal activities enraged her subjects, and she paid the ultimate price for her steadfast commitment to exposing crime. Guerin was assassinated by a Dublin criminal gang in 1996. Crime reporter Paul Williams described how 'no crime in gangland's blood-soaked history has so outraged a nation as the execution of Veronica Guerin.'[2] Williams aptly noted that this was 'an act of terrorism against society by a criminal organisation whose shady membership believed themselves untouchable and steps ahead of the law'.

Veronica Guerin was born on 5 July 1958 in Dublin, and she was raised in the family home at 26 Brookwood Avenue in Artane. Her father, Christopher, an accountant, and her mother, Bernie (née Parris), had five children. Guerin attended St Mary's Holy Faith Catholic School in Killester, where she completed her leaving certificate in 1976. Guerin was accomplished at sports and excelled in basketball and soccer, representing Ireland in both sports. After leaving school she initially worked for the Irish League of Credit Unions. The following year she joined her father's accountancy practice, Guerin, Reid and Company, in Gardiner Place. She worked with her father until his death in 1982.

Guerin had joined Ógra Fianna Fáil in 1978, becoming chair of the Dublin North Central branch the following year.[4] She was a keen supporter of Charles Haughey, a TD for her local constituency who had held various ministries up to that point. Guerin worked on a volunteer capacity for Fianna Fáil, at times writing election newsletters for Haughey. In 1979, Jack Lynch resigned as leader of Fianna Fáil, then in government, and Haughey was elected as the new party leader on 9 December. Two days later Haughey was elected as Taoiseach, after what Maume aptly describes as 'a bitter debate' in the Dáil.[5] In June 1981, following a general election, Fianna Fáil briefly lost power to an incoming collation government formed by Fine Gael and Labour. The 1980s were a politically difficult time in Ireland during a period of increased austerity and this was the first of five general elections that decade.

On 9 March 1982, Haughey was returned as Taoiseach in a short-lived Fianna Fáil government. During this time the government appointed Guerin to the governing body of the National Institute for Higher Education, now Dublin City University (DCU). She was employed by Fianna Fáil in 1983 and 1984 as a public relations advisor. In 1983, the New Ireland Forum was established to examine how a 'lasting peace and stability could be achieved in a new Ireland through the democratic process'.[6] The forum included members from the main parties in Ireland and Northern Ireland, including Fianna Fáil, Fine Gael, Labour, and the Social Democratic and Labour Party (SDLP). Guerin served as the Fianna Fáil secretary for the proceedings. When the forum concluded in May 1984, 'Guerin decided that, as she had no interest in standing for elected office, she would set up her own business rather than continuing as a Fianna Fáil employee.'[7]

That year, she established her own PR company, Guerin Public Relations Limited. On 21 September 1985, Guerin married Graham Turley, whom she met through Fianna Fáil. In 1988, she was awarded a diploma in marketing management from the Dublin Institute of Technology.[8] Guerin and Turley's only child, Cathal, was born in 1990. Guerin's business was unviable, and it was dissolved in 1992. By that time, she had begun contributing articles to the satirical magazine *The Phoenix*, where her friend Paddy Prendiville was the editor. This was Guerin's first professional entry into journalism, and she had a clear passion for the industry. Her political contacts became particularly useful.

Soon after her business was dissolved, Guerin became a freelance journalist for the *Sunday Business Post*, which had been founded by Damien Kiberd in 1989. She wrote a number of ground-breaking articles for this weekly newspaper from 1992 to 1993. Emily O'Reilly, former journalist and later European Ombudsman, described the paper as 'one of the few successes in Ireland in recent years. It specialises in business news, but also has a strong political core.'[9] From the outset, Guerin's business journalism focussed on uncovering scandals in the business world. She exposed problematic operations within the Aer Lingus Holidays company which, it transpired, was running at a loss although the company reported a profit annually when applying for the renewal of their operations licence.[10] Journalist Ursula Halligan described this story as 'an outstanding exposé of malpractice'.[11]

Guerin went to extreme lengths in her investigations. While researching the shady dealings of Goodman International, which went into receivership, she travelled to Cyprus to track down evidence that £25 million of company money had been deposited in a bank there.[12] In August 1992, while researching an article on phone tapping, Guerin was given a transcript of a telephone conversation between Fine Gael leader John Bruton and party member Michael Noonan.[13] The following month Guerin was given a recording of other conversations between Fine Gael members. The *Sunday Business Post* published details of these conversations. Guerin played no part in the illegal recordings, but she was part of a group of six journalists fined in July 1993 by the District Court in Dublin, after pleading guilty to illegally publishing and broadcasting the conversations.[14]

By the time of this court case, Guerin had joined the *Sunday Tribune* as a reporter. Her articles during her time at the *Tribune* were exceptional. In November 1993, a series of interviews by Guerin with Bishop Casey were published in the newspaper. The first wave of sexual scandals related to the Catholic Church in Ireland involved cases of parenthood. In 1992, it surfaced that Éamonn Casey, Bishop of Galway, had fathered a child with Annie Murphy in 1974. Added to this, Casey had used church funds to financially support Murphy and their son. The story sent shock waves throughout Catholic Ireland. Casey was ordered by the Vatican to leave Ireland, and he went to a rural parish in Ecuador as a missionary. Guerin travelled to Ecuador and contacted Casey; she succeeded in arranging a series of interviews with him. Veteran journalist Vincent Browne notes how these interviews offered 'the most intriguing . . . insights' into Casey and the workings of the Catholic church.[15] Casey later told the editor of the *Sunday Tribune* that 'he did the interviews solely because of Veronica's persuasiveness.'[16]

Guerin was by now a sought-after journalist, and she secured a post in the *Sunday Independent* in January 1994. Ursula Halligan maintains that the most spectacular exposé that Guerin had there 'was the revelation of the delay in the Attorney General's [Harry Whelehan] office in 1994, in handling the extradition application for Fr Brendan Smyth, accused of child sex abuse'.[17] When Guerin's article was published in the *Sunday Independent*, it caused considerable political controversy, leading to a split in the Fianna Fail–Labour government and the downfall of the Taoiseach, Albert Reynolds.

Organised crime on the streets of Dublin surged in the 1990s, and Guerin was increasingly attracted to investigating criminal activity. As Maume notes 'Guerin's journalism fed into a growing public fascination with Dublin's organised crime, stoked by the high-profile activities of Martin Cahill and the growth of a serious drugs problem in Dublin from the early 1980s.'[18] She succeeded in uncovering stories where others had failed because 'unlike other journalists, Guerin was prepared to approach criminals directly and pester them for interviews.'[19] She was a vocal opponent of the libel laws in Ireland, which she believed restricted a journalist's ability to reveal the criminal activity of individuals. In order to avoid such regulations Guerin, like other journalists at this time, began to use a sobriquet or nickname in her reporting. For example, Martin Cahill, a Dublin criminal who masterminded a series of high-profile robberies, became known simply as 'The General.'

Guerin's style of investigating by approaching criminals directly, eventually positioned her as a target. Shots were fired into her north county Dublin house on 7 October 1994, there were no injuries, but this was a harsh warning for her to curtail her investigations. On 30 January 1995 at just after 7 p.m., a man wearing motorcycle clothes called to her home. The man pointed a gun at Guerin's head before lowering his aim and shooting her in the leg. RTÉ news reported that 'the attack was presumed to be a warning from a crime gang not to push her investigations too far.'[20] Guerin's most recent investigation centred on a man suspected of masterminding a robbery at the Brinks Allied cash depository in Santry just days before. The armed robbery was carried out by a Dublin crime gang who stole an estimated £2.8 million, the largest robbery in the history of the Irish state to that date.

The attack on Guerin and warning may well have fazed her but only temporarily. Weeks later, she was interviewed by Pat Kenny on the *Kenny Live* television chat show. She insisted that she would continue with her work. After the attack, the *Sunday Independent* ordered the installation a state-of-the-art security system at her home. She was also given a Garda escort but requested that this be withdrawn as a police presence prevented her from approaching criminals to interview.

Guerin continued to report on crime and to interview criminals directly. On 14 September 1995, Guerin visited the home of John Gilligan, who had amassed a large fortune thought to be the proceeds of drug trafficking and other criminal activities. With no legal income, Gilligan owned Jessbrook Equestrian Centre in north Kildare. The premises was considered the largest indoor equestrian centre in Ireland at that time and cost an estimated €1.5 million to construct. Guerin arrived at Gilligan's home to question him about his earnings and the ownership of the equestrian centre. Paul Williams recounts that Gilligan instantly launched a violent attack on Guerin on his doorstep. Williams described how Gilligan punched her face and head, ripped her clothes and threatened to kill her and her family if she wrote about him.[21] Emily O'Reilly notes that 'Veronica was not frightened off, but the attack had a deeply traumatic effect on her.'[22]

Guerin later brought assault charges against Gilligan. The front page of the *Sunday Independent* that week carried the headline 'Gardaí investigate new attack on Guerin' above a report written by Liam Collins.[23] The article noted that Guerin declined to comment on the assault but that the day after the attack she had received a call on her mobile phone from Gilligan's wife, who claimed that she was legally separated from Gilligan and that she, not her husband, owned the equestrian centre. The article concluded, 'Ms Guerin's investigative work in the past has also led to death threats being issued against her.'[24]

In December 1995, the Committee to Protect Journalists (CPJ) honoured Guerin with an International Press Freedom Award due to the fact that 'she had been repeatedly targeted for physical attacks, a shooting, and death threats because of her incisive, continuing investigation into Ireland's criminal underworld.'[25] The CPJ is an independent organisation based in New York that promotes the freedom of the press globally and 'defend[s] the right of journalists to report the news safely and without fear of reprisal'.[26] In her acceptance speech, Guerin mentions a fellow recipient of the award that year, Fred M'membe, who was known for his editorship of the largest newspaper in Zambia, the *Post*. M'membe's work was often curtailed through threat of imprisonment, and in 2010 he was imprisoned for four months' hard labour for contempt after publishing an op-ed on the state's prosecution of a journalist.[27]

In her speech, Guerin also mentions the case of investigative journalist Liz Allen, who was facing the threat of seven years in prison for breaching the Official Secrets Act. Allen had published a story in the *Irish Independent* citing a leaked garda bulletin which showed that Gardaí had a north inner city Dublin gang under surveillance as they believed the gang was organising a robbery. The surveillance operation was stood down just weeks before the Brinks Allied robbery took place. The article implied that the Gardaí knew that a large-scale robbery was about to happen but that they took no action to stop it. Allen was later found guilty in the district court, but she received only a small fine.

Guerin comments in her speech that 'It is very unusual to hear that an Irish reporter has been shot or intimidated.' While she had already been shot once, her comment was indeed accurate: it was rare for a journalist in Ireland to be attacked in this way. Tragically, Guerin was shot again, just months after giving this speech. On 26 June 1996, she was returning from the district court in Naas, county Kildare, where she faced a speeding charge. It is believed that she was followed from the court. As she drove down the Naas Road, she stopped at a red traffic light at around 1.05 p.m. A motorcycle pulled up near her. The pillion passenger dismounted and approached her car and shot her six times. Guerin died instantly.

Some national newspapers carried the shocking story of Guerin's murder in their afternoon editions. The *Evening Herald,* a sister newspaper of the *Sunday Independent,* replaced their front page with the story and the stark headline 'Veronica Guerin shot dead' in bold typeface. The lead article covered half of the front page, while numerous articles relating to the murder and previous attacks on Guerin were contained in the inside pages.[28] The following day, newspapers and other media, in Ireland and abroad, were packed with the shocking story of Guerin's murder. Guerin's colleagues at the *Irish Independent* penned a number of pieces under the main heading 'Veronica Guerin: Murder of a reporter'.[29] The author and journalist, Bruce Arnold's contribution appeared under the headline 'Can our protectors live up to Veronica's courage?'[30]

The Minister for Justice, Nora Owen, had just returned to her hotel room in NewYork when she was informed that Guerin had been shot dead.[31] Having met with US secretary of state Madeleine Albright, Owen was preparing a speech for the United Nations on international drug crime.[32] She reacted swiftly to supress the activities of crime gangs in Ireland. Most notably, she oversaw the establishment of the Criminal Assets Bureau (CAB) on 15 October 1996. The bureau has the power to seize money and goods earned through illegal activity. Chief Superintendent Fachtna Murphy was appointed as Head of the CAB with former serious crime squad officer Felix McKenna second in command. This force acted swiftly. In November 1996, CAB officers moved in to seize Gilligan's equestrian centre and home. As Maume notes, Guerin's murder also 'led to the passage of legislation that restricted bail and the right to silence for those charged with crimes, [and] the establishment of a witness protection programme'.[33]

Immediately following Guerin's murder, a number of arrests were made. Charles Bowden, a member of Gilligan's gang, turned state's evidence and became the first person to avail himself of the newly established witness protection programme. Bowden named Patrick 'Dutchy' Holland as the person who received the gun used to shoot and kill Guerin. Holland was never convicted of the murder; he died in 2009 in a UK prison while serving a sentence for conspiracy to kidnap. Another gang member, Brian 'The Tosser' Meehan, was identified by Russell Warren, who also turned state's evidence. Meehan was named as the driver of the motorcycle that approached Guerin on the Naas Road. Meehan fled to Amsterdam but was extradited back to Ireland, where he was charged with her murder. Meehan was the only person sentenced for Guerin's murder.

John Gilligan left Ireland the day before the shooting, and it was believed that he ordered the murder of Guerin. He was arrested twelve months later at an airport in the United Kingdom with $500,000 in cash. He was imprisoned in Belmarsh prison in London for money laundering. The Irish authorities engaged in a three-year battle to have Gilligan extradited to Ireland to face trial for Guerin's murder. A trial at the Special Criminal Court in Dublin lasted 43 days and concluded in March 2001. The no-jury trial was heard by three judges, who deliberated on the evidence given by almost 200 witnesses, including John Dunne, Charles Bowden and Russell Warren, who were all then in the witness protection programme. Gilligan was found not guilty of the murder of Guerin, but he was convicted of drug trafficking and sentenced to 28 years, the longest sentence ever given for drugs offences in Ireland.[34] An appeal reduced the sentence to 20 years and he was released in 2013.[35]

In the aftermath of her death, some questioned the responsibility of her employers to protect Guerin. In the conclusion to her book assessing Guerin's life and death, Emily O'Reilly, summarises this controversy stating: 'Veronica Guerin died because a murderous, dangerous criminal and his colleagues shouted stop first, instead of the people who were firstly in charge of her, and secondly benefitting enormously from the stories she wrote for them.'[36] What is unquestionable is that Guerin is remembered globally for her 'fearless pursuit of the truth as an investigative journalist and for her refusal to be intimidated'.[37]

Guerin became the subject of several American television documentaries. In 1997, Steve Kroft reported on the Irish journalist's murder on *60 Minutes*. She inspired two films. In the 1999 film, *Though the Sky Falls*, Joan Allen plays a character based on Guerin. In 2003, Joel Schumacher directed *Veronica Guerin*, a film based on Guerin's life, work and her death. Cate Blanchett starred in the title role; Brenda Fricker was cast as Guerin's mother.

Guerin was among those honoured by the International Press Institute (IPI) on the occasion of the Institute's fiftieth anniversary in 2000. She was included in the 50 World Press Freedom Heroes at the IPI's World Congress in Boston. On 22 June 2001, a bronze bust of Guerin was unveiled by Taoiseach Bertie Ahern. The memorial bust was designed by sculptor John Coll and was placed in the gardens of Dublin Castle. An inscription under the bust reads, 'Be not afraid. Greater justice was her ideal and it was her ultimate achievement. Her courage and sacrifice saved many from the scourge of drugs and other crime. Her death has not been in vain.' The sculpture was erected on behalf of Independent Newspapers (Ireland) Limited and the National Millennium Committee.

13. Veronica Guerin Statue, gardens of Dublin Castle. Photographer Corse-calvi.

In 2007, the School of Communications at DCU established the Veronica Guerin Memorial Scholarship in her memory.[38] On 25 June 2011, to commemorate the fifteenth anniversary of her death, a plaque was unveiled on the wall of her secondary school in Killister. The plaque reads, 'Veronica Guerin: In loving memory of a courageous and loyal past pupil, St Mary's Secondary School, 1971–1976.'[39] Veronica Guerin was undoubtedly courageous, and her speech remains as evidence of her work and of her determination.

'I really am both humbled and honoured to receive this award, particularly because of the company that I am keeping here. The other recipients, I certainly feel, are more deserving than myself. I am accepting this award on behalf of myself and particularly on behalf of my colleagues in the *Sunday Independent,* who have encouraged me and supported me in my investigative work whilst I have been working in the paper.

It is very unusual to hear that an Irish reporter has been shot or intimidated. Unfortunately, because of the ever-rising crime problems in Ireland, a number of reporters – not just myself – have been subjected to death threats and to intimidation on a daily basis. So, for my colleagues in other newspapers and in the broadcast media, I'm grateful that the CPJ have decided to honour an Irish and European journalist.

Unfortunately, in Ireland, journalists there also have to face the threat of possible imprisonment. And I welcome this opportunity to highlight the appalling case of a colleague of mine who works in the *Irish Independent.* And she, too, is facing – like Fred M'membe, here – she's facing a possible gaol sentence. And the reason that she's facing possible imprisonment is because she published a document which was widely circulated within the police force in Ireland about the suspects of the bank robbery which I reported on the day before my shooting. Now, Liz Allen is my colleague who's facing a possible gaol sentence. She's – it's alleged – breach[ed] the Official Secrets Act. . . . We write under ridiculous restrictive laws in Ireland. It's a wonderful country, great place to visit, but unfortunately for journalists the most difficult thing that we have to work within are our restrictive libel laws. It's difficult for our publishers because they're the people who have to pay the lawyers the massive amounts of money on a daily basis in courts.

These are the issues that I feel that I have to highlight here. It's not the fact that journalists may be shot. But it is the legitimate restrictions that we work within. And I thank you, I thank the Committee for the Protection of Journalists for giving me the opportunity to highlight this.

I really am humbled and honoured to accept this award. In doing so, I want to thank two people who have encouraged me, despite an incredibly difficult last twelve months. And they are my husband, Graham, and my son, Cathal. Because I can assure you that if they hadn't supported me, I wouldn't be doing it.

Thank you very much.'[40]

ELEVEN

Nuala O'Faolain

1940–2008

Speech on *Are You Somebody*
Barnes & Noble booksellers, New York

18 MARCH 1998

'*The emptiness had been transformed by the act of publishing.*'

Nuala O'Faolain became one of the most respected social and political commentators of modern Ireland. She was also one of the most loved public personalities in Ireland. Her career spanned six decades, during which time she was a successful academic, filmmaker, producer and journalist. The pinnacle of her career was as a best-selling author, which began when she published her cutting-edge memoir *Are You Somebody?* in 1996. The book caused a sensation in Ireland because of her honesty about her childhood and openness about her sexuality.

O'Faolain was born on 1 March 1940 in Clontarf on the north side of Dublin. She had eight siblings, and although her father was a prominent journalist and broadcaster, O'Faolain and her siblings spent their childhood living in abject poverty. Her father, Terry Phelan (Tomás O Phaloin), used the pseudonym Terry O'Sullivan in his professional life. The name was taken from his wife's maiden name. O'Faolain's mother, Kathleen (née O'Sullivan), was a civil servant but was required to give up work when she married. Her mother was an avid reader and had 13 pregnancies during her marriage.

O'Faolain's father was a journalist with the *Irish Press* and the *Sunday Press* newspapers for a number of years. In 1954, when the *Evening Press* national paper was launched, he wrote a column 'The night reporter'. His column was hugely successful and evolved into the 'Dubliner's diary', which historian Paul Rouse notes 'ran for more than twenty years, offering a pot-pourri of social, cultural, and political life in the city'.[1] Terry was a broadcaster for Radio Éireann and worked for RTÉ for several decades, including on his own programme, 'Musical quiz'. Terry O'Sullivan led an unconventional life, which is a theme in Nuala O'Faolain's memoir. He had numerous extramarital affairs that produced at least two other children, one of whom was also called Nuala.

O'Faolain's mother, Kathleen, was left alone for long periods, rearing nine children with little support either financially or emotionally, while her husband socialised in the city. O'Faolain describes how her mother's life was a reflection of the time, as '1940s Ireland was a living tomb for women.'[2] When O'Faolain's father was at home, he mocked his wife and the condition of the house. There was an increasing level of violence in the relationship, and Kathleen numbed her emotions with alcohol. O'Faolain's mother spent every afternoon until late at night drinking in her local pub, leaving her children to fend for themselves. O'Faolain's childhood shaped her writing and indeed much of her behaviour in her later life. She blamed her parents for the premature death of two of her brothers from alcoholism. O'Faolain's childhood and her parents are a central theme in her memoir, *Are You Somebody?*

O'Faolain's education was greatly disturbed. She attended seven different national schools, including ones at Malahide, Baldoyle, Laytown and Balbriggan.[3] At the age of 13, she was expelled from school because the nuns discovered she was consorting with a married man.[4] Her mother enrolled her at St Louis' Convent boarding school in Monaghan, which she attended from the age of 14. O'Faolain later recalled, 'I have no doubt that being sent to this school was the biggest stroke of luck in my life.'[5] She sat her leaving certificate when she was 17 and later successfully completed the entrance and scholarship exams for UCD. She began university at the age of 18 but she was not a committed student. She failed to attend her first-year exams, choosing instead to canvass for Noel Browne's National Progressive Democrat Party during a by-election.

After dropping out of UCD, O'Faolain moved to London for a time and worked as a domestic in a hospital there. She was desperately lonely and unhappy in London. After a year, she managed to re-sit her exams and return to UCD with the financial support of the respected writer Mary Lavin, who had also studied at UCD. O'Faolain graduated in 1961 with a BA in English. The following year she won a scholarship to study mediaeval English at the University of Hull. Then she won a further scholarship to attend Oxford, where she completed a B.Phil. On completing her studies, O'Faolain secured a lectureship in the department of English at UCD.

In 1970, O'Faolain moved back to London and worked as a producer for the BBC on Open University programmes. This was a particularly exciting time for producing educational films. The Open University archive contains 77 films produced by O'Faolain on a wide range of topics, from *Gathering oral evidence in Belfast* to *An Irish poorhouse and its district, 1845–1851*.[6] O'Faolain was especially proud of producing *Germinal* in which John Berger examines what is at stake in Émile Zola's novel, 'relating it to the experience of miners in a Welsh pit community of the early 1970s'.[7] The film was broadcast 'between the miner's strike of 1972 and the Three Day Week of 1974'.[8] O'Faolain and Berger became lovers during this time. He was by then a famous writer and critic, having come to public attention through his television series *Ways of Seeing*, broadcast in 1972. O'Faolain was in a ten-year relationship with the art critic Tim Hilton, whom she left the day before they were set to get married, *c.* 1974.

O'Faolain returned to Ireland in 1976 and took up a job as a producer for RTÉ in 1977. She had a nervous breakdown after her father died of leukaemia on 5 December 1980, and she checked herself into St Patrick's hospital for treatment. Her mother, whose continuing alcoholism blighted her relationship with her children, died alone in the bathroom of her home on 29 September 1985. O'Faolain's early years back in Dublin were marked by heavy drinking and instability until she met the journalist and feminist Nell McCafferty. McCafferty had a stabilising effect on O'Faolain, and the two had a relationship for nearly 16 years. McCafferty helped O'Faolain control her drinking and to take control of her own life. O'Faolain described their partnership as 'by far the most life-giving relationship of my life'.[9] She continued working at RTÉ, producing programmes such as *Women Today* with presenter Marian Finucane; the two remained close friends for the rest of their lives. In 1985, O'Faolain won a Jacobs Award for producing *Plain Tales*, a series focussing on women's experiences.

The following year, O'Faolain was offered a column in the *Irish Times*, which was a turning point in her career. O'Faolain's columns, published weekly, covered an array of social and political topics. The author June Caldwell best describes O'Faolain's articles:

> The supreme achievement of these columns was both to explain the huge double standards encrusted in Irish life, and to confront her audience with their complicity. In 1997, for instance, on the death of the paedophile priest Brendan Smyth, who raped hundreds of children over the course of four decades, Nuala held up a tarnished mirror to her public. She wrote that 'they went on calling him "Father" in this culture; even though he embodied the worst wickedness anyone could think of, the notion of taking his title from him, or tacitly agreeing not to use it, was not entertained'.[10]

In 1987, O'Faolain won the A. T. Cross Woman Journalist of the Year.[11] O'Faolain's columns gained wide attention; not surprisingly, she was approached by numerous publishers to produce a volume of these articles. As O'Faolain notes in her speech in this section, she thought this was a lazy form of publishing and declined. Then she was approached by a recently established independent press in Dublin. Established in 1992, New Island was then a small press. O'Faolain agreed to publish with New Island but insisted on writing an introduction to give readers something new. Her introduction grew in word count and resulted in a forthright and uncompromising memoir.

Are You Somebody? The Life and Times of Nuala O'Faolain was published in September 1996. The book initially included her memoir followed by a selection of O'Faolain's *Irish Times* columns. O'Faolain appeared on the *Late Late Show* on 18 October 1996 for a candid interview with presenter Gay Byrne. That interview exhibits just how sensational the content of her book was, at the time of publication. Byrne opened by stating, 'To say that I am astonished and amazed at the revelations in this book is to put it mildly.'[12] Byrne continued by noting that O'Faolain had revealed in her memoir that she had slept with 'a fairly lengthy list' of men. O'Faolain responded by explaining how, 'I belonged, I think people still do, to a culture where the idea was that you were to grow up to find someone to love, then they'd love you. End of story'.[13] She went on to describe how she had spent decades searching for Mr. Right to no avail. In an honest exchange, O'Faolain challenged the notion that women should save themselves for marriage, questioning, 'does it not become reasonable for a woman to sleep with a fella or two'.[14]

The RTÉ studio audience responded positively to O'Faolain as did the Irish public. The following week *Are You Somebody?* entered the Irish bestseller list for paperback non-fiction and in the category of Irish published.[15] The book would remain a best seller in Ireland for 20 weeks. Irish newspapers were awash with commentaries on her television appearance; most commentators were in awe of her courage in revealing her personal life. Columnist Eddie Coffey was 'struck by the courage she showed in exposing her childhood and private life to the nation in the way she did'.[16] He concluded that 'despite (or maybe because of) many years that she would prefer to forget, she remains one of the most "human" writers around and can bring this to bear on a very wide range of subjects.'[17]

The commentary on her writing continued to be very positive. Liz Ryan, books editor with the *Evening Herald*, observed, 'Nuala is a vivid, slightly elegiac writer and, off her journalistic leash, she flows and bubbles like the Shannon.'[18] O'Faolain was certainly off her journalistic leash and she thrived. She became a full-time author from this point. *Are You*

Somebody? continued to climb the best-seller list and took the top place on 8 November 1996. Before the year was out, *Are You Somebody?* had gone to a third print run, and O'Faolain was in demand across the country for book signings.[19] The book was described as 'one of the most commercially successful Irish books of 1996'.[20]

Her book drew attention from foreign publishers. O'Faolain was approached by an English publisher; Sceptre, an imprint of Hodder & Stoughton, published a new version in 1997. The British version did not include the *Irish Times* columns, and so O'Faolain wrote what she describes in her speech as an afterword. An American volume was first published by Henry Holt in February 1998. The American version dropped the question mark from the title and added a new subtitle: *The Accidental Memoir of a Dublin Woman*, which was apt for reasons explained in O'Faolain's speech. The back cover included high praise for O'Faolain's memoir from the most prestigious Irish writers, including Frank McCourt, Roddy Doyle, Colm Tóibín and Edna O'Brien. O'Brien wrote that the book is 'a remarkable memoir, poignant, truthful, and imparting that quiet wisdom which suffering brings'.[21]

O'Faolain went to America in March 1998 for a week-long tour to publicise the book; she said it was 'the most exhausting and most exhilarating week of my life'.[22] *Are You Somebody* quickly hit the best-seller lists in the *Boston Globe* and the *San Francisco Chronicle*.[23] Then a rave review by journalist Zoe Heller was published in the *New York Times*, announcing that:

> . . . what O'Faolain exemplifies is that rare and much underrated quality – a sense of proportion. As a result, while her story incorporates many of the familiar features of the 20th-century Irish narrative – booze, religious repression, sexual guilt – it avoids the affectations and subverts the sentimentalities that often afflict a certain sort of self-consciously 'Oirish' literature.[24]

O'Faolain appeared on NBC's popular television programme *Good Morning America* on St Patrick's Day along with Frank McCourt. McCourt had published *Angela's Ashes: A Memoir* in September 1996, for which he won America's most prestigious literary award, the Pulitzer Prize, in 1997. The day after this television appearance, O'Faolain gave the speech in this section to an audience at Barnes & Noble booksellers, in New York. Her talk was introduced by McCourt. Sales of O'Faolain's book spiralled in New York, and it hit the best-seller list. O'Faolain was now an outstanding success, selling over one million copies of her book.

O'Faolain remained in Dublin, and she was now financially prosperous. She was thoughtful with her new wealth and bought her younger brother a house in Dublin; despite her support, her brother died prematurely a few years later. Initially, O'Faolain continued writing columns for the *Irish Times*; she was later granted leave from the newspaper to take up a fellowship at Glucksman Ireland House at New York University (NYU). She moved to Manhattan and taught a course on famous Irish memoirs at NYU. In 2002, O'Faolain resigned from the *Irish Times*. She wrote a column for the *Sunday Tribune* from 2005 to 2008 but focussed on writing books.

14. Nuala O'Faolain, publicity photograph for *My Dream of You*, 19 February 2001. Photograph by Perry Odgen. Courtesy of Mairead Brady.

While in New York, O'Faolain started writing a novel that went to a publishing auction. The prestigious New York publisher Viking won with a bid of $1 million for the publication rights. Her first novel, *My Dream of You*, was published in 2001 and became a best seller. Her next best-selling book, *Almost There*, published in 2003, was a memoir that focussed on her years after *Are You Somebody* was released. Her historical fiction novel *The Story of Chicago May* was published in 2005 and won the Prix Femina prize the following year.[25] In 2006, she was awarded an honorary doctorate by the Open University.[26]

O'Faolain was writing her third novel, *Best Love Rosie*, when she learnt that she was terminally ill. She returned to Ireland for treatment. On 12 April 2008, she met her friend Marian Finucane in Galway to record an interview about her terminal illness and imminent death. The interview was shockingly honest and heart-breaking. The *Irish Independent* recently published a full transcript of the interview, which they described as 'one of the most heart-rending and candid moments on *The Marian Finucane Show*'.[27]

O'Faolain died at Blackrock Hospice in Dublin on 9 May 2008. The *Evening Herald* dedicated its front page to a tribute to O'Faolain the following day.[28] All of the main national newspapers reported on O'Faolain's death; the *Irish Independent* announced that 'Nuala O'Faolain was one of a generation of Irish women journalists who were as notable for their campaigns for women's rights as for their remarkable writing skills. Even among that colourful company, she stood out for her sharp intelligence and unique writing.'[29] Her funeral mass was held at the Church of the Visitation in Fairview before the congregation proceeded to Glasnevin crematorium on 13 May 2008. As was expected, the church was packed with those paying tribute to O'Faolain, among them notable politicians, presenters and authors, including Nell McCafferty and Marian Finucane.

O'Faolain's final novel, *Best Love Rosie*, was posthumously published by New Island Books in March 2009. In his review of the book, author Ian Sansom declared that the book is 'best read as a long addendum to the interview [with Finucane]. . . . It is a summation, a record of a brilliant mind attempting to come to rest.'[30] In 2010, *A More Complex Truth*, a compilation of O'Faolain's *Irish Times* columns, was published with an introduction by writer and journalist Fintan O'Toole.[31] The volume was published in America the following year under the title *A Radiant Life*.[32]

In 2011, Marian Finucane produced and narrated a documentary dedicated to her friend, *Nuala: A Life and Death*. In May 2018, New Island Books published a commemorative edition of *Are You Somebody?* with an introduction by acclaimed author June Caldwell. This edition was republished again in 2020 and in 2021. In August 2022, New Island Books reissued O'Faolain's second memoir, *Almost There*. This edition has a new foreword written by the prestigious Irish author and Booker Prize winner, Anne Enright. Enright describes O'Faolain as 'brilliant, incisive and very charming'.[33] An article in the *Irish Independent* claimed that Nuala O'Faolain's 'memorial will be her writings, and the bleak courage with which she confronted life and death'.[34] The following speech remains as a testament not only to her deep intelligence but also to her quick wit and charming personality.

'I'm going to explain the title. You see this title: *Are You Somebody?* The Irish edition has a question mark. It is based on – sometimes I used to be on the television in Ireland, and then I might be in a bar a few nights later, and there'd be maybe a few women out for a few scoops. You'd see them talking to each other and looking at me, and then one of them would wobble across and stick her nose right into my nose and say, "Are you somebody?" [Laughter.] And that's a very important question, like. Am I somebody? And if so, what type of a body would I be? was a question, it turned out, I had to ask myself, like, in my fifties. And also "are you somebody?" neatly got rid of what I knew would be the reaction in Dublin to my saying nothing about myself at all, which was, "Who does she think she is?" You know. [Laughter.] And I wanted them to know that I knew I was nobody just as much as they knew I was nobody. Right? [Laughter.] So that was the general title, and then *The Accidental Memoir of a Dublin Woman*, that is absolutely true.

You see, I don't know or care about whether fiction has given way to the memoir genre or all that stuff. What happened to me was, you see, I write this column, and from time to time, very small publishers would come to me, and they'd ask could they collect old opinion columns, not because anyone at all wanted to read them but because it's a quick, cheap piece of bookmaking. Slap a cover on it – looks like a book. And it's so despicable a form of publication that even I said no. [Laughter.] But there I was two years ago, and I had nothing, it seemed to me. . . . And this very nice man asked me, and his little company was so small it consisted of him, another man that nobody knew what he was doing in Ireland anyway, and a little girl on a course, you know. And so, I said yes.

And then because I was ashamed, I said I'll write an introduction, then at least there'd be something new. And he said, "Oh, that's a good idea." And he must have envisaged something like a page and a half long. And, of course, I put it out of my mind, because I didn't want to write. I look on writing as hard work, and I don't want to do it. And it was due in March, so by April, I had stopped answering the phone, in case it was him. [Laughter.] Polite as he was, he did keep mentioning it. [Laughter.]

I was stuck, you see. An opinion column sort of is supposed to issue from some kind of solid Mount Ararat, you know, and you're supposed to know your politics and your ideology from which you're writing your opinions. But when I examined myself for these great things, I didn't have them. All I had – the only thing that formed my opinions – was my life. So, I knew that I couldn't say anything in my introduction except maybe something personal, to say this is what I experienced, and *that's* why I believe x or y! But I couldn't write something personal. I couldn't write the first sentence. I had written loads and loads of impersonal columns – a little bit personal, but never anything that went me, me, me, because it's terribly hard for a middle-aged Irish woman, however confident she may appear, to make that claim, you know, and say, "I can begin a sentence with *I*." And I couldn't do it. It was like a physical barrier.

So, I signed up for a writing course. And I went on this writing course down on Parnell Square. Six Wednesday nights. Sixty quid. And I was [en]raged, and I thought, "This bloody book is costing me money." [Laughter.] And I went on the writing course, and it was full of these brilliant writers. I mean it was a shock. . . . there were the usual quiet, like, housewives writing dynamically interesting poetry and short stories and all, so that wasn't helping me. [Laughter.] But the fourth week, the fourth week, the woman in charge of us gave us an exercise – *ecker*. . . . We had to write something that happened in a bathroom. . . .

So, that week, I remembered that my mother had died on the floor of the bathroom. And I suppose somebody who knew about therapy would think, "Oh, yeah, that's obvious. That is how you begin." But I didn't know that. I wrote my 2,000 words about mammy and her death. After that, then I just wrote the bits leading up to that, and then I wrote the bits leading after that. And it got longer and longer and longer, and the poor fella that had asked for the introduction was horrified. . . .

We met for a cup of coffee, and he said to me, "We're thinking of printing 2,500 copies." And I said, "I absolutely beg you not to, because every time I pass a book shop they'll be for sale outside for sixpence." [Laughter.] Great trays of remaindered ones, and everybody will know the eejit I made of myself in my middle age. [Laughter.] And he said, "Well, I'll ring the printer." And I went with him to the phone, and we rang the printer. And the printer refused to print fewer than 2,500. He said it wasn't worth his while, you know, doing the thing. . . .

Just before it came out, I met this friend of mine, and she said, "When's your book coming out?" And I said, "It isn't a book. And it's not coming out. [Laughter.] It's trickling out backwards. I hope nobody's going to notice." And she said, "Nonsense!" She said, "A book can only either come out or not come out." She said, "And if you wrote it, it's *yours*." She said, "Stand by it." So, I saw the justice of that, and I did stand by it in the sense that I rang up the main chat show and told them that the fella who does the chat show is mentioned in it about fifteen times. And so it was on that show, so then everyone heard of it. And believe me, my publishers weren't then and are not now in the phone book. [Laughter.] I didn't know that anything had happened. I went walking with the dog the day after the chat show, and wasn't Eason's the booksellers ringing up looking for 10,000 copies? But they had nobody to ring up. I didn't answer the phone. [Laughter.] They couldn't find the publisher. So, when I say *accidental* I mean "accidental". . . .

However, let me just say that it did mean something to people, because it definitely did; because I started getting letters back from people that read it. And you could see that the moment had been exactly right, to admit to a certain kind of sorrow, and that there was people out there so sorrowing that they wanted to talk back to me. And so they did, and this dialogue continues.

And then, after a while, a company in England published it. . . . I was so intimidated by the English people that I opened my big mouth again, and I said, "I'll write an afterword." And then I was back to not answering the phone in case it was the English people looking for the afterword. [Laughter.] But I did write an afterword, and the reason I did is not that this book is going to be called P.S., P.S., P.S., and every year I'm going to write another bit. It's that it was no sooner out than it wasn't the truth anymore: that the solitude it described and the, you know, the emptiness had been transformed by the act of publishing it. So that I couldn't leave it out there as the record because it wasn't the record, because life had had that one last kick in the tail ready – not to mention *this* kick in the tail, which I haven't even begun to come to terms with.

So, I wrote this afterword anyway to get them off me back. And I centred it around a thing that had really happened, which was Good Friday, I had gone into a church. On Thursdays in Ireland, they say on the radio what's the best seller. . . . But anyway, . . . that Thursday – Holy Thursday last year – I had been there, and I had gone off it. And that seemed to be good – that I was finished with it now.'[35]

TWELVE

Nuala Ní Dhomhnaill

b. 1952

Speech by the Chair of Poetry, 'Níl cead isteach ag an bpobal
(Public access denied)'
Queen's University, Belfast

DECEMBER 2001

'Níl againn ach scéalta (Stories are all we have).'

Nuala Ní Dhomhnaill is one of the most distinguished female poets
who writes solely in the Irish language. Her work has been central to re-
invigorating the Irish language in modern poetry. The highly regarded
poet Theo Dorgan attests that Ní Dhomhnaill 'is by far the most widely
translated Irish language poet of her generation, perhaps of all time'.[1] Ní
Dhomhnaill's writing is translated into many languages, including English,
French, German, Polish, Italian, Norwegian, Estonian and Japanese. These
translated works have brought Ní Dhomhnaill's literature to a global
audience.

Nuala Ní Dhomhnaill was born in Lancashire in 1952 to Irish parents.
Her father spoke Irish in their household. When she reached five years of
age, Ní Dhomhnaill went to live with her aunt in the Gaeltacht town of
Dingle in county Kerry.[2] Two years later she moved to Nenagh, county
Tipperary, to live with her parents. She began writing poetry when she was
in school. A teacher encouraged Ní Dhomhnaill to attend the first ever
Cumann Merriman, which was being held in her hometown of Nenagh
in January 1969. The Scoil Gheimhridh Merriman (Merriman Winter
School) is held in Irish and examines topics related to Irish language and
literature. Ní Dhomhnaill found herself among the most prestigious Irish-

language writers and musicians of the time. Speakers that year included the writer and translator Máirtín Ó Cadhain; the poet and journalist Seán Ó Ríordáin; and the poet Máirtín Ó Direáin. The latter two were described by Irish scholar Caoimhín Mac Giolla Léith as part of 'a new generation of modern poets in Irish, distinct in outlook and ambition from most of the revivalist poets who preceded them'.[3] Ní Dhomhnaill read her poems, and afterwards she received praise from the Irish poet and actor Caitlín Maude.[4]

Later that same year, Ní Dhomhnaill entered an *Irish Times* poetry competition. Her poem 'Sobhairíní i Samhain' was selected as a winner and was published in the *Irish Times* on 6 August 1969.[5] No language was specified for entries in the poetry competition. It was apparently assumed that poems would be entered in English since the main judge, Charles Monteith, director of the publishers Faber and Faber, did not understand Irish. Monteith noted at the end of his assessment in the *Irish Times* that as 'I can't, alas, read Irish, I'm not able to say anything about Nuala Ní Dhomhnaill's "Sobhairíní i Samhain."'[6] The fact that a major national Irish newspaper assumed entries for a poetry competition would be submitted only in English is a reflection of how Irish-language literature was marginalised. Ní Dhomhnaill attended University College Cork, where she studied Irish and English. While at university, Ní Dhomhnaill played a central role in Irish-language societies.

When asked in an interview with Theo Dorgan why people are letting the Irish language die, Ní Dhomhnaill explained that 'the famine had a lot to do with it and we associated Irish with poverty and hunger. . . . A lot of us haven't made the transition to the fact that you can actually be multilingual.'[7] Ní Dhomhnaill's poetry, her teaching and her public engagements have re-awakened an interest in Irish-language literature. She has held fellowships at the most prestigious universities, including as the Burns Chair of Irish Studies at Boston College, the Humboldt Chair of Irish Studies at Villanova University, and the Naughton Fellow of Irish Studies at the University of Notre Dame.

Ní Dhomhnaill was awarded the Ireland Chair of Poetry from 2001 to 2004. This esteemed chair was established through the Ireland Chair of Poetry Trust founded in 1998 in celebration of Seamus Heaney winning the Nobel Prize for Literature. Heaney was awarded the Nobel Prize in 1995 'for works of lyrical beauty and ethical depth, which exalt everyday miracles and the living past'.[8] The trust appoints a poet of distinction to hold the chair for a three-year period. During their tenure, the chair is connected to each of the three universities associated with the trust – Queen's University Belfast, Trinity College Dublin and University College Dublin – for one year. This is an all-Ireland collaboration overseen by the

Arts Council of Northern Ireland and the Arts Council/An Chomhairle
Ealaíon of Ireland. During their period of residency, the chair mentors
students and delivers public talks, which culminate in a formal lecture.
Heaney described how 'the Ireland Professor of Poetry is an honour as well
as an office. To hold this professorship is to stand as a representative of the
art within the Irish university system. The post is intended to manifest the
value of poetry within our cultural and intellectual life, north and south.'[9]

The first Ireland Chair of Poetry, John Montague, held the position
from 1998 to 2001.[10] Ní Dhomhnaill was the second person appointed,
holding the chair from 2001 to 2004. In the December of her first year,
Ní Dhomhnaill delivered the speech in this section, 'Níl cead isteach ag
an bpobal: Tírdhreach liteartha neamhaitheanta na Gaolainne (Public
access denied: Or the unrecognised literary landscape of Irish)', at Queen's
University, Belfast. Lilliput Press published *The Poet's Chair* in 2008 to
celebrate the tenth anniversary of the Ireland Chair of Poetry.[11] The volume
collected the first nine annual lectures, including three by Ní Dhomhnaill, a
foreword by Seamus Heaney and a preface by Donnell Deeny, the founding
chairman of the Poetry Trust. The volume was successful, and UCD
Press later produced individual volumes of each poet's public lectures. Ní
Dhomhnaill's volume was published in 2017, with the subtitle adapted
from the title of this speech, *Cead Isteach (Entry Permitted)*.[12] The Chair
of the Arts Council's Board of Trustees, Sheila Pratschke, described how
'in these absorbing lectures, [Ní Dhomhnaill] discusses the importance of
place in Irish literature and the need to preserve important sites of Irish
literary activity.'[13]

The fact that Ní Dhomhnaill discussed the importance of the Irish
language and sites of Irish literary landscape at a university in Belfast was
significant. Until May 2022, Northern Ireland, unlike Scotland and Wales,
did not have a law protecting the indigenous language of the land. The
Welsh Language Act of 1993 puts the Welsh language on an equal footing
with English in Wales. The Gaelic Language (Scotland) Act 2005 provided
a legislative framework for the use of Gaelic by public sector bodies in
Scotland. The issue of establishing an Irish Language Act on a par with
the Republic of Ireland, making the Irish language equal to the English
language in Northern Ireland, caused much political controversy.

The Northern Ireland Assembly at Stormont provided a devolved
government for Northern Ireland in accordance with the Good Friday
(Belfast) Agreement in 1998. A section in the agreement focused on
'economic, social and cultural issues', noting particularly that 'all
participants recognise the importance of respect, understanding and
tolerance in relation to linguistic diversity, including in Northern Ireland,
the Irish language, Ulster-Scots and the languages of the various ethnic

communities, all of which are part of the cultural wealth of the island of Ireland.'[14] When Ní Dhomhnaill delivered her talk at Queen's University, little to no action had been taken to promote or cherish the Irish language in Northern Ireland.

The Northern Ireland Executive was suspended less than a year after Ní Dhomhnaill's speech. In October 2002, the Sinn Féin offices at Stormont were raided as part of an investigation into an alleged IRA spy ring. The Northern Ireland Secretary, John Reid, suspended devolution, and Northern Ireland was again governed through Westminster. In an attempt to restore a devolved government at Stormont, the Northern Ireland (St Andrews Agreement) Act 2006 was agreed by the British and Irish governments and the main political parties in Northern Ireland. That agreement included a strategy relating to the Irish language, stating, 'The Executive Committee shall adopt a strategy setting out how it proposes to enhance and protect the development of the Irish language.'[15]

After the signing of the St Andrews Agreement, the Democratic Unionist Party (DUP) leader Ian Paisley and Sinn Féin's Martin McGuinness entered a power-sharing government in 2007. However, the executive failed to legislate for the protection of the Irish language in Northern Ireland. In 2017, McGuinness resigned in protest over the renewable heat incentive scandal, which saw costs for the DUP's scheme spiral; Stormont again collapsed. Sinn Féin leader Gerry Adams later stated that 'there won't be an assembly without an Acht na Gaeilge [Irish Language Act].'[16] The issue of an Irish language act remained controversial in Northern Ireland, and a number of protests were staged by An Dream Dearg (The Red Group), most recently on 21 May 2022, when thousands of protesters marched from Cultúrlann on the Falls Road to Belfast City Hall.[17]

Following the Northern Ireland elections in 2022, the DUP refused to enter a power-sharing government and Stormont remained in a state of suspension. On 25 May 2022, the Identity and Language (Northern Ireland) Bill was introduced to the UK Parliament aiming to deliver 'a balanced package of language and identity measures' including 'official recognition of the status of the Irish language in Northern Ireland.'[18] While the introduction of this bill is historically significant, it is just the beginning of a process to promote cultural pluralism in Northern Ireland. Ní Dhomhnaill's Irish-language poetry and her public talks remain culturally and politically significant. Her speech at Queen's University explains, with clarity, the importance of place in Irish literature and for the Irish language. The sites mentioned by Ní Dhomhnaill in her speech include areas across the entire island of Ireland.

Ní Dhomhnaill is recognised as the predominant champion of Irish-language literature. She has received several awards, including the

Lawrence O'Shaughnessy Award for Poetry, the American Ireland Fund Literary Award and the Seán Ó Ríordáin Award, which she won for four of her Irish poetry collections. Ní Dhomhnaill was awarded an honorary degree, a Doctor in Letters (Litt.D), from Trinity College Dublin on 6 July 2007 and an honorary Doctorate of Literature from University College Dublin on 16 June 2011. Ní Dhomhnaill has published numerous volumes of poetry, including *An Dealg Droighin* (1981), *Féar Suaithinseach* (1984), *Rogha Dánta/Selected Poems* (1986, 1988, 1990), *Pharaoh's Daughter* (1990), *Feis* (1991), *The Astrakhan Cloak* (1992), *Spíonáin is Róiseanna* (1993), *In the Heart of Europe: Poems for Bosnia* (1998) and *Cead Aighnis* (2000).

As well as her vast literary contributions, Ní Dhomhnaill supports other Irish female poets through major scholarly contributions. Most notably, Ní Dhomhnaill edited the contemporary poetry section in the *Field Day Anthology of Irish Writing*. When Seamus Deane edited three volumes of *The Field Day Anthology of Irish Writing*, female writers were sadly lacking. Field Day agreed to add two further volumes; volumes 4 and 5, *Irish Women's Writing and Traditions*, were published in 2002.[19] These substantial volumes, edited by eight main editors and a host of sub-editors, remain the most comprehensive account of Irish women's writing. Ní Dhomhnaill explained why she took on the role of a sub-editor: 'When I first took it upon myself to make this selection, back in the early 1990s, I did so out of a sense of moral outrage at the way women poets were being treated in Ireland. It seemed obvious to me that the rules of the game for men and women poets were different.'[20]

15. Nuala Ní Dhomhnaill, i mBéal Feirste, 3 April 2009, Contributor Ériugena.

Ní Dhomhnaill's poetry is on the leaving certificate syllabus, an accolade which ensures that second-level students in Ireland are familiar with her work. In 2018, she was the first woman to be awarded the Zbigniew Herbert International Literary Award, a distinction in the global literary world. Yurii Andrukhovych, a member of the international jury for the award, justified their decision stating that:

> We have to recognise Nuala Ní Dhomhnaill as someone who is like a fearless agent of a universal reanimation service of the Gaelic language. Defending the right to exist of her 'small language', Nuala Ní Dhomhnaill defends – at the same time – the right of Irish women to self-sufficient creativity, for a highly individual, sharply critical approach to the 'masculine' social reality of her country.[21]

In recognition of her work, Ní Dhomhnaill is a member of Aosdána, which is a premier Irish honour granted to those in the creative arts. Only those writers and artists whose 'work has made an outstanding contribution to the creative arts in Ireland' are honoured with this lifetime membership.[22] Membership is limited to 250 people, and members are selected by peer nomination and election. Nuala Ní Dhomhnaill remains a champion of Irish-language literature, most evident through her writing and her speeches. An extract from Ní Dhomhnaill's speech at Queen's University follows in Irish, with an English translation by her below.

'Ba mhaith liom a shamhlú gurb é an leagan ceart Gaolainne ar an Ollúnacht seo ná Ollamh Fódla. Gabhann an t-ainm sin siar i bhfad i réimsí na staire agus na miotaseolaíochta. Deir *Leabhar Gabhála Éireann* go raibh a leithéid d'Ollamh ann. Cailleadh sa bhliain 1390 RCh é agus is in Uisneach atá sé curtha. Chreid na luathársaitheoirí chomh daingean sin sa neach miotaseolaíochta seo gur dhein Macalister tochailt ar a uaigh, más fíor. Níor thángthas ar chorp ar bith san uaigh, ar ndóigh. Níor neach ceart é an tOllamh Fódla ach neach a fáisceadh as an miotaseolaíocht. Ach ní shin le rá nach ann dó go láidir mar mheafar. Meafar ab ea é. Meafar is ea é. Is cuid de réimse miotaseolaíochta agus samhlaíochta na hÉireann é, a d'fhág a mharc ar an litríocht riamh anall, go dtí an lá inniu féin. Is gné é seo atá cosúil go maith leis an gCúigiú Cúige a mhol Mary Robinson le linn a hUachtaránachta.

Is cóir mar sin agus is ceart má tá fáil ar a uaigh in aon áit gur in Uisneach a gheofaí í, croílár tíreolaíochta agus spioradáltachta na hÉireann, lár an Chúigiú Cúige. Is é imleacán na hÉireann é, arb ionann é agus an chloch i lár shuíomh beannaithe Delphi na Gréige – *omphalos* nó imleacán an domhain. Agus go deimhin tá *omphalos* in Uisneach. Is cloch an-aisteach í go dtugann muintir na háite "The Cat's Stone" uirthi sa Bhéarla agus go dtugtar Aill na Míreann uirthi sa Ghaolainn; glacaim leis gurb é an focal céanna é "mír" agus "curadhmhír", an chuid ab fhearr den fheoil go mbíodh na seanlaochra ag troid go bás ar a son. Seasann an mhír seo do chúig cúigí na hÉireann a tháinig le chéile ar an mball seo, de réir an tseanchais.

Bhí grianghraf den leacht neamhshuaithinseach seo, nach gallán, dolmain ná uaigh é, in eagrán den leabhar *Aimsir Óg* a tháinig amach le déanaí agus ina bhfuil saothar le céad scríbhneoir Gaolainne. Is maith liom a shamhlú go bhfuil cuspóir leis seo go léir. Is maith liom a shamhlú go bhfuil ceangal éigin idir céad scríbhneoir Gaolainne a bheith ann agus leac uaighe Ollamh Fódla. Fé mar a d'éirigh sé aníos ionainne. Fé mar ba sinne go léir a chuid leanaí.

Bhain go leor scríbhneoirí leas as an gcloch seo. Is cuid de chosmeolaíocht phearsanta James Joyce í. Mar sin féin, agus is pointe é seo a bheidh á dhearbhú arís agus arís eile agam sa léacht seo, is beag le rá é i gcomhthéacs an tsuímh féin in Uisneach, i gContae na hIarmhí. Tá fána bheag ann, mar is léir ón ainm Uisneach, ón nGaolainn "uisinn". Tugann an Duinníneach "a temple of the head" air chun nach gceapfaí gur teampall nó foirgneamh é. Tá comhartha beag dubh is bán in aice leis agus "Uisneach" scríofa air ach ní thugtar a thuilleadh eolais don taistealaí neamhairdiúil ná d'éinne eile a bheadh ag gabháil na slí. Cén fáth gur dóigh liom gur mór an trua é seo? Cén fáth gur dóigh liom gur sampla maith is ea é de rúnoidhreacht na hÉireann nach léir in aon chor í don ghnáthshaoránach? B'fhéidir gurb amhlaidh is fearr é. B'fhéidir gurb é an rud deireanach ar fad atá uainn ná Ionad Oidhreachta ar an suíomh seo, rud a léireodh ní arbh fhearr leat a bheith clúdaithe le tost is mistéir, ní a chaithfeadh daoine aonair a aimsiú chun go mbeadh sé ina shuíomh oilithreachta inmheánach dóibh, mar a déarfá.

Mar b'fhéidir an rud céanna a rá fé Ráth Cruachan, tamaillín suas an bóthar i gContae Ros Comáin. An uair dheireanach a thugas cuairt ar an áit úd ní fhaca mé ach sreanganna agus feochadáin. Arís bhí comhartha beag taobh leis an ráth a dúirt go raibh cónaí anseo ar go leor de Ríthe Chonnacht. Ní luaitear Meadhbh. Ní luaitear Ailill. Ní luaitear an Táin. Ní luaitear an comhrá cáiliúil idir an bheirt agus seo sampla de le go dtuigfí cad tá i gceist:

"Is fíorbhriathar é a 'níon ó"[,] arsa Ailill, "is maith an bhean bean dea-fhir."

"Is maith cheana"[,] arsa an iníon, "ach cén fáth duit sin a rá?"

"Tá", arsa Ailill, "gur fearr tusa inniu ná an lá a thógas-sa thú."

"Ba mhaith mise romhat"[,] arsa Meadhbh.

Agus fé mar a deir siad, "Chuadar ón bhfocal beag go dtí an bhfocal mór le chéile":

"Cibé a imreann méala nó meirtne nó mearbhall ortsa nil éiric ná eineachlann ann duitse ach a bhfuil domsa", arsa Meadhbh, "mar is fear an tionchar mná atá ionat."

A thuilleadh maslaí sa dá threo. Ansin:

"Mar sin féin", arsa Meadhbh, "is mó mo mhaithsa ná do mhaithsa."

"Is ionadh liom sin", arsa Ailill, "mar níl neach is mó seod agus maoin agus ollmhaitheas ná mise agus tá a fhios agam nach bhfuil."

[O'Rahilly]

Níl aon chúlántacht anseo. Níor shuáilce í an chúlántacht i measc na Sean-Ghael, bíodh an meon athraithe ó shin nó ná bíodh.

Bhuaigh Ailill i ndeireadh na dála, go sealadach, mar is aige atá an Finnbheannach agus níl a chómhaith ag Meadhbh. Bíodh sin mar atá, tugann sí fé sheilbh a fháil ar an Donn Cuailnge, rud a chuireann tús leis an eachtra ar fad agus le téacs na Tána, an rud is cóngaraí d'eipic náisiúnta atá againn.

Nach cuma mura bhfuil macallaí na Tána le clos thart ar Ráth Cruachan mar atá sé inniu? Tar éis an tsaoil níl iontu ach scéalta. Scéalta fánacha a d'oirfeadh, mar a dúirt na manaigh féin a bhreac síos iad, *ad delectationem stultorum*, "le haghaidh sult na n-amadán". Ach sin é go díreach é. Níl againn ach scéalta. Insímid scéalta dá chéile le bheith beo agus chun leanúint orainn. Agus bhí suímh chomh hoiriúnach do na scéalta sin in Éirinn againn le fada an lá gur mór an trua nach féidir iad a aithint. Cuimhním agus ríméad ar leith orm ar rud éigin a thit amach nuair a bhí an dara hiníon againn, Ayse, thart ar a haon déag. An lá áirithe seo chuir sí ceist orm: "Tás agat, a Mham, na scéalta sin go léir sa Táin – Deirdre agus Naoise agus Cú Chulainn agus an stuif sin ar fad – ar tharla sé sin go léir?" "Bhuel is scéalta breátha iad agus fiú munar tharla siad tá siad chomh maith sin mar scéalta gur chóir gur tharla." Ach pé acu ar tharla nó nár tarla, ar a laghad ar bith tá a fhios againn an áit inar tharla siad." "Is cén áit ab ea é sin?" "In Eamhain Mhacha." "Tá a leithéid d'áit ann mar sin?"

Agus dúrtsa go raibh a leithéid d'áit ann go deimhin agus go raibh sé ann i gcónaí – tamall lasmuigh d'Ard Mhacha i dTuaisceart Éireann – agus má bhí fonn uirthi dul ann go raghaimis ann chun é a fheiscint. Rud a dheineamar. An chéad deireadh seachtaine tar éis don tsíocháin briseadh amach, thugamar seáp ó thuaidh agus roinnt cairde inár dteannta agus bhí saol an mhadra bháin againn. Ar an mbóthar abhaile bhí an trácht go hainnis timpeall na Teorann, ach fuaireamar amach nach raibh bac ná moill orainn toisc líon mór na ndaoine a bhí amuigh agus an fonn céanna orthu is a bhí orainn féin, is é sin cuid d'Éirinn nach bhfacamar cheana, nó nach bhfacamar i gceart, a aimsiú.

Sean-nath calctha a bhaineann leis an litríocht in Éirinn ná í bheith gafa le háiteanna. Cúis mhaith ba dhóigh leat go marcálfaí na háiteanna sin ar cuid dlúth den litríocht iad. Is dócha gur i mBinn Umha gar go leor dúinne anseo, a chónaigh éinín dil na Sean-Ghaolainne, Int én bec ro léic feit, lon dubh Loch Lao.

Agus ar ndóigh cathair liteartha nótáilte is ea Baile Átha Cliath. Ach i mBaile Átha Cliath féin, braithim easnamh. Gné iomlán liteartha in easnamh. Gné liteartha na Gaolainne. Sampla beag. Thuas ag Ardeaglais Naomh Pádraig tá plaic mhór tiomnaithe do na "Writers of Dublin". Tá scata ainmneacha luaite ann ach níl oiread is scríbhneoir Gaolainne amháin ina measc. Ba chuma liom ach an chuid seo de Bhaile Átha Cliath, go háirithe sna Libirtí taobh leis, ba nead scríbhneoireachta agus scoláireachta Gaolainne í chomh fada siar le tús an ochtú haois déag. Lárnach ann bhí an file agus an scríobhaí Seán Ó Neachtain, fear a rugadh i gContae Ros Comáin ach a bhog go Baile Átha Claith agus é ina fhear óg, áit a gcaithfeadh sé an chuid eile dá shaol. Rugadh a mhacsan, Tadhg Ó Neachtain, sa bhliain 1671. Chaith sé a shaol ar fad sna Libirtí agus áit chruinnithe a bhí sa tigh aige, ar dtús in Cole Alley, agus níos déanaí i Sráid an Iarla, ag scríbhneoirí agus scoláirí na Gaolainne, go dtí gur theip ar radharc an fhile sna 1740í. I ndán dá chuid "Sloinfead Scothadh na Gaoidhilge Grinn" ainmníonn sé fiche is a sé scoláire Gaolainne a bhí ag saothrú leo i mBaile Átha Claith agus máguaird. Bheadh aithne ag Déan mór na hArdeaglaise, Jonathan Swift, ar go leor acu agus chuadar i bhfeidhm air – a fhianaise sin an leagan atá aige de "Pléaráca na Ruarcach". . . .

Dá réir sin, is den tábhacht é ná deinimis dearmad ar an ngníomhaíocht liteartha *in situ* agus tá súil agam go mbeidh ardmheas ar na céadta bliain de ghníomhaíocht liteartha na Gaolainne mar ghné shuaithinseach de chultúr an phobail agus nach bhfágfar fé shainghrúpaí scolártha amháin í. Tá sé tábhachtach mar sin go n-éileofaí saorchead isteach ag cách sa traidisiún sin, ar ais nó ar éigean.

TRANSLATION

[I would like to think that the proper Irish translation of the Ireland Chair of Poetry is "Ollamh Fódla". This is a name that goes back a long way and stretches into the distant reaches of history and mythology. According to *Leabhar Gabhála Éireann* (*The Book of Invasions*), there was an Ollamh Fódla. He died way back in 1390 BC and is buried at Uisneach. Early antiquaries believed so implicitly in this obviously mythological entity that Macalister excavated his reputed grave. Of course, no body was found in the grave. Ollamh Fódla was never a real person, in that he was a mythological entity. But that doesn't make him any less real in metaphoric terms. He was a metaphor. He is a metaphor. He is a marker of a mythological and imaginative dimension of Irish life that has been expressed since time immemorial in literature, and as such is being readily expressed today. This is a dimension akin to that Fifth Province espoused by Mary Robinson during her presidency.

It is therefore apt that if his reputed grave is anywhere, it should be at Uisneach, the geographical and spiritual dead centre of Ireland, the centre of the Fifth Province, the *imleacán*, or bellybutton, of Ireland, equivalent to the stone at the centre of the sacred site of Delphi in Greece – the *omphalos*, or navel, of the world. And there is an *omphalos* in Uisneach. A distinctly weird-looking stone, locally called The Cat's Stone in English, and known in Irish as *Aill na Míreann*; *mír* being probably the same word as in *curadhmhír*, the champion's portion, which the ancient warriors were wont to fight about to the death. This portion refers to the five divisions of Ireland that supposedly come together at that spot.

A photograph of this unprepossessing monument, neither a *gallán* (standing stone), dolmen nor grave, appeared in a recent edition of *Aimsir Óg*, a book containing the work of one hundred Irish-language writers. I like to think it is there for a purpose, that the possibility exists of at least a hundred writers in modern Irish who are somehow connected with the gravestone of Ollamh Fódla. As if it were resurrected in us. As if we were somehow all his children.

This Cat's Stone has been important for many writers. It is a part of the personal cosmology of James Joyce. Nevertheless, and this is the point I will be making again and again in this lecture, it would be very hard to make anything of it on the actual site of Uisneach itself, in County Westmeath. The site has a slight gradient, as implied by its name, Uisneach, from the Irish *uisinn* or temple. Ó Duinnín calls this "a temple of the head", no doubt to distinguish it from a temple which might be a building or edifice. There is a small black-and-white sign nearby marking it as "Uisneach", but no extra information is given to the unwary traveller, or to anybody else who might come that way. Why do I think this is a pity? Why do I think that it is typical of the deeply coded heritage of Ireland, which is well-nigh invisible to the ordinary citizen? Maybe it is better so. Maybe the last thing on earth we want is a Heritage Centre on the site, making blatantly obvious what is best left half in mystery and silence, to be searched out by individuals, making it, as it were, a site of inner pilgrimage.

The same could be said for Ráth Cruachan, just slightly up the road in County Roscommon. On my last visit to the site there was nothing to see except razor wire and thistles. Again, a small sign beside the rath notes only that this was the dwelling place of many of the kings of Connaught. No Meadhbh. No Ailill. No mention of the Táin. No pillow talk. Here are a few snippets of the very same pillow talk (translation from the Táin by Thomas Kinsella) by way of showing what is at stake:

> "It is true what they say, love", Ailill said, "it is well for the wife of a wealthy man."

> "True enough", the woman said. "What put that in your mind?"

> "It struck me", Ailill said, "how much better off you are today than the day I married you."

> "I was well enough off without you", Meadhbh said.

And as they say in Irish, "*Chuadar ón bhfocal beag go dtí an bhfocal mór le chéile*", which you could translate as saying, "They started out with the small insults and went on to the big insults with each other":

"So if anyone causes you shame or upset or trouble, the right to compensation is mine", Meadhbh said, "for you're a kept man."

More insults each way. Then:

"It still remains", Meadhbh said, "that my fortune is greater than yours."

"You amaze me", Ailill said. "No one has more property or jewels or precious things than I have."

No false modesty here. The like was never considered a virtue in Old Irish; however mores may have changed in the meantime.

They end up with Ailill winning, temporarily, because he has the *Finnbheannach*, or white-horned bull, and Meadhbh doesn't have its equivalent. Undaunted, she sets out to get possession of the brown bull of Cooley, creating a pretext for the whole adventure of the *Táin*, the nearest we have to a national epic.

Why should it matter that the echoes of the *Táin* are not heard around modern Ráth Cruachan? After all they are nothing but stories, idle tales, suitable, as noted by the very monks who wrote them down, *ad delectationem stultorum*, "for the amusement of idiots". But that is my very point. Stories are all we have. Stories are what we tell each other to keep going, to keep alive. And in Ireland we have had such a suitable setting for these stories for so long that it is a pity not to recognise it. I remember with particular joy something that happened when my second daughter, Ayse, was about eleven. She came to me one day with a question: "You know, Mam, those stories about the *Táin* – Deirdre and Naoise and Cuchulainn and all that stuff? Did it really happen?" "Well, they are very good stories, and even if they didn't happen they are such good stories that they should have happened. But whether they happened or not, at least we know where they happened." "And where was that?" "At Eamhain Mhacha." "Is that really a place then?"

And it was with great aplomb that I insisted that yes, indeed it was a place and that i[t] was still there – Navan Fort, just outside Armagh in Northern Ireland, and that if she wanted we could go and see it. And we did. The first weekend that peace broke out we made a jaunt with some friends to Armagh and parts north and had the time of our lives. On the way home the traffic around the border was dreadful, but we discovered that there were no hold-ups, or slow-downs, or checkpoints involved. It was due to the sheer number of people who had had the same idea as ourselves, and were out to discover a hitherto not so well-known part of Ireland.

One of the timeworn clichés about literature in Ireland is that it is very much a literature of place. All the more reason, one would think, that we should mark the actual places that are so much a part of the literature. Cavehill, just beside us here in Belfast, is more than likely the dwelling of the first beloved bird of Old Irish, *Int én bec ro léic feit*, the blackbird of Loch Lao.

And Dublin of course is a noted literary city. But in Dublin itself, I notice an absence. A loss of a whole literary dimension. The literary dimension of the Irish language. A small example: up by St Patrick's Cathedral there is a large plaque dedicated to the "Writers of Dublin". It gives many names but not one single Irish-language writer is mentioned. I wouldn't mind, but this particular area of Dublin, especially the nearby Liberties, was a veritable hotbed of Irish writing and scholarship going back as far as the start of the eighteenth century. It centered on the poet and scribe Seán Ó Neachtain who, though born in County Roscommon, moved to Dublin as a young man and spent the rest of his life there. His son, Tadhg Ó Neachtain, born in 1671, lived all his life in the Liberties and his houses, first at Cole Alley, and later in Earl Street, were meeting places for Irish writers and scholars until his sight failed in the 1740s. His poem, "Sloinfead Scothadh na Gaoidhilge Grinn" ("I Will Name the Best of Clear Irish"), names twenty-six Gaelic scholars working in Dublin and thereabouts. Many of them would have been familiars of the great Dean of St Patrick's, Jonathan Swift, who profited from them, if his version of "Pléaráca na Ruarcach" ("O Rourke's Ructions") is anything to go by. . . .

We must not forget the importance of literary activity *in situ*, and I hope that the centuries of literary activity in Irish will be cherished as an important dimension of our popular culture and not left purely to the devices of the scholarly elite. Public access to that tradition, one way or another, will not be denied.]'[23]

THIRTEEN

Salome Mbugua

b. 1971

Address on the Irish Immigration Bill
Leinster House, Dublin

19 JUNE 2003

*'The child will have to contend with a culture into
which he or she has not been socialised.'*

On 23 June 2022, the Irish census office released the preliminary results of the recent census taken in April of that year. The population of Ireland had reached 5.1 million people. This is the first time since the 1841 census that the Irish population had risen to over five million.[1] The rise in population is partly due to a steady increase in positive migration figures over the past three decades. As well as contributing to the economic and social development of the country, the influx of international migrants into Ireland ensures greater diversity as new cultures are introduced into Irish society. Psychologist Victoria M. Esses explains how 'culture may include specific beliefs, attitudes, and customs, as well as values and behaviors.'[2] When different cultures interact, there are inevitable 'changes in both immigrants and members of the receiving society'.[3] A misunderstanding or even a clash of cultures has, at times, led to racist and sexist stereotyping of migrants in Ireland.

On 19 June 2003, Salome Mbugua addressed the Joint Committee on Justice, Equality, Defence and Women's Rights in Leinster House. Mbugua was invited to present a submission concerning a proposed immigration bill and the implications of the Supreme Court judgement on the rights of foreign-national parents of Irish-born children. She spoke with passion and lucidity on behalf of African women living in Ireland. Her speech, in this section, highlights how negative cultural stereotyping of African women, specifically around the issue of childbirth, had developed at this time in Ireland.

Salome Mbugua was born in a rural village in Kenya. Her father was a teacher and her mother was a farmer. Mbugua was one of nine children, and at the age of two she was baptised by Pat O'Toole, an Irish missionary priest from Mayo who was first appointed to work in Kenya in 1966.[4] After completing her secondary education, Mbugua studied social work at the Kobujoi Development Training Institute in the Nandi South District in Rift Valley Province. The institute was established by the Catholic Diocese of Kisumu as a social training centre. Mbugua described this time as 'a journey that brought [home] the reality of life, especially during my field placement where I worked with women in the largest slum in Kenya'.[5] Mbugua was later employed as a social worker by the Undugu Society of Kenya and worked to rehabilitate street girls from the slums of Nairobi. In 1994, with the help of Fr O'Toole, who had become a firm family friend, Mbugua secured a scholarship to pursue further study in Ireland. She attended a private third-level college, Kimmage Manor Development Study Centre, and graduated with a diploma in Development Studies.

While in Ireland Mbugua became connected to women's groups and youth programmes. She completed a work placement at St Michael's Family Resource Centre in Inchicore and became associated with a Foróige youth club in Cork. Mbugua met Eamonn Henry while studying at Kimmage Manor; the couple later married in Nairobi. Mbugua moved to Uganda in 1996 to work with Eamonn at the Irish Foundation for Cooperative Development. The Irish founded charity works to promote the livelihood of small farmers in developing countries by organising agricultural and food co-operatives. Mbugua worked as a gender equality officer and helped establish a community organisation, Women Enterprises Association of Rakai (WEAR), in 1997.[6] She describes how this organisation 'was formed to address the social and economic effects of HIV/AIDS and poverty in rural Uganda. This way women were able to access small loans and establish a better way of selling their agricultural products.'[7] WEAR proved to be a successful community model, expanding from 13 members to 327 members and 22 regional groups.

In 1998, Mbugua returned to live in Ireland. In August 2001, Mbugua established AkiDwA, a national network of migrant women living in Ireland. This was the first migrant women's organisation in Ireland, and as of 2022 it is a large and effective national organisation providing support around health and integration as well as targeted alliances to dismantle racism. AkiDwA or the full name Akina Dada wa Africa means sisterhood in Swahili.[8] AkiDwA was established with the help of Sister Joan McManus of the Catherine McAuley Centre in Dublin. The centre is run by the Sisters of Mercy and is dedicated 'to the development, education and well-being of women in need.'[9] One year after AkiDwA was founded, an immigration bill was introduced for consideration by the Irish government. The bill would amend the refugee act of 1996 and 'make provision in relation to the control of entry into the state of non-nationals'.[10]

Before the immigration bill was fully debated in the houses of the Oireachtas, a legal case came before the Supreme Court relating to the rights of foreign-national parents of Irish-born children. Two families brought a case against their deportation orders. Andrew Osayande, from Nigeria, had a son born in Ireland in November 2001. The Lobe family, a couple and their three children from the Czech Republic, had a fourth child in Ireland born in October 2001. Hilkka Becker, Chairperson of the International Protection Appeals Tribunal, observed that following a Supreme Court case in 1990, 'parents of children born in Ireland were routinely granted permission to remain in the state, without families necessarily having resided in Ireland for a long period or an offer of employment being in place.'[11] However, as Becker attests, as the numbers of immigrants into the Irish state grew, 'more parents lodged applications for permission to remain on the basis of their parentage of an Irish citizen child, [and] the Government began to refuse residence permit applications.'[12]

When the Lobe family and Osayande claimed asylum, the Refugee Applications Commissioner determined that both claims should 'be processed in other Member States . . . and that the applicants should be removed to those countries.'[13] Both of the applicants challenged these decisions calling for a judicial review but this was denied by the High Court. An appeal of the decision was heard in the Supreme Court. In January 2003, the Supreme Court found that 'non-national parents of Irish-born children and their foreign-national siblings are not entitled to remain in this country by virtue of having an Irish born child.'[14] The *Irish Independent* newspaper estimated that this ruling would affect up to 10,000 foreign-national adults and children, who could face deportation.[15]

A Joint Committee, established to advise the Oireachtas on the introduction of a new immigration law, now had to consider how the Supreme Court ruling would affect any proposed legislation. The committee members included TDs and Senators, who received submissions and presentations from related interest groups. Mbugua's speech to the committee was on behalf of AkiDwA. The committee had previously received presentations from Amnesty International, Comhlámh, the Irish Congress of Trade Unions, the Irish Council for Civil Liberties, the Irish Refugee Council, the Refugee Project and the Immigrant Council of Ireland. The meeting on 19 June 2003 was the last one in which the committee heard presentations from interest groups. This was Mbugua's sole opportunity to address the committee and speak for African women in Ireland before new legislation was introduced. She clearly explained how families and especially children would suffer if their non-national parents were deported from Ireland. Current citizenship laws in Ireland ensured that any child born on the island of Ireland was automatically entitled to Irish citizenship, although their parents were not.

The immigration bill was signed into law as the Immigration Act 2003 in July of that year. The act centred around carrier liability, making it illegal for a person or persons to bring an immigrant into Ireland without permission. Although carriers included drivers of private vehicles, the act mainly targeted airlines and ferry companies imposing responsibility on them to ensure passengers held the required documentation to enter their destination country. The act did not include articles relating to citizenship rights of children born in Ireland to foreign-national parents. This issue became the basis of a constitutional referendum the following year.

A referendum was held on 11 June 2004. Voters were asked to decide on a 27th amendment to the Constitution that people born on the island of Ireland 'will not have a constitutional right to be Irish citizens, unless, at the time of their birth, one of their parents is an Irish citizen or is entitled to be an Irish citizen'.[16] The proposed amendment was introduced under Taoiseach Bertie Ahern and the Fianna Fáil – Progressive Democrats coalition government. It was opposed by the Labour Party and Sinn Féin. Many human rights organisations in Ireland opposed holding the referendum. Denise Charlton, then CEO of the Immigrant Council of Ireland, 'denied that letting parents of Irish-born children stay here would lead to an abuse of the system.'[17] The key, Charlton explained, was establishing clear rules. A group of medical doctors, opposed to the amendment, warning that even holding this referendum was 'fuelling racism.'[18] Author and journalist Fintan O'Toole later described the referendum as a 'disgrace to Irish democracy. It was cooked up by the Fianna Fáil–Progressive Democrats government on the basis of scare stories about foreign women coming to Ireland to have their babies purely so that those children could then claim Irish citizenship.'[19] These scare stories were exactly what Mbugua warned the committee about in her speech.

The referendum saw an overwhelming support for the amendment, with just under 80 per cent of people voting that birth in Ireland should not grant automatic entitlement to citizenship. The Irish Nationality and Citizenship Act 2004 amended the act of 1956 and was signed into law on 15 December 2004. This change allowed the Oireachtas to 'pass legislation which governs how other people born in Ireland may become Irish citizens' and although automatic entitlement to citizenship was removed, Ireland continues to operate one of the most generous citizenship laws in Europe.[20]

Mbugua continues with her determined campaign on behalf of equality and justice in her role as CEO of AkiDwA. In order to develop her skills even further, she completed a master's degree in equality studies at University College Dublin and a PhD in international peace studies at Trinity College Dublin in 2021. Her PhD dissertation focussed on 'Integrating women into peacebuilding in the Democratic Republic of the Congo: A case study of Goma'.[21] In 2018, she was appointed to chair the working group National Action Plan on Women, Peace and Security. She serves as chair on the board of the Equality, Diversity and Inclusion project with the Public Appointment Services and is a Commissioner of the Irish Human Rights and Equality Commission,

Mbugua's work and that of the AkiDwA continues to focus on integration and 'helping migrants to participate fully in all aspects of social, cultural, economic, civic and political life in Ireland.'[22] Such campaigning is having an impact at local and national level. On 7 February 2017, the Office for the Promotion of Migrant Inclusion based in the Department of Justice launched the Migrant Integration Strategy. The strategy establishes a direction for all government departments to follow. The main vision of the strategy is to ensure that 'migrants are facilitated to play a full role in Irish society, that integration is a core principle of Irish life and that Irish society and institutions work together to promote integration. Integration is understood to be a two-way process that involves action by migrants as well as by Irish society.'[23] Stemming from the strategy, a Communities Integration Fund was established in 2017. In 2022, the fund continues to support local communities across the country to promote the integration of migrants and refugees. Cultural and sports organisations in Ireland are now stepping up the campaign to ensure greater inclusion of migrant communities. The Gaelic Athletic Association (GAA) employed Ger McTavish as the National Diversity and Inclusion officer, in 2019. The GAA continues to develop a policy of using Gaelic games for cultural integration and social inclusion. In March 2020, McTavish launched the first GAA Responding To Racism educational and awareness campaign.[24]

Cultural integration into Irish communities has become a priority focus in 2022 when the invasion of Ukraine forced large numbers of people to seek refuge in Ireland. The Children's Rights Alliance published a report in March 2022 advising on the integration of Ukrainian children and young people arriving in Ireland.[25] That report includes a section on cultural integration and supports the ethos of the United Nations Convention on the Rights of the Child that 'children who are in an ethnic, religious or linguistic minority should not be denied the right to enjoy their own culture, practice their own religion and to use their own language.'[26] While it is fundamentally important that migrant children 'have the right to free participation in cultural life and the arts' in Ireland.[27]

Unfortunately, racism remains in Ireland and often it is connected to what Mbugua describes as cultural stereotyping. Mbugua is a prime example of someone who shatters the disturbing racist stereotype of African women who move to Ireland to give birth and live off the state.[28] Mbugua came to Ireland as a young educated woman, to further her studies. Since her arrival Mbugua has contributed vastly towards the improvement of Irish society both at community and at political level. Her speech is a vivid reminder of how dangerous cultural stereotyping can be. Indeed, Irish people are quick to condemn their own cultural stereotyping as drunk and aggressive *Paddys*.

16. Salome Mbugua. Photograph courtesy of Salome Mbugua.

'We wish to highlight the need for an immediate and fair system of hearing cases and, where necessary, reopening cases of non-national parents of Irish-born children. AkiDwA feels that a general amnesty granting leave to stay to non-national parents of Irish-born children before the Supreme Court judgment would be the fairest way of dealing with all the complexities of each individual case. The reasons for this position will become more apparent, especially when we look at the implications for the Irish-born children. We feel that humanitarian consideration should be given in the cases of all children born after the judgment. . . . AkiDwA contends that negative racist and sexist stereotypes of Africans, including African women, have developed around the issue of childbirth. There is a perception that the primary concern of African women when giving birth was to obtain leave to stay and to live off the welfare system. Nothing could be further from the truth. African women have no desire to be dependent on a welfare system. They do, however, want to be granted the opportunity to make a positive contribution to society, to earn a living, support themselves and their families in Ireland and their extended families–some in their home countries and others in safer locations. The women who gave birth when in Ireland were obviously of a child-bearing and sexually active age. Unlike Europe, where the average family comprises approximately two to three children, the standard African family has five to six.

AkiDwA is working to address the fact that not all African women entering Ireland knew how and where to access family planning while others found discussing such issues with strangers culturally inappropriate. The underlying issue that we wish to highlight is the need to ensure that those hearing the cases do not do so with negative baggage.

We wish to highlight the need for the rights of the child to be protected. Although AkiDwA represents the position of African women it believes that the group that will be most affected by the recent Supreme Court ruling comprises Irish-born children. In the current climate in which deportation orders are being issued against the parents of these children, we envisage three possible scenarios that could emerge. In each case it is likely that there will be a negative outcome for the child, unless he or she has good luck.

In the first scenario, the parents of the child are deported and take their child with them. The child, an Irish citizen, will not, in most instances, be able to receive dual citizenship. The right of the child to an identity in a new land would be denied. Likewise, the capacity of the State to afford the child protection to an acceptable degree will be limited. The parents of the child would have entered Ireland in a vulnerable position and would be returned home more vulnerable and to greater poverty and insecurity than that which they experienced when they arrived. The child will have to contend with a culture into which he or she has not been socialised and will have reduced life options. In the event of parental separation or divorce, a question arises over jurisdiction in deciding on the fate and well-being of the child – in most African traditions, priority is given to men to take their children if they so choose, implying that the mother will lose out again.

In the second and third scenarios, the parents are deported and choose to leave the child behind. While this may seem like neglect it will actually be quite a logical decision and will only be taken after the parents have painstakingly weighed up the options and considered what might be best for the security, protection and long-term future of the child. In the second scenario, the child will become a ward of State and will most likely be assigned to residential care, foster care or put up for adoption. Each option will have a developmental and psychological impact on the child and possibly his or her guardians.

In the third scenario, it is quite possible that parents facing deportation will use a variation of the extended African family and use an existing network of parents with leave to stay to care for the Irish-born children. In this scenario, which I believe is quite possible, there would be a disproportionate number of children to guardians. The decision to entrust a child to parents with leave to stay will most likely be made by and between men but will impact on women as primary carers. Given the disproportionate number of children to parents, the degree of care and attention needed by the children will be reduced.

. . . There are specific forms of violence against which women are not protected in many African societies – for example, female genital mutilation and death sentences for alleged adultery. Moreover, domestic violence is also accepted as the norm in many African societies. These, however, are not covered by the terms of the Geneva Convention as interpreted when asylum cases are heard. Nonetheless, they do warrant consideration on humanitarian grounds. As I stated, most African societies do not give priority to the mother in the case of a dispute on child custody. We believe this is wrong and represents a further reason why the Irish State needs to protect both Irish-born children and their mothers by granting leave to stay. Overall, we feel that everyone's best interests would be served by creating an enabling environment for African women and that investment in such a society would result in positive returns for all.

AkiDwA believes that a general amnesty should be given to all parents of Irish-born children before the Supreme Court ruling. Failing this, these and all individual cases after the ruling should be examined immediately on the basis of the legal entitlements of Irish citizens, including Irish-born children, social justice and humanitarian considerations, protection of the rights of the child and with due consideration for the concerns of women. AkiDwA believes that an enabling society should be established whereby Africans and their Irish-born children can make a positive contribution to society rather than be left in a state of dependence.'[29]

FOURTEEN

Maureen O'Hara

1920–2015

Speech at the Irish Film & Television Academy Awards
Burlington Hotel, Dublin

1 NOVEMBER 2004

'To have been born in Ireland is the greatest gift God can give you.'

Maureen O'Hara was the most successful Irish woman in the Hollywood film industry. Her career spanned six decades, during which time she starred in over 60 films, including classics such as *Rio Grande*, *The Brave and The Beautiful*, *How Green Was My Valley*, *Miracle on 34th Street* and the famous American romantic comedy set in Ireland, *The Quiet Man*. In 2004, Gay Byrne presented her with the Lifetime Achievement Award from the Irish Film & Television Academy, and O'Hara gave the speech in this section.

Maureen FitzSimons was born on 17 August 1920 at the family home, 32 Upper Beechwood Avenue in Ranelagh, Dublin. Her father, Charles Stewart Parnell FitzSimons, was from Kells in county Meath. He managed a clothing company, and he bought shares in Shamrock Rovers Football Club, an Irish association football club based in Tallaght, county Dublin. Her mother, Marguerita (Rita) (née Lilburn), was from Dublin; she was a clothes designer and an actress and singer. Maureen was the second oldest of six children.

O'Hara attended the girls' primary school on John Street West and completed her secondary education at the Sisters of Charity in Milltown, Dublin. In her autobiography, written with the support of her manager, John Nicoletti, she described her first school performance at the age of six. She was 'bitten by the acting bug that night' and 'wanted to become the greatest actress of all time!'[1] Her parents enrolled her in Ena Burke's Drama School, and she joined the Rathmines Theatre Company. From a young age, she won numerous amateur acting competitions, and she later took professional roles in radio dramas for 2RN (later Radio Éireann).[2]

When she turned 14, Maureen was accepted into the Abbey theatre, where she was initially given walk on parts in performances. At the age of 17, the American actor and singer Harry Richman noticed her in an Abbey production and recommended her for a screen test. Maureen's mother accompanied her to London for a screen test at Elstree Studios that, according to Maureen, did not go well. She described how the studio team 'transformed me with heavy makeup. . . . I looked like a ten-dollar hooker.'[3] However, a later meeting at Mayflower Pictures, a British-based film production company established by actor Charles Laughton and producer Erich Pommer, was an immense success. Laughton offered her a seven-year contract with the film production company. He changed her name to Maureen O'Hara, believing this was a better name to appear on film posters and credits. In 1939, at the age of just 18, she starred alongside Laughton in her first major film role in *Jamaica Inn*, a film based on Daphne du Maurier's novel and directed by Alfred Hitchcock.

On 13 June 1939, O'Hara married a production team member, George Brown, in England before she left for America to film *The Hunchback of Notre Dame*. She played a leading role as Esmerelda, and the film became a major box office success. As O'Hara notes in her speech in this section, shortly after her arrival in America, the Second World War broke out, and she was not allowed to leave America, nor was Brown allowed to enter the country. In her autobiography, O'Hara describes the marriage as a bad decision, and she did not see Brown again after their wedding day. Their marriage was annulled on 15 September 1941.[4] Her career in the film industry was already on an upward trajectory, and she signed with MCA, the largest talent agency in Hollywood.

In December of 1941, O'Hara married again, this time to an American dialogue director, William Price. The marriage lasted for 10 years, during which time O'Hara had her only child, a daughter Bronwyn, in 1944. Price was an abusive man with a drinking problem. Their daughter took her mother's maiden name, FitzSimons. Also in 1941, O'Hara starred in *How Green Was My Valley*. This was the first of five films she worked on with the Irish American director John Ford. The film had the biggest budget in 20th Century Fox's history; it won five Academy Awards. O'Hara collaborated with Ford for twenty years, and historian Liz Evers notes, 'A significant portion of O'Hara's 2004 memoir is devoted to recalling her intense and often troubled friendship with Ford, the son of emigrants from Spiddal,

Co. Galway. She became a regular visitor to his home and spent many weekends with the Ford family aboard their yacht, "the Araner.""[5]

Ford began his directing career during the silent film era. His films became more successful when sound was introduced, and *talkies* became a feature of the film industry by the 1930s. Film director John Sayles describes how Ford used this format to introduce 'a tension between the visual storyteller and the loquacious, poetically sentimental Irish yarn-spinner'.[6] O'Hara's entry on the Hollywood scene coincided with the rise of Technicolor, which demanded the use of brighter colours in films. Technicolor greatly enhanced O'Hara's red hair, green eyes and pale skin, which helped make her one of the most successful Hollywood actors of the 1940s and 1950s. She became known as the Queen of Technicolour, with one reviewer of the 1950 film *Comanche Territory* noting, 'framed in Technicolor, Miss O'Hara somehow seems more significant than a setting sun.'[7]

17. Maureen O'Hara and her mother from *Modern Screen* magazine, February 1948.

On 25 January 1946, O'Hara received her official citizenship of America. She remained proud of her Irish birth throughout her life. She initially refused to accept her American citizenship papers because they had been altered to show her nationality as British. Prior to 1948, when Ireland declared a republic and left the British Commonwealth, there was often a dispute about Irish citizens being British subjects. Britain officially acknowledged the end of Ireland's dominion status through the Ireland Act 1949; up till that point many official records in America, including O'Hara's citizenship papers, declared people from Ireland as British nationals. O'Hara went to the district court of Los Angeles to argue that her papers should be rectified to note her nationality as Irish. She won this right and became the first Irish citizen to gain American citizenship with her nationality noted as Irish rather than British.[8]

In 1952, *The Quiet Man*, directed by John Ford, was released. O'Hara played her most famous role as Mary Kate Danaher opposite John Wayne as Sean Thornton. The film was a critically acclaimed success and showcased the glorious countryside of Cong in county Mayo, named as the fictional Inisfree. The film won two Academy Awards; Ford won Best Director, and Winton Hoch won Best Cinematography. The film has endured the test of time, and in October 2002 a collector's edition DVD was released that included the documentary *The Quiet Man: The Joy of Ireland*, which features interviews with O'Hara on the making of the film.

18. Maureen O'Hara and Barry Fitzgerald, lobby card for *The Quiet Man*, 1952. Republic Pictures.

In August 1952, O'Hara divorced William Price and had a romantic relationship with the Mexican lawyer and politician Enrique Parra for the next 15 years, although they never married. O'Hara met Parra when she travelled to Mexico City for the Mexican Film Festival. She continued to star in many popular films throughout the 1960s, including *The Parent Trap* and in *Mr. Hobbs Takes a Vacation* with Jimmy Stewart.

O'Hara married for the final time on 12 March 1968 to former US Air Force Brig. Gen. Charles F. Blair. O'Hara described how:

> From the day we were married, Charlie and I were inseparable. Just standing beside him, I felt his strength – physical, mental, spiritual – and that made me feel secure and content. We were a dynamite couple, and within months of being married it was fireworks between us that never stops.[9]

The couple moved to the Virgin Islands, and Blair founded an inter-island airline there. On 8 September 1970, Conor Beau FitzSimons, her grandson, was born. O'Hara retired from Hollywood in 1973 after starring in *The Red Pony*, a film produced for television, with Henry Fonda. The film won the Peabody Award for Television Excellence.[10]

In 1970, O'Hara and her husband purchased Lugdine Park, a large house set on 35 acres of land overlooking Glengarriff Bay in county Cork. The land was originally owned by the founder of the *Irish Independent* newspaper, William Martin Murphy, whose son William Lombard Murphy built a house there in 1935. In 1978, eight years after buying the property, Blair was tragically killed in a plane crash. He was buried with full military honours at Arlington National Cemetery. O'Hara took over as president of her husband's airline company. The following year in 1979, she was again hit by tragedy when her closest friend, the actor John Wayne, died. O'Hara sold the airline shortly after Wayne's death.

In 1990, film director Chris Columbus persuaded O'Hara to return to acting, when he wrote *Only the Lonely* with her in mind. She starred alongside John Candy as his overbearing Irish mother, Rose Muldoon, in the film, which was released in 1991. Over the next decade, O'Hara starred in three television films produced by the Polson Company for the American network CBS: *The Christmas Box*; *Cab to Canada*; and, most appropriately, her last appearance was in the film titled *The Last Dance*. In 2004, O'Hara published her memoirs, and that same year she received the highest accolade from the recently established Irish Film and Television Academy (IFTA). The all-Ireland organisation aims to stimulate 'original and creative production work, and [encourage] excellence through recognition, education and leadership in film and television'.[11] IFTA holds two annual awards ceremonies: the IFTA Film and Drama Awards and the

IFTA Gala Television Awards, which honour and celebrate excellence in outstanding Irish creativity. In 2004, IFTA voted to present O'Hara with the Lifetime Achievement Award.

The awards ceremony that year was held at the Burlington Hotel in Dublin, and before O'Hara received her award from presenter Gay Byrne, a video tribute was played. A selection of actors, admirers and collaborators recounted O'Hara's glittering career; speakers included Steven Spielberg, Chris Columbus, Milo O'Shea and Hayley Mills. Columbus declared:

> Maureen O'Hara changed my life as a film director. She was one of the most professional, responsible actors I've ever met. She gave our film a realistic, touching and honest performance. She enriched my creative hunger with her knowledge of film history, relating stories about my heroes, people like John Ford, Charles Laughton and John Wayne. I will spend my life cherishing the memories of the time we spent together on the *Only the Lonely* film set. Thanks to my friendship with Maureen O'Hara, my world is a much richer place.[12]

O'Hara then gave the speech in this section, recounting her entry into the film industry and her love for Ireland. The audience responded enthusiastically, as evidenced by the cheering and applause throughout. Her sense of humour and good nature is particularly evident in her speech. In 2005, just months after she received the IFTA award, O'Hara suffered a stroke. She had kept Lugdine Park at Glengarriff as a holiday home, and she moved there that year.

When O'Hara's health deteriorated further in 2012, she moved to live with her grandson, Conor, in Idaho. She died in her sleep from natural causes at home in Boise, Idaho, on 24 October 2015, at the age of 95. She was buried next to her husband, Blair. O'Hara's coffin was carried to her grave by a US Air Force honour guard, and Catherine O'Connell sang 'The Isle of Innisfree', the main song from *The Quiet Man*.[13] During her lifetime, O'Hara received many other awards and tributes, including a star on the Hollywood Walk of Fame in 1960; an honorary degree from NUI Galway in 1988; and a fellowship of the British Film Institute in 1993. In 2012, she was given the freedom of the town of Kells, her father's birthplace. In November 2014, having never won an Oscar, O'Hara was presented with an Honorary Academy Award for her contribution to Hollywood at the Academy of Motion Picture Arts and Sciences Governors Awards in Los Angeles. She was presented with her Oscar by Irish actor Liam Neeson and by Clint Eastwood, after which she received a standing ovation from those in attendance. O'Hara sang the final words of the Irish ballad 'Danny Boy' and thanked Charles Laughton, John Wayne and John Ford for helping her career.

O'Hara continues to be recognised in Ireland and further afield for her long and illustrious acting career. In 2020, O'Hara was rated the top Irish actor of all time by film critics of the *Irish Times*.[14] In April 2022, a life-sized statue of Maureen O'Hara by sculptor Don Cronin was installed at Glengarriff then removed from its site 48 hours later.[15] The statue received negative criticism online, with many people stating that it was not an accurate portrayal of the beautiful O'Hara. The statue was removed at the request of the sculptor. The films and speeches of Maureen O'Hara, the Queen of Technicolour, remain as testimony to her vibrant personality and to her love of her country.

'To have been born in Ireland is the greatest gift God can give you. [Cheers.] Yes, it is. And to be proud of that is the greatest gift you can return to God and give to the country of our birth. [Applause.] I know many of you think I boast of Ireland too much. *I* don't think so, and that's what's really important to me. [Laughter and applause.]

I started in the theatrical business when I was six years of age. And I entered all the feises in Ireland. I won the Rathmines Feis. . . . I won every feis in Ireland.[16] And I was always very proud of it. I was a theatre snob, and I never intended to have anything to do with movies. [Laughter.] But Charles Laughton saw me working and signed me to a seven-year contract and took me to America. I made my first film in London called *Jamaica Inn*, and he took me to America to make *The Hunchback of Notre Dame* with him.

And then war broke out, and none of us who went out – people like David Niven and everything – went out to America, we were not permitted back under the law of war. And so I stayed in the United States of America and was very lucky to have met all the wonderful directors I did, including an old devil called John Ford. [Applause and whistling.] And the first picture I made with that great, distinguished director was the film in Wales, *How Green Was My Valley*. And I was very thrilled and really blessed to have been given all of the support and everything that I did get. And I was very proud to have made one of the first great film[s] made in Ireland that did so much for Ireland.

But there was one, many years ago, and I don't know if any of you are as old as I am and consequently old enough to remember the wonderful film that was made called *The Araner*. Nobody remembers it? It was a great Irish film when I was a little girl. I don't know if *all* of you know how old I am. I do – unfortunately. [Laughter.] I had a sister who said, "Old age is a terrible thing, particularly when it strikes you when you are so young." [Laughter and applause.] I am *84* years of age. [Cheers and applause.] And if any of you young gentlemen would like to come up here and have a little battle, I know who'd win . . . me! [Laughter and applause.]

But, anyway, I guess enough is enough, and really all of you who are in the theatrical profession, the television profession or the movie profession keep really working. Never forget you represent to the whole world this small, great, fabulous country. [Applause.] . . .

I'd like to say hello to my daughter, who is with me tonight, Bronwyn, who was named for the part played by Anna Lee in *How Green Was My Valley*. . . .

Thank you for the award tonight. I can't tell you how much I appreciate it. It's just a wonderful gift from Ireland to an Irish woman, and she appreciates it. [Applause.]'[17]

FIFTEEN

Lydia Foy

b. 1947

Speech at Dublin LGBTQ+ Pride
Westin Hotel, Dublin

23 JUNE 2013

'I was a threat to stability and family life and the Church.'

On 14 June 2022, Dublin Pride terminated their media partnership with the national broadcaster, RTÉ. Dublin Pride organise hundreds of events throughout Pride LGBTQ+ month, culminating in a parade and a march on the final Saturday of June. RTÉ had been the official media partner of Pride for the previous three years; their role was to represent LGBTQ+ people positively across the media forums of radio, television and online. A correspondent for *Gay Community News* (*GCN*), Han Tiernan, described how the move to terminate the partnership 'was prompted by a series of transphobic discussions which were broadcast on RTÉ's popular phone-in radio programme *Liveline*'.[1]

The discussions in question were hosted by RTÉ presenter Joe Duffy and began on 9 June 2022 when a person phoned the show to argue that the word *woman* should not be removed from maternity legislation. That change of language was proposed to ensure inclusivity for transgender and non-binary parents. The discussion continued on-air for a number of days, during which numerous people expressed anti-transgender sentiments. Feminist activist Ailbhe Smyth noted that, 'it is not the role of our national broadcaster to enable or encourage hate speech of any kind.'[2] Ultimately, the radio discussions highlighted that there are transphobic groups and individuals in Ireland, not unlike many other countries. In his report on the series of discussions on *Liveline*, the radio columnist for the *Irish Times*, Mick Heaney, stated that 'transgender rights have become a bitterly contested frontline in the culture wars elsewhere, with Republican-controlled states in the US passing anti-trans laws and, closer to home, the author JK Rowling facing fierce online responses to her views.'[3]

Transgender rights activists across the globe have spent decades campaigning to gain basic human rights, and in many countries activists have succeeded in securing fundamental legal changes. However, this minority group still face public attack, questioning even their right of existence. Lydia Foy is the predominant trans rights activist in Ireland, and she led numerous legal challenges regarding gender recognition. Foy launched a long and difficult campaign in 1993, following her sex reassignment surgery, to have her female gender reflected on her birth certificate. On 23 June 2013, Foy was invited to give an address as part of the Pride celebrations in Dublin that year. Her speech, in this section, was on the topic of redefining the norm. In it, Foy describes her personal and legal journey to obtaining a birth certificate with her correct gender identity as female.

Lydia Foy was born on 23 June 1947 in Westmeath. Foy graduated from UCD with a Bachelor of Dental Surgery in 1971 and practised as a dentist. In 1977, Foy married and had two children born in 1978 and 1980. In her speech, Foy discusses how she attempted to conform; marriage and parenthood was one such route to social acceptance. In 1989, Foy suffered a total collapse, after years of psychological deterioration. She was referred to Dr Frank O'Donoghue, a psychiatrist specialising in psychosexual matters. O'Donoghue diagnosed Foy as a 'core transsexual'.[4] Foy obtained a second and a third medical opinion from two psychiatrists in England who confirmed a diagnosis of gender dysphoria. The condition of gender dysphoria is described by the Mayo Clinic as 'the feeling of discomfort or distress that might occur in people whose gender identity differs from their sex assigned at birth or sex-related physical characteristics'.[5]

In order to ensure that people with gender dysphoria could seek access to essential health care and treatment, a medical diagnosis was included in the *Diagnostic and Statistical Manual of Mental Disorders*, published by the American Psychiatric Association. The stresses involved in diagnosis took a heavy toll on Foy's marriage, and she left the family home in 1990; a judicial separation from her wife followed on 13 December 1991. On 25 July 1992, Foy completed full gender reassignment surgery under consultant urologist, Michael Royle.

In March 1993, Foy applied to the office of the registrar general for a new birth certificate to reflect her gender as female. Her request was refused, and she legally changed her name by deed poll to Lydia that same year. Although Foy could now obtain some official documentation such as a driving licence in her female name, her birth certificate was still required for many professional and official purposes. The fact that her birth certificate identified her sex as male was the cause of much distress. Foy persisted in seeking a new birth certificate from the registrar until 1997. In April 1997, she initiated High Court proceedings to compel the registrar to issue her with a new birth certificate. The case came before the High Court in October 2000 and was heard by Justice Liam McKechnie.

The High Court judgement was finally delivered on 9 July 2002; McKechnie rejected Foy's claim due to the lack of legislation on the matter. Ultimately McKechnie found that the Registrar did not have the power to alter the original register. He called on the government to address the issue of gender recognition for those who are transgender in Ireland. Just two days after Foy's High Court judgement, on 11 July 2002, the European Court of Human Rights found in favour of Christine Goodwin, a trans woman from the United Kingdom, who sought to have her birth certificate rectified. The judgement in the Goodwin case noted that 'The stress and alienation arising from a discordance between the position in society assumed by a post-operative transsexual and the status imposed by law could not be regarded as a minor inconvenience arising from a formality.'[6] In response to the finding that the UK had violated Article 8 and Article 12 of the European Convention on Human Rights, the British government introduced the Gender Recognition Act 2004, which ensured that transgender people could have their new gender acknowledged, including through the issuing of a new birth certificate.

On 30 July 2002, Foy appealed the High Court decision to the Supreme Court. While she waited for a hearing date, the European Convention on Human Rights Act 2003 was signed into law in Ireland on 30 June 2003. In November 2005, Foy applied once more to the registrar for a new birth certificate, citing the European Convention Act. The registrar again refused to issue a new birth certificate, and Foy brought a new case to the High Court. This time Foy sought 'a declaration under the ECHR Act that Irish legislation was incompatible with the European Convention regarding the registration and issue of birth certificates'.[7] The new case was heard by judge McKechnie, who heard Foy's original High Court case in 2002. McKechnie delivered his judgement on 19 October 2007 and found that the Irish government was violating Article 8 of the European Convention. He also voiced his frustration that the Irish government had failed to take any action regarding the legal position of transgender people since the 2002 High Court case. The Irish state appealed the findings to the Supreme Court.

19. Lydia Foy and David Norris at the launch of Dublin Pride, 9 June 2010. Photograph by Neil Ward.

In May 2010, the Gender Recognition Advisory Group (GRAG), an inter-departmental working group, was established to advise the government on a legal framework for the recognition of the acquired gender of trans people. The following month, the state withdrew its Supreme Court appeal. In July 2011, GRAG published its recommendations to the Minister for Social Protection. Two years after the recommendations were published, the government had failed to take any action regarding gender recognition. On 27 February 2013, Foy, supported by the human rights group Free Legal Advice Centres (FLAC), announced that she would take a case against the government due to their lack of action. By the time Foy gave the speech in this section, she was frustrated by the entire legal process and by the Irish government's clear violation of the European Convention on Human Rights. Her frustration is clear in her speech as she details the arduous legal and personal journey she had taken up to that point in time.

However, Foy's work was about to be rewarded. On 17 July 2013, less than one month after she delivered her speech, Joan Burton, the Minister for Social Protection, published the heads of bill for gender recognition. In November of that year, President Higgins invited members of the Transgender Equality Network of Ireland (TENI) and members of FLAC to a reception at Áras an Uachtarain, where they discussed the need for transgender rights in Ireland. Foy was part of the delegation and she described how 'the President gave us a warm reception and was very generous with his time . . . He was supportive of our work, and he spoke knowledgeably about the issues we face.'[8]

On 15 July 2015, the Gender Recognition Act was finally passed, and it was signed into law by President Michael D. Higgins the following week. The act recognises a change of gender, enabling those who are transgender to receive a new birth certificate to reflect their preferred gender. TENI welcomed this new legislation and noted that 'the Gender Recognition Act allows all individuals over the age of 18 to self-declare their own gender identity. Young people aged 16–17 can also apply to be legally recognised, though the process is more onerous.'[9]

Lawyer and Labour Party leader, Ivana Bacik, asserts that it was Foy's legal struggle which brought about this legislative change. Bacik notes that 'The Foy litigation is remarkable in many respects. It has had a clear and tangible effect in changing the law, and has generated extensive public debate and real legal change for transgender persons in Ireland'.[10] Foy was the first person in Ireland to receive her new birth certificate under this act.

In 2015, Foy was the recipient of the European Citizen's Prize, which is 'awarded to citizens or organisations having contributed to promoting better mutual understanding and closer integration between citizens or to facilitating cross-border or transnational cooperation within the EU'.[11] Foy was nominated for the award by Sinn Féin MEPs Martina Anderson, Lynn Boylan, Matt Carthy and Liadh Ní Riada. She was the subject of a radio documentary 'My Name is Lydia Foy', which first aired on RTÉ Radio One in 2011. In the documentary, her senior counsel, Bill Shipsey, described how 'There was something of the trailblazer about Lydia'.[12]

Over the course of her determined campaign, Foy lost her marriage, her family, her home and her job. She courageously stepped into the public arena to fight for justice for all transgender people in Ireland. Sara Phillips, in her role as CEO of TENI, said that 'there is still a need to ensure that . . . heroes like Lydia are documented and remembered. For the trans community, we must pledge for keeping this story alive in the minds of everyone, in the minds of society, but also in the minds of our own community.'[13] The following speech is a vivid reminder of how one person can stand up to a legal and political system to successfully challenge and redefine the norm.

'Redefining the norm sort of got me a little bit confused as to what exactly I was going to talk about . . . and I just came up with a few little things there. The norm is not a norm until you have actually seen it for a while and got used to it basically. . . . It means you have to be visible or even luminous at times, because what happens is, it can be difficult for the first minority to be exposed to a stodgy majority. They can be entrenched in the perceived security of predictability and sameness. Unpredictability brings out the alertness of fight or flight. And it is a sort of a basic, animalistic survival instinct. . . . So, what I am going to talk about, redefining the norm, it definitely was the norm years ago.

I was born in 1947 when the first basics of the human rights conventions were being thought about. . . . So 1947, I think it was, Eleanor Roosevelt was getting the convention together.[14] You can think of all the way through to 2003, when the European Convention of Human Rights was re-enforced, and it was meant to be put into proper practice and meant that we shouldn't have the need to get to Strasbourg anymore. Everything should be conformed to the European Convention of Human Rights, and any legislation even should have been immediately enacted basically. But we seem to be very cumbersome in doing legislation in Ireland, so I got leave for judicial review. I was born transgender, and I was trying to conform, I was not brave, I didn't understand gay pride or anything like that or Stonewall. I thought if you just try to conform and maintain a low profile . . . So, I had to learn the hard way that maintaining a low profile in a majority situation doesn't work, so I redefined the norm. . . .

I was told that I was going to upset society: "I could turn Irish society into a lunatic asylum." Actually, that's a quote. . . . I was treated very, very badly by the courts – that were closed. These were in camera proceedings . . . they could do what they wanted under that system. . . . I was trying to educate myself and get a little stronger with my pen. . . .

I said what I'm looking for – the right to reply – these weren't even open to me, but I started getting a little bit, you know, backed into a corner and getting to fight back. The first thing I did, I went into the registrars and asked for my birth cert, a basic cert of identity. When I went in, they said they didn't want to know. I actually got a little bit stubborn and said, "Look, if you're turning me down, I want something in writing." This was 1993, which is twenty years ago; I was turned down. Finally, after years, the only representation I could get to address the way I had been treated, I had been treated like a criminal basically for years, but the only little segment of hope was given as a judicial review. This means that I had to pretty much take it on all on my own, and yet I couldn't get to Strasbourg or anywhere else. . . . So, somebody who is already under pressure, not qualified in law, has to try and change the law. . . .

I was put through the mill, and even when the High Court said, "Yes, we are in breach of the European Convention of Human Rights", what happened? The government appealed the court's decision, so the government was just about in contempt of the court finding. Even the court had been so cumbersome and obstructive, and now the government were actually appealing the decision of the High Court. And that appeal happened for a number of months, and they finally got through their appeal.

A couple of days after the first time I was turned down, there was a case, the Goodwin case in England, and they were found to be – just two days too late for me – . . . in breach of the European Convention of Human

Rights. So, finally, they told me that they agreed they were in breach of the European Convention of Human Rights. But would you believe it, well, it's about six years now since that was declared and agreed, what the government set down. About six years. They told me that it was a priority and they are still stalling. The only country in Europe that hadn't done something about the issue was Malta, and they got their act together.

We had what was called the GRAG [Gender Recognition Advisory Group] report, and that was published in 2011. Which was meant to get things organised, get a gender recognition panel set up. So, the delay now has actually seriously undermined the European Convention of Human Rights. . . . We haven't got our own act together. We're in breach of this convention, and we're sort of bringing the European Convention into disrepute. And the strange thing about it is that I'm actually the first ever to get the declaration of the European Convention of Human Rights. And I had the most difficult job twenty, twenty-five, thirty years back . . . I had every obstruction . . . I made every mistake in the book. I came out of court, and I was told that I could upset Irish society, that, you know, I was a threat to stability and family life and the Church, and I was blamed for absolutely everything. . . .

But, anyway, just to tell you that we are breaching the European Convention of Human Rights for just about seven years now. . . .

Thank you for your attention.'[15]

Sixteen

Edna O'Brien

b. 1930

Speech at the Dublin One City One Book launch
Mansion House, Dublin

27 February 2019

'Poetry and great writing unites us.'

In 2019, *The Country Girls Trilogy* by Edna O'Brien was chosen as the One City One Book.[1] Annually since 2006, a distinguished book, connected with Dublin, is chosen for this honour. This programme was introduced by Dublin City Council and is led by Dublin City Libraries with partners UNESCO City of Literature; the Department of Culture, Gaeltacht, Sport and Media; and New Island Books. In 2019, there followed a series of events celebrating Edna O'Brien and her three remarkable debut novels. Associated events included a stage adaptation of *The Country Girls*, performed in the national theatre, the Abbey, and at venues in Cork, Galway and Limerick. O'Brien gave numerous interviews and public talks, including the speech in this section in the Mansion House in Dublin.

The One City One Book organisers declared that 'Quite simply, *The Country Girls* is a twentieth-century literary masterpiece which anticipates and puts into effect a feminist revolution all of its own.'[2] O'Brien is acknowledged by many as the greatest living Irish writer. When her first book, *The Country Girls*, was published in 1960, she received international acclaim, but her work was banned and her books were burned in Ireland; she was subjected to personal attack through threatening letters, and her family was vilified in their local community.

Josephine Edna O'Brien was born on 15 December 1930 to parents Michael and Lena (née Cleary) O'Brien at the family home of Drewsborough House in the village of Tuamgraney in county Clare. She was the youngest of four children. O'Brien attended Scariff National School and completed her secondary education as a boarder at the Convent of Mercy School in Loughrea, county Galway. After completing school, O'Brien moved to Dublin, where she worked in a pharmacy during the day and attended lectures in the evening at the Pharmaceutical College in Dublin. She was awarded a licence as a pharmacist in 1950.

Dublin opened access to the literary world for O'Brien; she read voraciously and began writing small items for newspapers. She met writers, including Ernest Gébler; he was 20 years her senior and previously had been married with a child. O'Brien married Gébler in 1954 against her parents' wishes. The couple had two sons: Carlo and Sasha Gébler. The family moved to London in November 1958, and O'Brien, feeling a sense of alienation in London, began to write. She received a £50 advance payment from the publisher Ian Hamilton. Remarkably, O'Brien finished writing *The Country Girls* in just three weeks.

The Country Girls trilogy was completed with the publication of *The Lonely Girl* in 1962 and *Girls in Their Married Bliss*, published in 1964.[3] The novels chart the lives of two friends from a rural village in the west of Ireland: Caithleen Brady (Cait) and Bridget Brennan (Baba). The trilogy follows the women as they move from a rural environment to Dublin city and later when they emigrate to London. O'Brien's husband was jealous of her literary talent, and the marriage declined further after her success. O'Brien described how, on 24 September 1962, she walked away from marriage 'because it was undeviatingly punishing and grim'.[4] O'Brien fought for three years for custody of her children, which she finally received. She remained in London and raised her two children on her own.

All three of O'Brien's novels were banned by the Irish Censorship Board. Her novels shocked Irish society because she dared to write about women's sexuality in frank and open terms. O'Brien's literature was and remains ground-breaking. The celebrated Irish author Eimear McBride explains how 'the moral hysteria that greeted the book's [*The Country Girls*] first appearance has since ensured that both it, and O'Brien, have become era-defining symbols of the struggle for Irish women's voices to be heard above the clamour of an ultra-conservative, ultra-religious and institutionally misogynistic society.'[5] O'Brien's next two novels, *August Is a Wicked Month* (1965) and *Casualties of Peace* (1966), were also banned in Ireland.[6]

In December 1966, O'Brien travelled to Dublin to attend the first meeting of the Censorship Reform Society, a group established by writers and academics to challenge the Irish Censorship Board. O'Brien arrived at Dublin airport with copies of her five books; customs officers seized and confiscated her books, allowing her only to 'keep the sleeves of the books'.[7] O'Brien attended the meeting of the Censorship Reform Society, held at the Gate Theatre on 4 December 1966. The theatre was packed with interested parties and members of the public keen to hear about challenges to the censorship board. O'Brien spoke out against the harsh censorship rules enforced by the board. There were 13 speakers: 12 men and O'Brien. The other panel members included actor and co-founder of the Gate Theatre Micheál Mac Liammóir, dramatist Hugh Leonard, author James Plunkett, poet and Trinity College Dublin lecturer Brendan Kennelly, and journalists Bruce Arnold and Proinsias Mac Aonghusa.[8] Mac Liammóir noted that 'if the Censorship Board censored foreign works to the same degree as they did the works of Irish authors, some of the classics, including grand opera, would be banned.'[9] The audience heard that since the introduction of the publication censorship bill an average of one book per day had been banned in Ireland, over a 36-year period. While legislation had initially been introduced to ensure censorship of pornographic literature, Hugh Leonard condemned the current standards through which 'major works had been outlawed on the strength of a sentence or a paragraph marked by a reader who thought that life itself was an obscenity.'[10]

Historian Peter Martin maintains that by examining the 'early days of Irish censorship we can see how the pattern was set that led to the bizarre decisions of later years'.[11] Censorship in Ireland became a public focus and a political issue even before the Irish Free State was formally established in 1922. In November 1911, the Irish Vigilance Association (IVA) was formed. IVA campaigners were mainly members of Catholic organisations who received support from the religious hierarchy. Their focus was primarily against British publications thought to promote birth control and other supposedly obscene material. The Censorship of Films bill was introduced by Minister for Justice Kevin O'Higgins in 1923 after he came under pressure from a delegation of Catholic and Protestant dignitaries. This bill passed without much dispute, although the IVA then demanded consideration for censorship of printed matter.

In 1926, the Committee on Evil Literature was formed by the Irish government to examine the question of censorship of printed material. The committee did not include any women; five men were appointed by the Minister for Justice to 'consider and report whether it is necessary or advisable in the interest of public morality to extend the existing powers of the State to prohibit or restrict the sale and circulation of printed matter'.[12] The committee heard statements from a number of Catholic and Protestant organisations as well as from the IVA. In their final report, the committee recommended that stricter control of censorship was required for printed material and directed the government to take action. The Censorship of Publications Act was introduced in 1929, and a Censorship of Publications Board was established to advise on publications that should be banned. Within the first 13 years of its existence, the board banned 1,600 books.[13] A high percentage of books and other printed material were censored specifically for referring to birth control. The Censorship of Publications Act was updated in 1946, including further provisions for censorship; publications that contained crime were now also subject to censorship. The new act did, however, establish a system of appeal for the first time.

By the 1960s, censorship in Ireland was becoming indefensible as the system was flawed. The board did not work to clear guidelines and had not clearly defined what constituted obscene literature. Campaigners, including O'Brien, generated public discussion, and demand for a re-evaluation of the censorship laws intensified. Historian Donal Ó Drisceoil maintains that 'the controversies generated by the banning of works by John McGahern and Edna O'Brien in the 1960s helped fuel the movement for reform.'[14] When McGahern won the Macauley Prize for his first novel *The Barracks*, he took a career break from teaching to write his next book, *The Dark*. When *The Dark* was censored, McGahern was denied re-entry to his teaching post. Such decisions caused public outrage. O'Brien found a strong ally to support her campaign against censorship. Fr Peter Connolly, a Professor of English Language and Literature at Maynooth University, actively campaigned against the censorship system and was a staunch defender of O'Brien's literature.

Through pressure from O'Brien and others, the censorship bill was reformed in 1967, and 'there was a gradual unbanning of Irish books on the list over the next twelve years, and the marked end of censorship of Irish writers.'[15] O'Brien continues to publish and has published over 20 works of fiction, including novels, plays and short story collections. She has also written a number of non-fiction works. Her first non-fiction book, *Mother Ireland: A Memoir*, was published in 1976.[16] The volume contained seven autobiographical essays about her life in Ireland and her emigration to London. It was the subject of an episode of *Aquarius*, a British arts television series produced by London Weekend Television for ITV.[17] The episode, in which Russell Harty interviewed O'Brien about her relationship with Ireland, aired on 11 September 1976. O'Brien published her memoirs in 2012; the book was aptly entitled *Country Girl*.[18] That same year, a documentary, *Edna O'Brien: Life, Stories*, profiled O'Brien and her literature.

20. Edna O'Brien, speaking at the Hay Festival, Hay-on-Wye, 30 May 2016. Photographer Andrew Lih.

O'Brien has been the recipient of many prestigious awards and accolades, including the Irish PEN Lifetime Achievement Award, the Frank O'Connor prize and the American Arts Gold Medal. In 2006, she was awarded the Ulysses Medal by University College Dublin. In 2015, O'Brien received the highest literary accolade in Ireland when she was elected by members of Aosdána as a Saoi. This honour is granted 'for singular and sustained distinction in the arts', and no more than seven people can hold this title at any given time.[19] President Michael D. Higgins conferred on O'Brien the symbol of the office of Saoi, the gold Torc, at a ceremony on 15 September 2015 at the Arts Council on Merrion Square in Dublin. In his speech Higgins applauded O'Brien and her work, noting how she overcame hostility and malice:

Edna O'Brien has been and continues to be a fearless teller of truths, a celebrant of life's mysteries with their moments of beauty rescued from repression and the price of contradictions inherited and continued, the darkness as it is delivered, and defeated. She has continued to write, undaunted by culpable incomprehension, authoritarian hostility and sometimes downright malice. She has had the courage always to pursue the truth of the fit and the wonder between life and words in perfect works of art. In more than 20 books now, with Ireland and Irishness always in the background, she has striven to give us 'the beauty and sorrow of the larger world'.[20]

It is significant that O'Brien's trilogy was chosen as the One City One Book for 2019. The public are encouraged to read the book during the month of April, and associated events celebrate the chosen work. For the first ten years from its inception, only books by male authors were selected as One City One Book. The prestigious list of authors included James Joyce, James Plunkett, Oscar Wilde, Flann O'Brien and Jonathan Swift. It was not until 2016 that a female author's book was chosen: Lia Mill's historical fiction *Fallen*. O'Brien's speech, in this section, was delivered to a crowded launch reception for the One City One Book, at the Mansion House in Dublin. Her speech is a beautiful reflection on her writing career and her relationship with Ireland. She describes her home county of Clare, as the 'cradle' of her writing and Dublin as the place of her literary 'awakening.' Her speech provides a wonderful account of authors and books that have influenced and moved her.

In 2019, O'Brien was the focus of an episode of the BBC's cultural programme *Imagine,* which features prestigious artists and authors who shape the contemporary cultural world.[21] O'Brien continues to write urgent and unparalleled work. In 2019, she published her novel *Girl*.[22] The novel was inspired by the mass kidnapping of 276 schoolgirls in the Nigerian town of Chibok by Boko Haram jihadists in 2014. O'Brien, then aged 87, made two trips to Nigeria in 2016 and 2017 to speak with some of the young women who had escaped their abductors. O'Brien explained that she was driven to write this novel after reading an account in a newspaper of a young woman who was found wandering in Sambisa Forest in Nigeria: 'The girl had escaped her captors, but she had lost her mind and she was carrying a baby. I could not have written this novel if the violence and injustice done to this young woman and many others hadn't been moulded on to myself and my soul.'[23] *Girl* was hailed as 'a masterclass of storytelling' in a review in *The Guardian*.[24] The book was shortlisted for the Orwell Prize for Political Fiction and longlisted for the Women's Prize for Fiction in 2020.

In March 2021, O'Brien was appointed a Commander in Ordre des Arts et Lettres, the highest cultural distinction in France. The French culture minister, Roselyne Bachelot-Narquin, when presenting the award to

O'Brien in an online ceremony, stated that it is 'for being a legendary writer who has enriched Irish literature in inestimable ways and for nurturing French literature'.[25] Edna O'Brien's speech, in this section, exhibits just one aspect of her legendary status. In the words of Eimear McBride,

> O'Brien gave voice to the experiences of a previously muzzled generation of Irish women. Into bodies raised to the expectation of violence, rape, forced pregnancy, innumerable dangerous childbirths, domestic bondage and the ever-present risk of institutionalisation for intentionally, or unintentionally, bringing social shame on male relations, she breathed the radical oxygen of choice, desire and sensual delight.[26]

In September 2022, *Joyce's Women*, a play by Edna O'Brien written to celebrate the centenary publication of *Ulysses* premiered at the Abbey theatre. The Abbey announced that 'One of Ireland's greatest contemporary writers turns her attention to the life of one of the country's greatest novelists, in a powerful new play *Joyce's Women*.'[27] At the age of 92, Edna O'Brien continues to produce significant literary works and to showcase Irish culture in all its glory.

'I would like to thank UNESCO and Dublin One City One Book for the surprise honour of choosing *The Country Girls* as their book of the year. My apprenticeship as a writer began in this city, seventy-odd years ago, and therefore there is an added reason to rejoice.

Readers often ask me how I became a writer, and the truest answer is I don't fully know. Writing is both an accident and a deliberation. It lasts a lifetime and if you ask me, is it worth it, I would say yes. Yes, regardless of all the terrors along with the slings, arrows and fickle estimation of the literary establishment.

As a very young girl I wrote short pieces, mostly about nature. It was partly an escape from the world around me, and the immersion in it made me forget the weal and woes of our lives. Had I read Tolstoy's *Childhood, Boyhood and Youth*, I might of course have written with more depth, and given a truer life to my characters. There were no books in our house, or in any of the houses in the parish. Prayer books and a cooking book – Mrs Beaton – constituted the sparse library on every shelf. The prayer books, along with their frightening indoctrination, had graphic vignettes of Christ and the women who adored him and suffered on his behalf. This was not lost on me. I would go alone to our local chapel to do the Stations of the Cross, to meditate on the road to Calvary, not forgetting that it was a woman, a Veronica, who with her towel wiped the face of Jesus. In direct contrast there was a weekly paper, called the *Clare Champion*, in which the small crimes, beauty contests, quarrels between farmers over the right of way on this or that, and beaming advertisements for Show Bands, which made me wish for city life. At school we looked at a frayed map showing the rivers of the world, history books that understandably stressed the history and subjugation of our little land, and sometimes for relaxation our teacher, who was very highly strung, would read an essay from an anthology of English. One was a description of snow by the American author Thoreau, which far surpassed the snow that fell on our fields. We also learned a poem or two by W. B. Yeats.

To write I went out of doors, because I knew even then that it was a subversive occupation. I mostly wrote about our landscape, as the world of nature had an ongoing effect on me. How beautiful the smell and the freshness of our woods after rain, how utterly surprising that bog-lilies and wild iris would sprout on the surface of the murky bog lake, and how industrious to see stooks of turf stacked together, to dry out. Our workman, Torpey, praised himself excessively for the hard work he had done, while crying out for refreshments. His appetite was huge. Big hunks of bread with butter and jam and maybe a boiled egg or a rasher. On Saturdays, I would be sent to the bog with his lunch and a flask of tea, only to find him lolling in the sunshine. He seemed like a rascally fellow in the paintings of Peter Breugel the Elder, which I saw many years later, just lolling there, soaking up whatever nature brought. So these images, even at that young age, were fixed in my memory. But I had to write them. Nothing was permanent until it was set down in language, and that language had to be imbued with some whispers of magic. By writing these pieces, I was both escaping the real world and also immersing myself in it more intensely.

County Clare was the cradle of my writing, or rather its landscape, along with the stories known and covert of the people around me, but most of all the private woes behind our front gate and that avenue of thistles. There were touches of semi-grandeur, ornaments that my mother had brought from America, decorated china plates behind which were stuffed the bills that seemed to constantly come and alarm us. There were moments of great fear and moments of partial reconciliation all stacked up in me, like the little arcs of turf. But to convert that into literature was daunting.

It was in Dublin that I got to read books, and hence my education as such began. An awakening. Peadar O'Donnell, an editor of a literary magazine *The Bell*, showed me immense kindness, in that he was frank with me. I was not ready to write, because I had not read enough. In a sense it was then, without declaring it, that I swore I would become a writer. I went to bookshops on my half-day from the pharmacy where I worked as an apprentice. I copied lines from Faulkner into my notebook, those soaring Biblical sentences at which I positively levitated. In one bookshop there was a quotation from James Joyce on a big poster at the back of the counter. It concerned "a lady of letters in Leeson Street". I read Robert Frost's immortal couplet – "Two roads diverged in a wood, and I— / I took the one less travelled by". It was not that I forgot the yellow buttercups on our fields, and the rain that refreshed them, or the howling wind, the precursor of troubling things. It was that all my imagery and feelings were both present and enriched by reading these great authors. What I would say is that the impulse to write and the secret certainty of the vocation is already there, long before one comes to literature, but literature draws it out and gives it its life and its lustre. Not every steadfast reader becomes a writer. In fact writers are both a mystery to themselves and often an abomination to their family.

One day, by chance, I found what I have to liken to the Annunciation. I had gone to a second-hand bookshop on the quays overlooking the River Liffey. It was more ramshackle. Many of the books were outside in cardboard boxes, prey to the ever-faithful rain, and all were second-hand. At random, I picked up a short book with a yellow cover. It was called *Introducing James Joyce*, by T. S. Eliot. The page that I opened was from *Portrait of the Artist*, in which the festivities of a Christmas dinner are abruptly ended, as the two incendiary topics of sex and politics are raised and the harmony sabotaged. This was our house, or many of the houses I knew, and this was my first and most lasting introduction to the mysteries and particularities of writing. I sensed without knowing the silent transaction between reader and writer. I lived inside those two pages that I read and promptly bought the book for a mere four pence. I had begun, and it does not need retelling of what followed. *The Country Girls* trilogy caused indignation in my own land, a banning of course, and a rift, partly unexpressed, within my own people and my own family. It was thought that I had betrayed them, and maybe all fiction is a betrayal in that it sees and expresses things more mercilessly. For a while, I was something of a sensation, photogenic as was said, and probably on the path of perdition. My mother feared for my immortal soul. The book I had dedicated to her was put in an outhouse, a manger of sorts. I found it after her death. Were she alive today, I would be a bit braver by reading her a page or two from one of Chekhov's stories, and maybe she would decide that literature was a hoard of singular riches.

Not too long ago, I wrote an article asking if literature was a dying animal. I said I feared it was. Books are on the increase but that very holiness, that perseverance, that exigence, those ascensions are less in evidence. As for the oft-quoted phrase – "Poetry makes nothing happen" – it is true to some extent. But even when desolating, poetry is on the side of life, in contrast to the mad incendiary passions of despots and their brute adherents, the perpetrators of hate and of slaughter.

Poetry and great writing unites us even as the world marches towards its own demise.

My thanks to everybody and to Dublin for my rehabilitation.'[28]

SEVENTEEN

Lian Bell

b. 1978

Speech at the launch of the Waking The Feminists archive
National Library of Ireland (online)

21 JANUARY 2021

'A whirlwind year that changed Irish theatre and, by extension, Irish society.'

In October 2015, the Abbey announced its new season for the centenary year of the 1916 Easter Rising. As the national theatre of Ireland, the Abbey receives half of Ireland's public funding for theatre arts; yet the programme did not represent half the population of Ireland. The 'Waking The Nation' programme scheduled for 2016 included 10 plays, of which nine were written by male playwrights, seven would be directed by men and only three by female directors. The programme was not well received by many in the theatre industry. Angry responses to the male-dominated programme were posted on social media by a number of people, including Lian Bell, a designer and arts manager, and author Belinda McKeon. Bell explained why the programme was problematic, noting that 'The Abbey explicitly states in its mission statement that it exists to reflect Irish society and to put the artist at the centre of the work. For it then to so blatantly disregard women artists was for us a clear misuse of public money.'[1]

The Abbey's director, Fiach Mac Conghail, made what journalist Una Mullally described as a 'misguided choice to answer questions about the controversy off the cuff on Twitter. Lian Bell, Belinda McKeon and others were quick to interrogate him about the gender disparity in the Abbey's programme, to which he tweeted the very poorly thought out comment "them's the breaks".'[2] The controversy exploded online. Over the coming weeks, people working in Irish theatre posted personal statements that told a grim story of female under-representation and lower pay rates for women across the Irish theatre sector. The online campaign, led by Bell, soon attracted international attention. Hollywood actor Meryl Streep took to Twitter and, alongside fellow actor Christine Baranski, held a sign saying, 'I support Irish women in Irish theatre.'[3] Waking the Feminists (WTF) became 'a grassroots campaign calling for equality for women across the Irish theatre sector that ran from November 2015 to November 2016'.[4]

21. Lian Bell. Photographer, Róise Goan. Waking The Feminists collection, courtesy of the National Library of Ireland.

Lian Bell is a freelance arts manager and a designer for performance. She mainly works on 'one-off cultural events and stand-alone projects in all areas of the arts'.[5] Bell has a 'particular interest in artist development and in events that bring Irish artists in contact with their international counterparts'.[6] She has designed spaces for contemporary performances of dance and theatre artists and has won numerous awards. Bell graduated from Trinity College Dublin with a BA Hons in Drama and Theatre Studies.

She attended Central St. Martins, London, where she completed an MA in Scenography. She has also studied Visual Arts Practice at the National College of Art and Design in Dublin.[7] Bell has years of experience working in Irish theatre and was well placed to launch a campaign for gender equality within the industry.

22. The first Waking The Feminists public meeting at the Abbey Theatre, Nov. 2015. Photographer, Fiona Morgan. Waking The Feminists collection, courtesy of the National Library of Ireland.

On 12 November 2015, WTF held a public meeting at the Abbey theatre. Bell received a standing ovation when she took the stage. She outlined WTF's objectives, and then a number of women read their personal statements. The talks were chaired by Ivana Bacik, now the Labour Party leader, and producer Sarah Durcan. So many people turned up to support the campaign that the theatre was filled to capacity. Loudspeakers were set up outside the building on Abbey Street streaming the speeches to the crowd gathered outside. Author Sinéad Gleeson remarked, 'Up until a few people on social media raised objections about "Waking The Nation" and the gender imbalance everyone was holding their tongues. Today felt like a very special moment when the fear had gone and women spoke up.'[8]

In response, the board and director of the Abbey theatre issued a public statement setting out their commitment to establish a gender equality policy and ensure the inclusion of more work by women. While WTF campaigners welcomed this move, it was now clear that there was an under-representation of women across Irish theatre and not just in the Abbey. A group of theatre professionals outlined their campaign objectives:

1. A sustained policy for inclusion with action plan and measurable results
2. Equal championing and advancement of women artists
3. Economic parity for all working in the theatre[9]

A number of people in the group volunteered their time to help further the campaign objectives. Over the following year, the volunteers met with state-funded theatre organisations, 'encouraging them to make gender equality a reality through their policies and programming'.[10]

On International Women's Day in 2016, 8 March, a second public meeting was held by WTF. This time the event took place at Liberty Hall, the headquarters of the Services, Industrial, Professional, and Technical Union (SIPTU). Representatives from major state-funded theatres attended, including the Abbey, the Gate theatre, Druid Theatre Company, Rough Magic Theatre Company, Dublin Theatre Festival, Dublin Fringe Festival and the Project Arts Centre. After that meeting, WTF commissioned research to acquire figures on gender balance in Irish theatre. The research was conducted by a team of six researchers led by Brenda Donohue, a research assistant at the Educational Research Centre in St Patrick's College. The research was funded by the Arts Council and assessed organisations in Ireland that produced or presented theatre from 2006 to 2015.[11] In the foreword to the report, Bell described the substantial changes that had resulted from the WTF campaign in just one year:

> In the one short year of the campaign, we have seen some extraordinary shifts, both in the working practices of many of our major organisations, and in the openness with which we can discuss gender as an issue. Our national theatre has set itself far-reaching and carefully chosen guidelines on gender equality. Our major theatre organisations are working together to formulate gender equality policies. Our Minister for the Arts has called on all our National Cultural Institutions to have their own gender policies in place by next year. Programmes across the arts are beginning to reflect a new, deeper consideration for gender – and where they do not, they are being taken to task by their audiences.[12]

This was the first time that research on gender balance in Irish theatre had been conducted, and the results were, as Bell notes, 'stark'. For example, 'in six of the ten years studied, the Gate Theatre did not present a single play directed by a woman, that in 2008 the Abbey Theatre produced no play at all by a female writer, and that in the entire study, only 9% of productions employed female sound designers.'[13]

The WTF campaign centred on redressing such huge gender inequalities, and it accomplished seismic changes in just one year. A research report was now published, providing a basis to work from. The Abbey was now aware of their gender equality issues, and the board established their Guiding Principles on Gender Equality, the first initiative of its kind for a national theatre. Sarah Durcan, a core member of the WTF campaign, was appointed to the board of the Abbey, while the Arts Council appointed core WTF member Loughlin Deegan to their board.

In March 2017, Heather Humphreys, the Minister for Arts, Heritage, Regional, Rural and Gaeltacht Affairs, held a gender policy workshop with representatives from WTF and Irish national cultural institutions, also present were representatives from the Arts Council and the Irish Film Board. Humphreys directed all national cultural institutions to introduce gender policies by 2018. The minister stated that 'The role of women in contemporary arts and culture has been brought into sharp focus following the centenary year and in no small part due to the advocacy work of the Waking the Feminists movement.'[14] On 1 March 2022, Catherine Martin, in her role as Minister for Tourism, Culture, Arts, Gaeltacht, Sport and Media, reasserted her department's objective to ensure 'greater visibility of women in the arts, as participants and in content'.[15]

Bell was recognised for her determined campaign, which achieved positive change in a short space of time. She was given the Trinity College Law Society's Praeses Elit Award. She received the Outstanding Young Person Award from the Dublin branch of Junior Chamber International and the Trinity College Philosophical Society's Bram Stoker Award. Bell was presented with the Judge's Special Award at the *Irish Times* Theatre Awards for her work spearheading the WTF movement. A report in the *Irish Times* noted how a campaign 'initially born in protest of the Abbey Theatre's male-dominated programme for the centenary of the Rising . . . has quickly evolved into a considerable force for gender equality and economic parity in the performing arts'.[16] In July 2016, WTF was honoured with a Lilly Award in New York. This was a historic move, as 'the Lilly Awards honour the achievements of women in American theatre and never before has one been awarded to anyone outside the US; neither has one ever been given to an organisation.'[17]

The donation of the WTF archive to the National Library of Ireland was marked by an event that occurred online due to Covid-19.[18] In her role as campaign director, Bell gave the speech in this section to an online audience. Honouring the significance of this archive and the importance of the campaign, the Minister for Tourism, Culture, Arts, Gaeltacht, Sport and Media, Catherine Martin, was in attendance. Martin declared, 'This movement began in 2015 and grew to become a focused and highly-effective campaign, with worldwide reach, to address the under representation of women in the world of Irish theatre, and in Irish culture more widely.'[19] Then director of the National Library of Ireland, Sandra Collins, was quick to confirm that this 'archive is a comprehensive record of a campaign which shone light on under representation of women in the theatre industry; and continues today to bring about change in women's employment in the industry, on the stage, in production and direction'.[20]

'There's a strange feeling at marking a significant milestone in a collective, collaborative social campaign with each of us in our own rooms. Not to mention the irony of celebrating women in Irish theatre, at a moment when Irish theatre is essentially on pause. However, I feel like it is precisely because of this that the marking of this archive is important.

Theatre is the ultimate opportunity to feel and think collectively. Being together allows us to find our common ground. I recently attended a wonderful talk, online naturally, by Dr Aoife Monks called *"In defence of craft"*. She made the argument that one of the reasons costume workers, traditionally women, were often paid less than stage workers, traditionally men, was that the costume work was primarily done in the women's own homes. The men had more opportunity to work together in the theatre building, to share their experiences and to begin collectively to argue their worth. That is, of course, only part of the picture; the long-running discrepancy in payment to costume workers is often credited to the fact that women's work in general is undervalued.

Soon after #WakingTheFeminists began, I heard anecdotally that Dublin Theatre Festival had brought the daily costume rate for casual crew up to be equal to the daily technical rate. That is only one tiny example of the #WakingTheFeminists effect. You see, there is nothing more powerful than people gathering and talking with each other.

I first made contact with the National Library in June 2017 about setting up a #WakingTheFeminists archive. The work on the archive over the subsequent three and a half years has been a labour of love, but a hugely important final step in our campaign. We knew from the get go how important it was to ensure that #WakingTheFeminists was properly archived. We saw first-hand how easy it is for women's stories, women's voices, and women's achievements to be overlooked, and how quickly they fade. . . .

Between this digital archive and the physical archive that is now housed in the National Museum of Ireland, #WakingTheFeminists has taken its rightful place in our national story. We stand in solidarity with all women who have been denied the right to be remembered, whose stories are not told. This week, of all weeks, with the Mother and Baby Homes report being published, those women in particular and their children are in our minds.

Today many of us who were key to the #WakingTheFeminists campaign are here to mark this official remembering of our story, peering at computer screens in our separate rooms. We're also joined by some of the photographers who have generously included their work in the archive. I can't wait to raise a glass in person in celebration with you all. This archive, we hope, will inspire future historians, theatre makers and feminists, and we hope it will give a small insight into the workings behind a whirlwind year that changed Irish theatre and, by extension, Irish society.

I have a short text to read to you. It's an extract of the most recent addition to the archive, being emailed to me only a few days ago. On the morning of the first #WakingTheFeminists gathering at the Abbey, I was standing out the front of the building in a growing crowd of women, with press photographers amassing. I was told that a banner was on its way and that "Molly was cycling it over." I had no idea who Molly was, but I had faith. Molly O'Cathain now works as a professional set and costume designer, but at the time was a student at the Samuel Beckett Theatre in Trinity College. She writes:

. . . I ended up making the banner because Sarah Durcan called me one night. . . . I remember asking her, "How big should it be?" Answer: "As big as you can manage!" . . . I . . . hightailed it into Ikea to buy canvas. I went around to my mum's house late that night – she's a screen-printer and used to have a studio with a big table – called for back-up (Liadain Kaminska and John Gunning soon joined me). . . . We worked late into the night, and then the next morning I got two broom handles, sewed pockets for them and delivered it into the Abbey.

Molly's contribution gives a sense of the way things worked throughout the campaign. There was such goodwill, such absence of ego, and such a feeling that it was now or never. Someone was asked to help, jumped in with both feet, and used their skills to the maximum. The photographs with that banner, of course, became the iconic visual calling card for #WakingTheFeminists, used in the media across the world. And the rest, as they say, is well-documented and soon to be very well-archived history.'[21]

Notes

FOREWORD

1. See, Melissa Dinsman, "'A river is not a woman'": re-visioning *Finnegans Wake* in Eavan Boland's "Anna Liffey'", *Contemporary Women's Writing*, 7:2 (Jul. 2013), pp 172–89.

INTRODUCTION

1. Margaret Ward, *Unmanageable Revolutionaries: Women and Irish Nationalism* (London, 1995), p. 51.
2. The last Magdalene Laundry to close was operated by the Sisters of Our Lady of Charity on Sean MacDermott Street in Dublin. See Elizabeth Coppin's speech about her incarceration in Magdalene Laundries, where she was subjected to abuse and forced labour, in Sonja Tiernan, *Irish Women's Speeches: Voices That Rocked the System* (Dublin, 2021), pp 276–85.
3. See Catherine Connolly's speech on the launch of the Mother and Baby Homes report (2021), in Tiernan, *Irish Women's Speeches: Voices that Rocked the System* (Dublin, 2012), pp 286–95.
4. Nuala O'Faolain, *Are You Somebody?* (Dublin, 2021), p. xxi.

CHAPTER I – CHARPOLTTE STOKER

1. *Leitrim Observer*, 7 Dec. 2007.
2. Fióna Gallagher, 'Cholera: Fever, fear and facts: A pandemic in Irish urban history', *Dr Fióna Gallagher*, https://www.drfionagallagher.com/about.html, accessed 22 Mar. 2022.
3. W. Parker Stoker, 'Charlotte Stoker: A family perspective', *Bram Stoker Estate*, https://www.bramstokerestate.com/charlotte-matilda-blake-thornley, accessed 21 Mar. 2022.
4. Ben Griffin, *The Politics of Gender in Victorian Britain: Masculinity, Political Culture and the Struggle for Women's Rights* (Cambridge, 2012), p. 80.
5. Frances Power Cobbe, *Friendless Girls, and How to Help Them: Being an Account of the Preventive Mission at Bristol* (London, 1861).
6. Mary E. Daly, 'The society and its contribution to Ireland: Past, present and future', in *Journal of the Statistical and Social Inquiry Society of Ireland* 27 (1998), p. 33.
7. 'History of 1813–1851 census', *The National Archives of Ireland*, http://www.census.nationalarchives.ie/help/pre1901.html, accessed 23 Mar. 2022.
8. Fiona Fitzsimons, 'Deaf records', in *History Ireland* 25:4 (Jul./Aug. 2017), p. 29, https://www.historyireland.com/deaf-records/, accessed 22 Mar. 2022.

9. J. B. Lyons, 'Wilde, Sir William Robert Wills', in *Dictionary of Irish Biography* (www.dib.ie).

10. 'Discussion', in *Journal of the Statistical and Social Inquiry Society of Ireland* (Dublin, 1863), p. 458.

11. Ibid.

12. 'Third meeting', in *Journal of the Statistical and Social Inquiry Society of Ireland* (Dublin, 1864), p. 42.

13. Charlotte Stoker, *On Female Emigration from Workhouses* (Dublin, 1864), p. 5.

14. Michael Wainwright, 'Female suffrage in Ireland: James Joyce's realization of unrealized potential', in *Criticism* 51:4 (2009), p. 653.

15. Harry Ludlam, *A Biography of Bram Stoker, Creator of 'Dracula'* (London, 1977), p. 14.

16. *Irish Times*, 16 Sep. 1867.

17. Trinity College Dublin (hereafter TCD), Typescript transcription of an account of the cholera outbreak in Ireland in 1832, originally written by Charlotte Stoker, MS 11076/2/3.

18. Charlotte Stoker, 'Experience of the cholera in Ireland 1832', in *The Green Book: Writings on Irish Gothic, Supernatural and Fantastic Literature* 9 (2017), p. 11.

19. Ibid., p. 12.

20. Ibid., p. 15.

21. *Sligo Champion*, 29 Aug. 2001. Peter Treymane is a pseudonym for the historian and writer Peter Berresford Ellis.

22. Brian J. Showers, 'Editor's note', in *The Green Book: Writings on Irish Gothic, Supernatural and Fantastic Literature* 9 (2017), p. 6.

23. *Evening Herald*, 1 Apr. 1901.

24. 'Charlotte Matilda Blake Thornley Stoker', *Find a Grave*, https://www.findagrave.com/memorial/97436509/charlotte-matilda_blake-stoker, accessed 21 Mar. 2022.

25. *Irish Independent*, 1 Apr. 1901.

26. 'Did you know that the novel Dracula has Sligo connections?', *Sligo Walking Tours*, https://sligowalkingtours.com/sligo-dracula-tour/, accessed 22 Mar. 2021.

27. *Sligo Champion*, 2 Feb. 1973.

28. TCD, Stoker Family Papers, MS 11076.

29. '*JSSISI: Journal of The Statistical and Social Inquiry Society of Ireland*, 1847–', *TARA*, http://www.tara.tcd.ie/handle/2262/1080, accessed 22 Mar. 2022.

30. Charlotte M. B. Stoker, 'On the necessity of a state provision for the education of the deaf and dumb of Ireland', in *Journal of the Statistical and Social Inquiry Society of Ireland* (Dublin, 1863), pp 456–8.

CHAPTER 2 – MAUD GONNE

1. Margaret O'Callaghan and Caoimhe Nic Dháibhéid, 'MacBride, (Edith) Maud Gonne', in *Dictionary of Irish Biography* (hereafter *DIB*) (www.dib.ie).

2. Ibid.

3. Bureau of Military History (hereafter BMH), 1913–21, 'Statement by Madam Maud Gonne McBride', *Military Archives*, p. 1, https://www.militaryarchives.ie/collections/online-collections/bureau-of-military-history-1913-1921/reels/bmh/BMH.WS0317.pdf#page=1, accessed 25 Mar. 2022.

4. Ibid.

5. See Anna Parnell's speech in Sonja Tiernan, *Irish Women's Speeches: Voices that Rocked the System* (Dublin, 2021), pp 7–17.

6. BMH, 'Statement by Madam Maud Gonne McBride', p. 2.

7. O'Callaghan and Nic Dháibhéid, 'MacBride, (Edith) Maud Gonne', in *DIB*.

8. Anna MacBride White and A. Norman Jeffares (eds), *The Gonne–Yeats Letters, 1893–1938* (London, 1992), p. 12.

9. James Connolly, 'Socialism and Irish nationalism', in *L'Irlande Libre* (1897).

10. Karen Steele, *Women, Press, and Politics During the Irish Revival* (New York, 2007), p. 97.

11. Senia Pašeta, '1798 in 1898: The politics of commemoration', in *Irish Review* 22 (1998), p. 46.

12. A statue was eventually erected to Wolfe Tone in St Stephen's Green in 1967. Four years later it was attacked by the Ulster Defence Association and was later recast by sculptor Edward Delaney and re-erected on the same spot at the corner of the Green opposite the Shelbourne Hotel.

13. Karen Steele, 'Raising her voice for justice: Maud Gonne and the "United Irishman"', *New Hibernia Review/Iris Éireannach Nua* 3:2 (1999), p. 88.

14. Ibid., p. 94.

15. Maud Gonne, 'Famine Queen', *United Irishman*, 7 Apr. 1900.

16. Maud Gonne, 'Her subjects', *United Irishman*, 21 Apr. 1900.

17. Hanna Sheehy Skeffington, 'Constance Markievicz – Stray memories and reflections', *Irish Press*, 9 Feb. 1940.

18. Margaret Ward, *Unmanageable Revolutionaries: Women and Irish Nationalism* (London, 1995), p. 51.

19. Ibid.

20. Military Archives Ireland, Dublin, 'Irish Girls', Inghinidhe na hÉireann handbill, CD119/3/1.

21. Ibid.

22. *Irish Times*, 10 Sep. 1901.

23. *Freeman's Journal*, 9 Mar. 1899.

24. *Westmeath Examiner*, 18 Mar. 1899.

25. *Western People*, 25 Mar. 1899.

26. *Irish Daily Independent*, 14 Sep. 1901.

27. *Westmeath Independent*, 14 Sep. 1901.

28. P. J. Mathews, 'A poets' revolt: How culture heavily influenced the Rising and its leaders', *Irish Independent*, 21 Jan. 2016.

29. Ibid.

30. BMH, 'Statement by Madam Maud Gonne McBride', p. 6.

31. 'Witness Madam Maud Gonne McBride', document no W.S. 317, Bureau of Military History, 1913–21, www.militaryarchives.ie, accessed 20 Jul. 2022.

32. O'Rahilly styled himself on his more famous father The O'Rahilly who was killed during the hostilities of the Easter Rising.

33. *Irish Examiner*, 30 Apr. 1953.

34. O'Callaghan and Nic Dháibhéid, 'MacBride, (Edith) Maud Gonne', in *DIB*.

35. For further details on Gonne's life and legacy, see Trish Ferguson, *Maud Gonne* (Dublin, 2019); Margaret Ward, *Maud Gonne: Ireland's Joan of Arc* (London, 1990).

36. 'Lavin memorial: Unveiling of the monument', *Westmeath Independent*, 14 Sep. 1901.

CHAPTER 3 – ALICE STOPFORD GREEN

1. Alice Stopford Green, *The Making of Ireland and Its Undoing, 1200–1600* (London, 1908), p. ix.

2. John Richard Green, *A Short History of English People* (London, 1874).

3. John Richard Green and Alice Stopford Green, *A Short Geography of the British Islands* (London, 1879).

4. Biographical details from William Murphy, 'Green, Alice Sophia Amelia Stopford', in *Dictionary of Irish Biography* (hereafter *DIB*) (www.dib.ie).

5. John Richard Green, *The Conquest of England*, Alice Stopford Green (ed.) (London, 1883).

6. National Library of Ireland (hereafter NLI), Dublin, 'Letter from Florence Nightingale', 30 Jul. 1884, MS 43,326.

7. Morley served as Chief Secretary for Ireland in 1886 and again from 1892 to 1895. Alice Stopford Green, *Henry II* (London, 1888).

8. Mrs. J. R. Green, *Town Life in the Fifteenth Century: In Two Volumes* (London, 1894).

9. Angus Mitchell, 'Woman of the fifth province: Remembering Alice Stopford Green', in *Ríocht na Midhe* 32 (2021), p. 136.

10. Ibid.

11. See NLI, letters from R. I. Best, Alice Stopford Green Papers, MS 10,457.

12. See Mary Robinson's speech in Sonja Tiernan, *Irish Women's Speeches: Voices That Rocked the System* (Dublin, 2021), pp 195–206.

13. 'Address by the President, Mary Robinson, on the occasion of her inauguration as President of Ireland, 3rd December, 1990', *President of Ireland*, https://president.ie/en/media-library/speeches/address-by-the-president-mary-robinson-on-the-occasion-of-her-inauguration, accessed 5 Aug. 2022.

14. Angus Mitchell, 'Historical revisit: Mythistory and the making of Ireland: Alice Stopford Green's undoing', in *Irish Historical Studies* 44:166 (2020), p. 355.

15. Ibid.

16. *Freeman's Journal*, 14 Dec. 1908.

17. Ibid.

18. Ibid.

19. Ibid.

20. *Freeman's Journal*, 17 Dec. 1908.

21. *Freeman's Journal*, 14 Dec. 1908.

22. Mitchell, 'Historical revisit', p. 354.

23. Hiram Morgan, 'In search of Owen Roe O'Neill', in *History Ireland* 4:3 (Autumn 1996), p. 5, https://www.historyireland.com/in-search-of-owen-roe-oneill/, accessed 9 Aug. 2022.

24. Mitchell, 'Historical revisit', p. 358.

25. *The Harp*, Aug. 1909, as cited in Mitchell, 'Historical revisit', p. 360.

26. *Irish Homestead*, 11 Jul. 1908.

27. *The Sphere*, 29 Aug. 1908; *The Sphere*, 19 Sep. 1908.

28. Alice Stopford Green, *Irish Nationality* (London, 1911).

29. Ibid., p. 254.

30. Alice Stopford Green, *The Old Irish World* (Dublin, 1912), p. vi.

31. Murphy, 'Green, Alice Sophia Amelia Stopford', in *DIB*.

32. Sonja Tiernan, *Eva Gore-Booth: An Image of Such Politics* (Manchester, 2012), pp 186–7.

33. Ibid.

34. Alice Stopford Green, *Ourselves Alone in Ulster* (Dublin, 1918); Alice Stopford Green, *The Government of Ireland* (London, 1921).

35. Seanad Éireann debate, Vol. 3, No. 21, 26 Nov. 1924.

36. Ibid.

37. Alice Stopford Green, *History of the Irish State to 1014* (London, 1925).

38. NLI, Alice Stopford Green Papers, MS 10,427–10,465.

39. Alfred, Lord Tennyson, then Poet Laureate.

40. 'Mrs. J. R. Green's book: Brilliant address by the authoress', *Freeman's Journal*, 14 Dec. 1908.

CHAPTER 4 – NORAH DACRE FOX

1. Christopher Wiley and Lucy Ella Rose (eds), *Women's Suffrage in Word, Image, Music, Stage and Screen: The Making of a Movement* (London, 2021), p. 1.
2. Angela McPherson, 'A grandmother's legacy: The gift that keeps on giving?', in *Women's History Review* 30:4 (2021), p. 691.
3. Patrick Maume, 'Elam (Dacre Fox), Norah', in *Dictionary of Irish Biography* (hereafter *DIB*) (www.dib.ie).
4. *The Times*, 16 Oct. 1905.
5. WSPU, *Tortured Women: What Forcible Feeding Means: A Prisoner's Testimony* (London, 1914).
6. McPherson, 'A grandmother's legacy', p. 691.
7. The Women's Library (hereafter TWL), London, interview with Grace Roe at Green Cottage, Hastings Road, Pembury, Tunbridge Wells, 23 Sep. 1974, Oral Evidence on the Suffragette and Suffragist Movements: the Brian Harrison interviews, Ref: 8SUF/B/007.
8. TWL, printed ticket for WSPU event, Papers of Katie Gliddon, Ref: 7KGG/3/19.
9. *The Times*, 8 May 1914.
10. *The Suffragette*, 22 May 1914.
11. *New York Times*, 15 May 1914.
12. *Irish Times*, 6 Jul. 1914.
13. *The Times*, 14 Aug. 1918.
14. Norah Dacre Fox, *The Vitamin Survey: A Reply* [to Special Report no. 38 of the Medical Research Council, entitled 'Report on the present state of knowledge concerning accessory food factors-vitamines'] (London, 1934); Norah Dacre Fox, *The Medical Research Council: What It Is and How It Works* (London, 1935).
15. 'Oswald Mosley', *Encyclopaedia Britannica*, https://www.britannica.com/biography/Oswald-Mosley, accessed 6 Apr. 2022.
16. Julie V. Gottlieb, *Feminine Fascism: Women in Britain's Fascist Movement, 1923–1945* (London, 2021), p. 147.
17. Ibid., p. 149.
18. Norah Elam, 'Fascism, women and democracy', in *Fascist Quarterly* 1:3 (1935).
19. Gottlieb, *Feminine Fascism*, p. 150.
20. Maume, 'Elam (Dacre Fox), Norah', in *DIB*.
21. Susan McPherson and Angela McPherson, *Mosley's Old Suffragette: A Biography of Norah Dacre Fox* (n.p., 2011).
22. Ernest Jones (1819–1869) was an English poet and novelist. He was a chartist leader, supporting a working-class movement for political reform in Britain.
23. Norah Dacre Fox, 'A prisoner's speech', *The Suffragette*, 10 Jul. 1914.

CHAPTER 5 – SARAH PURSER

1. St. Enda's, Irish language secondary school, was established by Irish nationalist leader Patrick Pearse.
2. Female students were not accepted into to Trinity College Dublin until 1904.
3. Elizabeth Coxhead, *Daughters of Erin: Five Women of the Irish Renascence* (London, 1965), p. 129.

4. Oil on canvas, Size 59.8 x 41.3 in./152 x 105 cm. Christie's Catalogue: Country House Auction (25 November 2003).

5. Trinity College Dublin, Letters of Thomas MacGreevey, director of the National Gallery, MS 10381/81–182; partly cited in Coxhead, *Daughters of Erin*, p. 129.

6. Ibid., p. 131.

7. John N. O'Grady, 'Purser, Sarah Henrietta', in *Dictionary of Irish Biography* (hereafter *DIB*) (www.dib.ie).

8. Coxhead, *Daughters of Erin*, p. 132.

9. O'Grady, 'Purser, Sarah Henrietta', in *DIB*.

10. William Murphy, 'Martyn, Edward', in *DIB*.

11. 'An Túr Gloine', *Artist Biographies: British and Irish Artists of the 20th Century*, https://www.artbiogs.co.uk/2/organizations/tur-gloine, accessed 27 Apr. 2022.

12. Coxhead, *Daughters of Erin*, p. 136.

13. John B. Yeats was the father of writer W. B. Yeats, painter Jack B. Yeats, designer Susan 'Lily' Yeats, and publisher and painter Elizabeth 'Lollie' Yeats.

14. The Royal Society of Antiquaries of Ireland is now based at 63 Merrion Square, in a building acquired by the society in 1917.

15. National Library of Ireland (NLI), Dublin, 'A loan collection of pictures by Nathaniel Hone, R.H.A. and John Butler Yeats, R.H.A.', call number BB111.

16. Margarita Cappock, 'Lane, Sir Hugh Percy', in *DIB*.

17. Coxhead, *Daughters of Erin*, p. 136.

18. Ibid.

19. Ibid.

20. *Twenty-Fifth Anniversary Celebration: An Túr Gloine Stained Glass and Mosaic Works, 24 Upper Pembroke Street Dublin* (Dublin, 1928), NLI, Book A54.

21. Ibid., p. 18.

22. Stuart Park, 'A touch of the Irish in Karori', *New Zealand Glass*, 11 Jan. 2016, http://newzealandglass.blogspot.com/2016/01/a-touch-of-irish-in-karori. html#disqus_thread, accessed 27 Apr. 2022.

23. *Irish Times*, 8 May 1915.

24. Hugh Lane Gallery, https://www.hughlane.ie/current-collections/887-lanepictures, accessed 7 Jul. 2022.

25. *Friends of the National Collections of Ireland*, http://www.fnci.ie, accessed 27 Apr. 2022.

26. Danielle McLaughlin, 'Mespil revisited', in *The Stinging Fly* 37:2 (Winter 2017–18), https://stingingfly.org/2017/12/01/mespil-revisited/, accessed 27 Apr. 2022.

27. Coxhead, *Daughters of Erin*, p. 165.

28. 'Champion of the arts 1975', *RTÉ*, https://www.rte.ie/archives/2020/1007/1169951-artist-sarah-purser/, accessed 27 Apr. 2022.

29. *RTÉ Guide*, 19 Sep. 1975.

30. Purser attributes this quotation to the English author and art critic G. K. Chesterton. See G. K. Chesterton, *G. F Watts* (London, 1904), p. 60.

31. Sarah Purser, 'Miss Purser's reply', in *Twenty-Fifth Anniversary Celebration: An Túr Gloine Stained Glass and Mosaic Works, 24 Upper Pembroke Street Dublin* (Dublin, 1928), pp 8–13.

CHAPTER 6 – MARGARET (GRETTA) COUSINS

1. Jyoti Atwal, 'Margaret Elizabeth Cousins and transnationalism: An Irish suffragette as an anti-colonial feminist in Colonial India', in Jyoti Atwal, Ciara Breathnach and

Sarah-Anne Buckley (eds), *Gender and History: Ireland, 1852–1922* (London, 2022), p. 250.

2. James H. Cousins and Margaret E. Cousins, *We Two Together* (Madras, 1950), p. 25.

3. Henry A. Jeffries, *Derry–Londonderry: The Ulster Covenant and the 1916 Proclamation* (Derry, 2010), p. 3.

4. Frances Clarke, 'Cousins, James Henry Sproull', in *Dictionary of Irish Biography* (hereafter *DIB*) (www.dib.ie).

5. Diarmaid Ferriter, 'Fay, William George ("Wille")', in *DIB*.

6. See Maud Gonne section in this volume, pp 16-28.

7. *Irish Times*, 1 Apr. 2002.

8. Clarke, 'Cousins, James Henry Sproull', in *DIB*.

9. Atwal, 'Margaret Elizabeth Cousins and Transnationalism', p. 252.

10. Cousins and Cousins, *We Two Together*, p. 128.

11. Catherine Candy, 'The occult feminism of Margaret Cousins in Modern Ireland and India, 1878–1954', PhD diss., Loyola University, 1996.

12. See Hanna Sheehy Skeffington's speech in Sonja Tiernan, *Irish Women's Speeches: Voices that Rocked the System* (Dublin, 2021), pp 69–76.

13. Frances Clarke, 'Cousins, Margaret ("Gretta") Elizabeth', in *DIB*.

14. J. P. Finnan, *John Redmond and Irish Unity, 1912–1918* (New York, 2004), p. 125.

15. Sonja Tiernan, '"Challenging the headship of man": Militant suffragism and the *Irish Citizen*', in Mark O'Brien and Felix Larkin (eds), *Periodicals & Journalism in Twentieth-Century Ireland* (Dublin, 2014), pp 61–74.

16. For further information, see Sonja Tiernan, *Eva Gore-Booth: An Image of Such Politics* (Manchester, 2012).

17. Cousins and Cousins, *We Two Together*, p. 257.

18. Jyoti Atwal, 'Global lives: Margaret Cousins', *RTÉ*, https://www.rte.ie/centuryireland/index.php/articles/global-lives-margaret-cousins, accessed 19 Apr. 2022.

19. 'Rabindranath Tagore, Biographical', *Nobel Prize Organisation*, https://www.nobelprize.org/prizes/literature/1913/tagore/biographical/, accessed 19 Apr. 2022.

20. Atwal, 'Global lives'.

21. 'Rowlatt Acts', *Encyclopaedia Britannica*, https://www.britannica.com/event/Rowlatt-Acts, accessed 19 Apr. 2022.

22. Pierce A. Grace, 'Repression: The Amritsar massacre, 1919: The Irish connection', in *History Ireland* 4:18 (Jul./Aug. 2010), pp 24–5.

23. Margaret E. Cousins, *The Awakening of Asian Womanhood* (Madras, 1922), p. vi.

24. Ibid., p. 17.

25. Atwal, 'Global lives'.

26. Margaret E. Cousins, 'Presidential address', in *All-India Women's Conference, Eleventh Session* (Ahmedabad, 1936), p. 23.

27. Margaret Ward, 'Irish suffrage: Remembrance, commemoration, and memorialization', in Oona Frawley (ed.), *Women and the Decade of Commemorations* (Bloomington, 2021), p. 174.

28. Margaret E. Cousins, *The Music of Orient and Occident: Essays Towards Mutual Understandings* (Madras, 1935).

29. Margaret E. Cousins, *Indian Womanhood Today* (Allahabad, 1941; reprint 1947), p. 5.

30. Cousins and Cousins, *We Two Together*, p. 770.

31. Ibid., pp 582–3.

CHAPTER 7 – MAUREEN O'CARROLL

1. Mary J. Murphy, '"Little Mo": Maureen O'Carroll TD 1913–1984', *NUI Galway*, https://www.nuigalway.ie/coiscoiribe2015/features/little-mo/#, accessed 20 Apr. 2022.
2. *Irish Times*, 15 May 2021.
3. Ibid.
4. National Archives of Ireland (hereafter NAI), Dublin, 'Letter to the Taoiseach from Mrs Maureen O'Carroll, Honorary Secretary, Lower Prices Council', 3 Nov. 1947, Record 7256 from 'Women in 20th-century Ireland – 1922–1966: Sources from the Department of the Taoiseach database'.
5. NAI, 'Letter from Seamus Mac Ugo, Private Secretary to the Taoiseach, to O'Carroll', 11 Nov. 1947, Record 7258 from 'Women in 20th-century Ireland'.
6. *Evening Echo*, 21 Feb. 1951.
7. *Evening Herald*, 26 Jan. 1953.
8. *Irish Independent*, 10 Jul. 1953.
9. *Evening Herald*, 26 Sep. 1953.
10. *The Real Mrs. Brown*, a documentary produced and presented by Caroline Dalton, mixed by John Murphy and funded by the Broadcasting Authority of Ireland, aired on Newstalk, 27 Feb. 2018.
11. The national police service of the Republic of Ireland.
12. *The Real Mrs. Brown*, Newstalk, 27 Feb. 2018.
13. Mike Milotte, *Banished Babies: The Secret History of Ireland's Baby Export Business* (Dublin, 2012).
14. See Fergus Finlay, 'Professor Éamon de Valera Jnr: A hypocrite and baby thief at the heart of the Irish establishment', *Irish Examiner*, 9 Mar. 2021.
15. Department of Foreign Affairs, Adoption Policy Files, 345/164, cited in Moira J. Maguire, 'Foreign adoptions and the evolution of Irish Adoption Policy, 1945–52', in *Journal of Social History* 36:2 (Winter 2002), p. 389.
16. Valerie O'Brien and Sahana Mitra, 'An overview of adoption policy and legislative change in Ireland 1952–2017', Oct. 2018, p. 5, https://aai.gov.ie/images/Report_2_An_Overview_of_Policy_and_Legislative_Change_in_Ireland_1952_to_2017.pdf, accessed 17 May 2022.
17. *Irish Times*, 9 Mar. 1996.
18. Limerick County Hospital at Croom later became a Regional Orthopaedic Hospital when it was replaced by Limerick Regional Hospital in 1956.
19. 'Mother and Baby Homes Commission of Investigation: Final report', 30 Oct. 2020, p. 47, https://assets.gov.ie/118565/107bab7e-45aa-4124-95fd-1460893dbb43.pdf, accessed 22 Apr. 2022. See Catherine Connolly's speech in *Irish Women's Speeches: Voices That Rocked the System* (Dublin, 2021), pp 286–95.
20. Dáil Éireann debate, Vol. 159, No. 8, 18 Jul. 1956.
21. Ibid.
22. Ibid.
23. Ibid.
24. *Belfast Newsletter*, 19 Jul. 1956.
25. Dáil Éireann debate, Vol. 158, No. 4, 19 Jun. 1956.
26. Ibid.
27. Maguire, 'Foreign adoptions and the evolution of Irish Adoption Policy', p. 388.
28. O'Nolan also wrote as Flann O'Brien.
29. *Irish Times*, 30 Oct. 1956. Córas Iompair Éireann, is the main provider of public transport in Ireland.
30. *Irish Press*, 10 May 1984.

31. *Sunday Press*, 13 May 1984.
32. Brendan O'Carroll, *The Mammy* (Dublin, 1994).
33. *Irish Examiner*, 29 Jul. 2016.
34. Dáil Éireann debate, Vol. 159, No. 8, 18 Jul. 1956.

Chapter 8 – Máirín de Burca

1. T. F. O'Sullivan, *The Young Irelanders* (Tralee, 1944).
2. *Irish Examiner*, 2 Oct. 2010.
3. *The Journal*, 9 Jun. 2019.
4. *Sunday Independent*, 31 Oct. 1971.
5. See the speech by Nuala Fennell in *Irish Women's Speeches: Voices that Rocked the System* (Dublin, 2021), pp 150–9.
6. Sonja Tiernan, 'Levine, June', in *Dictionary of Irish Biography* (hereafter *DIB*) (www.dib.ie).
7. Irish Women's Liberation Movement, *Chains or Change?: The Civil Wrongs of Irishwomen* (Dublin, 1971).
8. *Irish Times*, 8 Mar. 2021
9. Ibid.
10. Ibid.
11. June Levine, 'The Women's Movement in the Republic of Ireland, 1968–80', in Angela Bourke et al. (eds), *The Field Day Anthology of Irish Writing: Volume 5* (Cork, 2002), p. 180.
12. Conor Hanly, 'Why were women absent from Irish juries for 50 years?', *RTÉ*, 19 Feb. 2020, https://www.rte.ie/brainstorm/2020/0219/1116230-ireland-women-juries/, accessed 23 Mar. 2021.
13. The annual Merriman winter school conference is held entirely in the Irish language and examines topics related to Irish language.
14. *Irish Times*, 29 Aug. 1980.
15. Ibid.
16. Eoghan Ó hAnluain, 'Merriman, Brian', in *DIB*.
17. *Five Red Roses – One for Every Syllable of Your Name*, dir. Cathal Black, script by Theresa Caherty and produced by Cathal and Catherine Black, 2018.
18. Jesse Jones, 'Made in stone: Jesse Jones celebrates activist Máirín de Búrca', *RTÉ*, 18 Dec. 2021, https://www.rte.ie/culture/2021/1214/1266792-made-in-stone-jessie-jones-celebrates-activist-mairin-de-burca/, accessed 3 May 2022.
19. See Jennie Wyse Power's speech on women on juries in *Irish Women's Speeches: Voices that Rocked the System* (Dublin, 2012), pp 86–93.
20. Speech reproduced with kind permission of Máirín de Burca.
21. *Women's View* 3 (Autumn 1980), pp 8–9.

Chapter 9 – Brenda Fricker

1. Details taken from an interview with Brenda Fricker published in the *Irish Independent*, 2 Jan. 2000.
2. '*Tolka Row*, TV Series 1964–68', *IMDb*, https://www.imdb.com/title/tt4139338/, accessed 5 May 2022.
3. *Kerryman*, 25 Nov. 1988.
4. *Irish Press*, 22 Nov. 1988.
5. Carmel Doyle, 'Brown, Christopher ("Christy")', in *Dictionary of Irish Biography* (www.dib.ie).

6. Christy Brown, *My Left Foot* (London, 1954).

7. *Ferndale Films*, https://www.ferndalefilms.com, accessed 6 May 2022.

8. *Irish Times*, 8 Apr. 2019.

9. Debbie McGoldrick, 'Harvey Weinstein's struck Irish gold with *My Left Foot*', *Irish Central*, 20 Oct. 2017, https://www.irishcentral.com/news/irishvoice/harvey-weinstein-brenda-fricker-my-left-foot, accessed 6 May 2022.

10. *Irish Independent*, 3 Feb. 2008.

11. *Irish Independent*, 18 Feb. 2015.

12. *Irish Times*, 8 Apr. 2019.

13. See Veronica Guerin's speech in this volume, pp 94-102.

14. *Irish Times*, 17 Feb. 2012.

15. *The Chronicle-Herald*, 11 Dec. 2012.

16. 'An Post stamps celebrate Ireland's Oscar® winners', *An Post*, https://www.anpost.com/Media-Centre/News/An-Post-stamps-celebrate-Ireland's-Oscar®-winners, accessed 6 May 2022.

17. *Killarney Today*, 11 Jan. 2020.

18. *Irish Sun*, 25 Mar. 2022.

19. Brenda Fricker, 'Brenda Fricker wins Supporting Actress: 1990 Oscars', *YouTube*, https://www.youtube.com/watch?v=wtj3RiwmTbg, accessed 6 May 2022. Speech reproduced by kind permission of Brenda Fricker.

CHAPTER 10 – VERONICA GUERIN

1. Patrick Maume, 'Guerin, Veronica', in *Dictionary of Irish Biography* (hereafter *DIB*) (www.dib.ie).

2. Paul Williams, *Evil Empire: John Gilligan, His Gang and the Execution of Journalist Veronica Guerin* (Dublin, 2001), p. xiii.

3. Ibid.

4. Maume, 'Guerin, Veronica', in *DIB*.

5. Patrick Maume, 'Haughey, Charles James (C. J)', in *DIB*.

6. 'Preface', in *New Ireland Forum Report* (Dublin, 1984), https://cain.ulster.ac.uk/issues/politics/nifr.htm#preface, accessed 11 May 2022.

7. Maume, 'Guerin, Veronica', in *DIB*.

8. Ibid.

9. Emily O'Reilly, *Veronica Guerin: The Life and Death of a Crime Reporter* (London, 1998), p. 29.

10. Ibid., p. 30.

11. *Magill*, 1 May 1998.

12. O'Reilly, *Veronica Guerin*, p. 31.

13. *Sunday Independent*, 1 Aug. 1993.

14. *Evening Herald*, 28 Jul. 1993.

15. *Magill*, 30 Nov. 2005.

16. *Magill*, 1 May 1998.

17. Ibid.

18. Maume, 'Guerin, Veronica', in *DIB*.

19. Ibid.

20. Sean Whelan, RTÉ News report, 30 Jan. 1995.

21. Williams, *Evil Empire*, pp 166–7.

22. O'Reilly, *Veronica Guerin*, p. 123.

23. *Sunday Independent*, 17 Sep. 1995.

24. Ibid.

25. 'Veronica Guerin', *Committee to Protect Journalists*, https://cpj.org/data/people/veronica-guerin/, accessed 12 May 2022.

26. 'What we do', *Committee to Protect Journalists*, https://cpj.org/about/, accessed 12 May 2022.

27. Committee to Protect Journalists, 'In Zambia, *Post* editor Fred M'membe sent to prison', *refworld*, 4 Jun. 2010, https://www.refworld.org/docid/4c15f0a65.html, accessed 12 May 2022.

28. *Evening Herald*, 26 Jun. 1996.

29. *Irish Independent*, 27 Jun. 1996.

30. Ibid.

31. *Irish Times*, 26 Jun. 2021.

32. See Nora Owen's speech in *Irish Women's Speeches: Voices that Rocked the System* (Dublin, 2021), pp 216–22.

33. Maume, 'Guerin, Veronica', in *DIB*.

34. *Irish Times*, 15 Mar. 2001.

35. *Sunday World*, 27 Jun. 2021.

36. O'Reilly, *Veronica Guerin*, p. 188.

37. Maume, 'Guerin, Veronica', in *DIB*.

38. 'Veronica Guerin', *Dublin City University*, https://www.dcu.ie/communications/veronica-guerin, accessed 12 May 2022.

39. *Sunday Independent*, 26 Jun. 2011.

40. Veronica Guerin, 'International Press Freedom Award acceptance speech', 1995, *American Rhetoric*, https://www.americanrhetoric.com/speeches/veronicaguerinbraveryaward.htm, accessed 1 Apr. 2022. Speech reproduced with kind permission of Jimmy Guerin, Veronica's brother.

Chapter 11 – Nuala O'Faolain

1. Paul Rouse, 'O'Sullivan, Terry', in *Dictionary of Irish Biography* (hereafter *DIB*) (www.dib.ie).

2. Nuala O'Faolain, *Are You Somebody?* (Dublin, 2021), p. 7.

3. Patrick Maume, 'O'Faolain, Nuala', in *DIB*.

4. O'Faolain, *Are You Somebody?*, p. 33.

5. Ibid., p. 39.

6. *Open University Digital Archive*, https://www.open.ac.uk/library/digital-archive/search/Nuala%20OFaolain/page2, accessed 18 May 2022.

7. William Fowler and Matthew Harle, 'John Berger: Radical broadcaster', *LUX*, 24 Oct. 2017, https://lux.org.uk/john-berger-radical-broadcaster/, accessed 18 May 2022.

8. Ibid.

9. O'Faolain, *Are You Somebody?*, p. 207.

10. June Caldwell, 'Foreword', in Nuala O'Faolain, *Are You Somebody?* (Dublin, 2021), pp vi–vii.

11. Ibid., p. vii.

12. 'Nuala O'Faolain's search for "Mr Right"', RTÉ Archives, https://www.rte.ie/archives/2015/0508/699637-nuala-ofaolains-search-for-mr-right/, accessed 20 May 2022.

13. Ibid.

14. Ibid.

15. *Evening Herald*, 25 Oct. 1996.

16. *Nationalist and Leinster Times*, 25 Oct. 1996.

17. Ibid.
18. *Evening Herald*, 25 Oct. 1996.
19. *Southern Star*, 14 Dec. 1996.
20. *Connacht Tribune*, 20 Dec. 1996.
21. Nuala O'Faolain, *Are You Somebody* (New York, 1998).
22. *Irish Times*, 18 Apr. 1998.
23. Ibid.
24. *New York Times*, 15 Mar. 1998.
25. Nuala O'Faolain, *Almost There: The Onward Journey of a Dublin Woman* (London, 2003); Nuala O'Faolain, *The Story of Chicago May* (London, 2005).
26. *The Journal*, 12 May 2008.
27. *Irish Independent*, 2 Jan. 2020.
28. *Evening Herald*, 10 May 2008.
29. *Irish Independent*, 12 May 2008.
30. *The Guardian*, 11 Jul. 2009.
31. Nuala O'Faolain, *A More Complex Truth* (Dublin, 2010).
32. Nuala O'Faolain, *A Radiant Life* (New York, 2011).
33. *Irish Times*, 13 Aug. 2022.
34. *Irish Independent*, 12 May 2008.
35. Nuala O'Faolain, '*Are You Somebody*', C-SPAN, 18 Mar. 1998, https://www.c-span.org/video/?104060-1/are-somebody, accessed 8 Apr. 2022. The extract from this speech is reproduced by kind permission of Mairead Brady.

Chapter 12 – Nuala Ní Dhomhnaill

1. 'Nuala Ní Dhomhnaill – Imprint: Writer in profile', 2000, *Irish Film Institute*, https://ifiarchiveplayer.ie/imprint-nuala-ni-dhomnaill/, accessed 19 May 2022.
2. Gaeltacht, Irish speaking area.
3. Caoimhín Mac Giolla Léith, 'Ó Direáin, Máirtín', in *Dictionary of Irish Biography* (www.dib.ie).
4. 'Nuala Ní Dhomhnaill – Imprint: Writer in profile.'
5. *Irish Times*, 6 Aug. 1969.
6. *Irish Times*, 7 Aug. 1969.
7. 'Nuala Ní Dhomhnaill – Imprint: Writer in profile.'
8. 'The Nobel Prize in Literature 1995', *Nobel Prize Organisation*, https://www.nobelprize.org/prizes/literature/1995/summary/, accessed 23 May 2022.
9. Seamus Heaney, 'Remarks on the occasion of John Montague's appointment to the post of Ireland Professorship of Poetry, 14 May 1998', in John Montague, Nuala Ní Dhomhnaill and Paul Durcan, *The Poet's Chair: The First Nine Years of the Ireland Chair of Poetry* (Dublin, 2008), p. vii.
10. Montague was an esteemed poet and lecturer who co-founded Claddagh Records and was for a time president of Poetry Ireland.
11. John Montague, Nuala Ní Dhomhnaill and Paul Durcan, *The Poet's Chair: The First Nine Years of the Ireland Chair of Poetry* (Dublin, 2008).
12. Nuala Ní Dhomhnaill, *Writings from the Ireland Chair of Poetry: Cead Isteach / Entry Permitted* (Dublin, 2017).
13. Ibid., p. viii.
14. *The Belfast Agreement: An Agreement Reached at the Multi-Party Talks on Northern Ireland* (London, 1998), p. 19.
15. S. 28D, inserted by the Northern Ireland (St Andrews Agreement) Act 2006 (c. 53).

16. 'Gerry Adams: "No assembly without Irish language act"', 30 Aug. 2017, https://www.bbc.com/news/uk-northern-ireland-politics-41095799, accessed 23 May 2022.

17. *Irish Independent*, 21 May 2022.

18. Identity and Language (Nothern Ireland) Bill, [HL]: Explanatory Notes, 25 May 2022, https://bills.parliament.uk/publications/46556/documents/1817, accessed 8 Jul. 2022.

19. Angela Bourke, Siobhán Kilfeather, Maria Luddy, Margaret Mac Curtain, Gerardine Meaney, Máirín Ní Dhonnchadha, Mary O'Dowd and Clair Wills (eds), *The Field Day Anthology of Irish Writing, Volume 4 and Volume 5: Irish Women's Writings and Traditions* (Cork, 2002).

20. Nuala Ní Dhomhnaill, 'Contemporary poets', in Bourke et al. (eds), *The Field Day Anthology of Irish Writing, Volume 5*, p. 1290.

21. 'Gaelic poet Nuala Ní Dhomhnaill wins the Zbigniew Herbert International Literary Award 2018', *Culture PL*, https://culture.pl/en/article/gaelic-poet-nuala-ni-dhomhnaill-wins-the-zbigniew-herbert-international-literary-award-2018, accessed 23 May 2022.

22. 'Welcome to Aosdána', *The Arts Council*, http://aosdana.artscouncil.ie, accessed 23 May 2022.

23. Ní Dhomhnaill, *Writings from the Ireland Chair of Poetry*, pp 1–5, 15, 16–20, 31. Irish and English versions by Nuala Ní Dhomhnaill and reproduced by kind permission of the author.

Chapter 13 – Salome Mbugua

1. Central Statistics Office, 'Press Statement Census of Population 2022 – Preliminary Results', 23 Jun. 2022, https://www.cso.ie/en/csolatestnews/pressreleases/2022pressreleases/pressstatementcensusofpopulation2022-preliminaryresults/, accessed 5 Jul. 2022.

2. Victoria M. Esses, 'Immigration, Migration, and Culture', in *Oxford Research Encyclopedia of Psychology*, 28 Mar. 2018, https://oxfordre.com/psychology/view/10.1093/acrefore/9780190236557.001.0001/acrefore-9780190236557-e-287, accessed 8 Jun. 2022.

3. Ibid.

4. Salome Mbugua, 'Opinion: Equality and social justice for women is my life's work', in *The Journal*, 23 May 2014.

5. Szabolcs Karikó, 'Salome Mbugua & Melanie Lynch', *Herstory*, https://www.herstory.ie/movementblog/1, accessed 8 Jun. 2022.

6. Ibid.

7. Ibid.

8. AkiDwA, https://akidwa.ie, accessed 7 Jun. 2022.

9. AkiDwA, https://akidwa.ie/obituary-sister-joan-mcmanus/, accessed 21 Jun. 2022.

10. 'Immigration Bill 2002, No. 9C of 2002', *Houses of the Oireachtas*, https://data.oireachtas.ie/ie/oireachtas/bill/2002/9/eng/ver_c/b9c02d.pdf, accessed 8 Jun. 2022.

11. Hilkka Becker, 'Commentary on Lobe v Minister for Justice, Equality and Law Reform', in Máiréad Enright, Julie McCandless and Aoife O'Donoghue (eds), *Northern/Irish Feminist Judgements: Judges' Troubles and the Gendered Politics of Identity* (London, 2017), p. 263.

12. Ibid.

13. Ibid., p. 264.

14. *Irish Independent*, 24 Jan. 2003.

15. Ibid.

16. Referendum Commission, *The Referendum on Irish Citizenship* (Dublin, 2004), https://www.refcom.ie/previous-referendums/irish-citizenship/27th-amendment-Citizenship-guide.pdf, accessed 9 Jun. 2022.

17. *Irish Independent,* 20 May 2004.

18. *Irish Times,* 1 Jun. 2004.

19. *Irish Times,* 16 Jul. 2019.

20. Referendum Commission, 'Irish Citizenship: Referendum on the Twenty-Seventh Amendment of the Constitution Bill 2004 (Irish Citizenship)', https://www.refcom.ie/previous-referendums/irish-citizenship/, accessed 2 Aug. 2022.

21. Salome Mbugua Henry, 'Integrating women into peacebuilding in the Democratic Republic of the Congo: A case study of Goma', PhD diss., Trinity College Dublin, School of Religion, 2021.

22. AkiDwA, https://akidwa.ie/our-work/#integration, accessed 20 Jun. 2022.

23. 'The Migrant Integration Strategy', Office for the Promotion of Migrant Inclusion, http://www.integration.ie/en/isec/pages/migrant_integration_strategy, accessed 5 Jul. 2022.

24. 'Zero tolerance for racism in Gaelic Games', GAA, https://www.gaa.ie/my-gaa/community-and-health/social-inclusion/responding-to-racism, accessed 5 Jul. 2022.

25. Children's Rights Alliance, 'Initial submission on the reception and integration of Ukrainian children and young people arriving in Ireland', 15 Mar. 2022.

26. UN Convention on the Rights of the Child, 20 Nov. 1989, 1577 UNTS 3 (UNCRC), Article 30.

27. Ibid.

28. For discussion on the Irish government's and the public's responses to pregnant asylum seekers, see Eithne Luibhéid, *Pregnant on Arrival: Making the Illegal Immigrant* (Minneapolis, 2013).

29. 'Joint Committee on Justice, Equality, Defence and Women's Rights', Vol. 1, No. 29, 19 Jun. 2003, *Houses of the Oireachtas,* https://www.oireachtas.ie/en/debates/debate/joint_committee_on_justice_equality_defence_and_womens_rights/2003-06-19/2/, accessed 8 Jun 2022. Speech reproduced with kind permission of Salome Mbugua.

CHAPTER 14 – MAUREEN O'HARA

1. Maureen O'Hara with John Nicoletti, *'Tis Herself: An Autobiography* (New York, 2004), p. 13.

2. Liz Evers, 'O'Hara, Maureen', in *Dictionary of Irish Biography* (www.dib.ie).

3. O'Hara, *'Tis Herself,* p. 20.

4. Evers, 'O'Hara, Maureen', in *DIB.*

5. Ibid.

6. John Sayles, 'John Ford', in *Britannica Academic, Encyclopædia Britannica,* 2 Oct. 2019, academic-eb-com.ezproxy.otago.ac.nz/levels/collegiate/article/John-Ford/34846, accessed 13 Jun. 2022.

7. *New York Times,* 24 Oct. 2015.

8. 'Maureen O'Hara makes immigration history', *Maureen O'Hara Magazine,* http://moharamagazine.com/Immigration.htm, accessed 10 Jun. 2022.

9. O'Hara, *'Tis Herself,* p. 252.

10. Ibid., p. 259.

11. 'About the Academy', *The Irish Film & Television Academy,* https://www.ifta.ie/academy/index.html, accessed 13 Jun. 2022.

12. Chris Columbus, 'Maureen O'Hara, recipient of the IFTA Lifetime Achievement

Award in 2004 full unedited speech', *YouTube*, https://www.youtube.com/
watch?v=bZiJxw9IjAI, accessed 20 May 2022.

13. *Irish Central,* 10 Nov. 2015.

14. *Irish Times,* 13 Jun. 2020.

15. *Irish Times,* 22 May 2022.

16. The Irish word *feis, festival* in English, is used to describe local competitions in
music, drama and dancing in Ireland.

17. Maureen O'Hara, 'Maureen O'Hara, recipient of the IFTA Lifetime
Achievement Award in 2004 full unedited speech', *YouTube*, https://www.youtube.
com/watch?v=bZiJxw9IjAI, accessed 20 May 2022. Speech reproduced by kind
permission of Elga Liliana FitzSimons, with many thanks to Margaret O'Shaughnessy
at Foynes Flying Boat Museum for facilitating contact.

CHAPTER 15 – LYDIA FOY

1. Han Tiernan, 'RTÉ releases statement in response to termination of Dublin Pride
partnership', *GCN*, 15 Jun. 2022, https://gcn.ie/rte-releases-statement-response-
dublin-pride/, accessed 21 Jun. 2022.

2. Qtd in Alice Linehan, 'RTÉ Liveline criticised for enabling transphobic hate
speech', *GCN*, 14 Jun. 2022, https://gcn.ie/rte-liveline-enabling-hate-speech/,
accessed 21 Jun. 2022.

3. *Irish Times,* 17 Jun. 2022.

4. High Court Judgement, 'Foy -v- An t-Ard Chláraitheoir & Ors', [2007] IEHC
470, 19 Oct. 2007.

5. Mayo Clinic Staff, 'Gender dysphoria', *Mayo Clinic*, https://www.mayoclinic.org/
diseases-conditions/gender-dysphoria/symptoms-causes/syc-20475255, accessed 21
Jun. 2022

6. Christine Goodwin v. the United Kingdom [GC] – 28957/95, Judgment 11.7.2002
[GC], Jul. 2002.

7. 'Dr. Lydia Foy', *TENI*, https://teni.ie/gender-recognition/dr-lydia-foy/, accessed
22 Jun. 2022.

8. *Pink News,* 12 Nov. 2013.

9. 'Gender Recognition', *TENI*, https://teni.ie/gender-recognition/, accessed 22 Jun.
2022.

10. Ivana Bacik, 'Commentary on Foy v An t-Ard Chláraitheoirin,' in Máiréad
Enright, Julie McCandless and Aoife O'Donoghue (eds), *Northern/Irish Feminist
Judgments: Judges' Troubles and the Gendered Politics of Identity* (London, 2017), p.
581.

11. 'Lydia Foy receives the European Citizen's Prize 2015 from the European
Parliament', *European Parliament*, 18 Jun. 2015, https://www.europarl.europa.eu/
news/en/press-room/20150603AVI62403/lydia-foy-receives-the-european-citizen-
s-prize-from-the-european-parliament, accessed 22 Jun. 2022.

12. 'My Name is Lydia Foy', *Doc on One*, RTÉ Radio One, first broadcast on 2 July
2011, https://play.acast.com/s/documentary-on-one/mynameislydiafoy, accessed 17
Aug. 2022.

13. Qtd in Hayley Halpin, 'Lydia Foy: The woman at the heart of securing transgender
rights in Ireland', *The Journal*, 9 Jun. 2018, https://www.thejournal.ie/lydia-foy-flac-
report-4060076-Jun2018/, accessed 27 Jun. 2022.

14. Eleanor Roosevelt, first lady of the United States 1933–1945, was a dedicated
champion of civil rights. In 1948, she led representatives from 50 United Nations
states to formulate a list of human rights that all individuals should be entitled to.

The Universal Declaration of Human Rights was announced in December 1948, including 30 rights and freedoms. The declaration continues to form the basis for international human rights law. Amnesty International UK, 'What is the Universal Declaration of Human Rights?' https://www.amnesty.org.uk/universal-declaration-human-rights-UDHR , accessed 28 Jul. 2022.

15. Lydia Foy, 'Dr Lydia Foy', 23 June 2013, *YouTube*, https://www.youtube.com/watch?v=FuDYZVdWRKU&t=74s, accessed 11 Apr. 2022. Speech extract reproduced by kind permission of Lydia Foy. With many thanks to Sara Phillips former chair of TENI for facilitating contact.

CHAPTER 16 – EDNA O'BRIEN

1. Edna O'Brien, *The Country Girls Trilogy* (London, 2017).
2. '*The Country Girls Trilogy*', *One Dublin One Book*, http://www.onedublinonebook.ie/books/the-country-girls-trilogy/, accessed 4 Jul. 2022.
3. Edna O'Brien, *The Lonely Girl* (New York, 1962); *Girls in Their Married Bliss* (London, 1964).
4. *Edna O'Brien: Life, Stories*, a documentary produced by Icebox Films and directed by Charlie McCarthy, 8 May 2012.
5. Eimear McBride, 'Foreword', in Edna O'Brien, *The Country Girls Trilogy* (London, 2017), pp ix–xx.
6. Edna O'Brien, *August Is a Wicked Month* (London, 1965); *Casualties of Peace* (London, 1966).
7. *Irish Times*, 5 Nov. 2018.
8. *Evening Herald*, 5 Dec. 1966.
9. Ibid.
10. Ibid.
11. Peter Martin, 'Irish censorship in context', in *Studies: An Irish Quarterly Review* 95:379 (Autumn 2006), p. 261.
12. Committee on Evil Literature, *Report of the Committee on Evil Literature* (Dublin, 1926), p. 2.
13. Donal Fallon, 'The Irish Vigilance Association and the war on "Evil Literature"', *Dublin InQuirer*, 3 Apr. 2019.
14. Donal Ó Drisceoil, '"The best banned in the land": Censorship and Irish writing since 1950', in *The Yearbook of English Studies* 35 (2005), p. 146.
15. Ibid.
16. Edna O'Brien, *Mother Ireland: A Memoir* (London, 1976).
17. '*Mother Ireland*', *Aquarius*, directed by Derek Bailey, London Weekend Television, aired 11 Sep. 1976.
18. Edna O'Brien, *Country Girl* (London, 2012).
19. 'Saoi', *Aosdána: The Arts Council*, http://aosdana.artscouncil.ie/saoi/, accessed 5 Jul. 2022.
20. Michael D. Higgins, 'Speech at the conferring of Torc on Edna O'Brien, Imogen Stuart and William Trevor', *President of Ireland*, https://www.president.ie/en/media-library/speeches/speech-at-the-conferring-of-torc-on-edna-obrien-imogen-stuart-and-william-t, accessed 5 Jul. 2022.
21. 'Edna O'Brien: Fearful . . . and Fearless', *Imagine*, produced and directed by Katy Homan, BBC, aired 7 Jul. 2019.
22. Edna O'Brien, *Girl* (London, 2019).
23. *The Guardian*, 25 Aug. 2019.
24. *The Guardian*, 6 Sep. 2019.

25. *The Journal*, 7 Mar. 2021.

26. McBride, 'Foreword', pp xvi–xvii.

27. Abbey Theatre, https://www.abbeytheatre.ie/whats-on/joyces-women/, accessed 6 Jul. 2022.

28. Adapted by Edna O'Brien from a speech given at the Mansion House at the launch of *The Country Girls* as the Dublin One City One Book on 27 February 2019. This speech is reproduced by kind permission of Edna O'Brien.

CHAPTER 17 – LIAN BELL

1. Quoted in Elana Gartner, 'Waking The Feminists: The gender parity revolution in Irish theatre', *Women and the Arts*, 27 Apr. 2017, https://www.womenarts.org/2017/04/27/waking-the-feminists-the-gender-parity-revolution-in-irish-theatre/, accessed 23 Jun. 2022.

2. *Irish Times*, 29 Oct. 2016.

3. *The Guardian*, 12 Nov. 2015.

4. 'About the campaign', *#WakingTheFeminists: Equality for women in Irish theatre*, http://www.wakingthefeminists.org/about-wtf/how-it-started/, accessed 23 Jun. 2022.

5. 'About', *Lian Bell*, http://lianbell.com/about, accessed 23 Jun. 2022.

6. Ibid.

7. 'Lian Bell', *ISSSD*, https://isssd.ie/project/lian-bell/, accessed 23 Jun. 2022.

8. *The Guardian*, 12 Nov. 2015.

9. Ibid.

10. Ibid.

11. Brenda Donohue, Ciara O'Dowd, Tanya Dean, Ciara Murphy, Kathleen Cawley and Kate Harris, *Gender Counts: An Analysis of Gender in Irish Theatre 2006–2015* (Dublin, 2017).

12. Ibid., p. 5.

13. Ibid.

14. Irish Government News Service, 'Minister Humphreys hosts gender policy workshop with Cultural Institutions', *MerrionStreet*, 22 Mar. 2017, https://merrionstreet.ie/en/news-room/releases/minister_humphreys_hosts_gender_policy_workshop_with_cultural_institutions.html, accessed 23 Jun. 2022.

15. Dáil Éireann debate, Vol. 1018, No. 7, 1 Mar. 2022.

16. *Irish Times*, 6 Mar. 2016.

17. '"Waking The Feminists" wins prestigious US theatre award', *RTÉ*, 20 Jul. 2016, https://www.rte.ie/news/2016/0524/790524-waking-the-feminists-award/, accessed 23 Jun. 2022.

18. National Library of Ireland (NLI), Dublin, '#WakingTheFeminists Collection, 2015–2018', Manuscripts Reading Room, MS 50,778.

19. '#WakingTheFeminists digital archive acquired', *National Library of Ireland*, https://www.nli.ie/en/list/latest-news.aspx?article=9453f42c-e3b0-4085-8452-c1f19bde8c0c, accessed 23 Jun. 2022.

20. Ibid.

21. Lian Bell, '#WakingTheFeminists archive launch speech', *YouTube*, 22 Jan. 2021, https://www.youtube.com/watch?v=eCMs7z7TUYc, accessed 23 Jun. 2022. Extract of speech reproduced by kind permission of Lian Bell.

Bibliography

Atwal, Jyoti, 'Margaret Elizabeth Cousins and transnationalism: An Irish suffragette as an anti-colonial feminist in Colonial India', in Jyoti Atwal, Ciara Breathnach and Sarah-Anne Buckley, eds, *Gender and History: Ireland, 1852–1922* (London: Routledge, 2022), pp 248–64.

Bacik, Ivana, 'Commentary on Foy v An t-Ard Chláraitheoirin', in Máiréad Enright, Julie McCandless and Aoife O'Donoghue, eds, *Northern/Irish Feminist Judgments: Judges' Troubles and the Gendered Politics of Identity* (London: Bloomsbury Publishing, 2017), pp 579–600.

Becker, Hilkka, 'Commentary on Lobe v Minister for Justice, Equality and Law Reform', in Máiréad Enright, Julie McCandless and Aoife O'Donoghue, eds, *Northern/Irish Feminist Judgments: Judges' Troubles and the Gendered Politics of Identity* (London: Bloomsbury Publishing, 2017), pp 263–82.

The Belfast Agreement: An Agreement Reached at the Multi-Party Talks on Northern Ireland (London: The Stationery Office, 1998).

Bourke, Angela, Siobhán Kilfeather, Maria Luddy, Margaret Mac Curtain, Gerardine Meaney, Máirín Ní Dhonnchadha, Mary O'Dowd and Clair Wills, eds, *The Field Day Anthology of Irish Writing, Volume 4 and Volume 5: Irish Women's Writings and Traditions* (Cork: Cork University Press, 2002).

Brown, Christy, *My Left Foot* (London: Secker and Warburg, 1954).

Candy, Catherine, 'The occult feminism of Margaret Cousins in Modern Ireland and India, 1878–1954', PhD diss. (Chicago: Loyola University, 1996).

Cappock, Margarita, 'Lane, Sir Hugh Percy', in *Dictionary of Irish Biography* (www.dib.ie).

Clarke, Frances, 'Cousins, James Henry Sproull', in *Dictionary of Irish Biography* (www.dib.ie).

Clarke, Frances, 'Cousins, Margaret ("Gretta") Elizabeth', in *Dictionary of Irish Biography* (www.dib.ie).

Cobbe, Frances Power, *Friendless Girls, and How to Help Them: Being an Account of the Preventive Mission at Bristol* (London: Emily Faithfull & Co., 1861).

Committee on Evil Literature, *Report of the Committee on Evil Literature* (Dublin: Stationery Office, 1926).

Connolly, James, 'Socialism and Irish nationalism', in *L'Irlande Libre* (Paris, 1897).

Cousins, James H. and Margaret E. Cousins, *We Two Together* (Madras: Ganesh & Co., 1950).

Cousins, Margaret E., *The Awakening of Asian Womanhood* (Madras: Ganesh & Co., 1922).

Cousins, Margaret E., *The Music of Orient and Occident: Essays Towards Mutual Understandings* (Madras: B. G. Paul & Co., 1935).

Cousins, Margaret E., 'Presidential address', in *All-India Women's Conference, Eleventh Session* (Ahmedabad: S. R. Vasavada, 1936), pp 23–32.

Cousins, Margaret E., *Indian Womanhood Today* (Allahabad: Kitabistan, 1941; reprint 1947).

Coxhead, Elizabeth, *Daughters of Erin: Five Women of the Irish Renascence* (London: Secker & Warburg, 1965).

Dacre Fox, Norah, *The Vitamin Survey: A Reply* (London: London and Provincial Anti-Vivisection Society, 1934).

Dacre Fox, Norah, *The Medical Research Council: What It Is and How It Works* (London: London and Provincial Anti-Vivisection Society, 1935).

Daly, Mary E., 'The society and its contribution to Ireland: Past, present and future', in *Journal of the Statistical and Social Inquiry Society of Ireland*, 27, 1998, pp 33–46.

Dinsman, Melissa, '"A river is not a woman": re-visioning Finnegans Wake in Eavan Boland's "Anna Liffey", *Contemporary Women's Writing*, 7:2, Jul. 2013, pp 172-89.

Donohue, Brenda, Ciara O'Dowd, Tanya Dean, Ciara Murphy, Kathleen Cawley and Kate Harris, *Gender Counts: An Analysis of Gender in Irish Theatre 2006–2015* (Dublin: #WakingTheFeminists, 2017).

Doyle, Carmel, 'Brown, Christopher ("Christy")', in *Dictionary of Irish Biography* (www.dib.ie).

Elam, Norah, 'Fascism, women and democracy', in *Fascist Quarterly*, 1:3, 1935, pp 290–8.

Evers, Liz, 'O'Hara, Maureen', in *Dictionary of Irish Biography* (www.dib.ie).

Ferguson, Trish, *Maud Gonne* (Dublin: UCD Press, 2019).

Ferriter, Diarmaid, 'Fay, William George ("Wille")', in *Dictionary of Irish Biography* (www.dib.ie).

Finnan, J. P., *John Redmond and Irish Unity, 1912–1918* (New York: Syracuse University Press, 2004).

Fitzsimons, Fiona, 'Deaf records', in *History Ireland*, 25:4, Jul./Aug. 2017, p. 29.

Gottlieb, Julie V., *Feminine Fascism: Women in Britain's Fascist Movement, 1923–1945* (London: I. B. Tauris & Co., 2021).

Grace, Pierce A., 'Repression: The Amritsar massacre, 1919: The Irish connection', in *History Ireland*, 4:18, Jul./Aug. 2010, pp 24–5.

Green, John Richard, *A Short History of English People* (London: Macmillan, 1874).

Green, John Richard, *The Conquest of England*, Alice Stopford Green, ed. (London: Macmillan, 1883).

Green, John Richard and Alice Stopford Green, *A Short Geography of the British Islands* (London: Macmillan, 1879).

Green, Mrs. J. R., *Town Life in the Fifteenth Century: In Two Volumes* (London: Macmillan, 1894).

Griffin, Ben, *The Politics of Gender in Victorian Britain: Masculinity, Political Culture and the Struggle for Women's Rights* (Cambridge: Cambridge University Press, 2012).

Irish Women's Liberation Movement, *Chains or Change?: The Civil Wrongs of Irishwomen* (Dublin: Irish Women's Liberation Movement, 1971).

Jeffries, Henry A., *Derry–Londonderry: The Ulster Covenant and the 1916 Proclamation* (Derry: Derry City Council, 2010).

Ludlam, Harry, *A Biography of Bram Stoker, Creator of 'Dracula'* (London: New English Library, 1977).

Luibhéid, Eithne, *Pregnant on Arrival: Making the Illegal Immigrant* (Minneapolis: University of Minnesota Press, 2013).

Lyons, J. B., 'Wilde, Sir William Robert Wills', in *Dictionary of Irish Biography* (www.dib.ie).

MacBride White, Anna and A. Norman Jeffares, eds, *The Gonne–Yeats Letters, 1893–1938* (London: Hutchinson, 1992).

Mac Giolla Léith, Caoimhín, 'Ó Direáin, Máirtín', in *Dictionary of Irish Biography* (www.dib.ie).

McPherson, Angela, 'A grandmother's legacy: The gift that keeps on giving?', in *Women's History Review*, 30:4, 2021, pp 688–700.

McPherson, Susan and Angela McPherson, *Mosley's Old Suffragette: A Biography of Norah Dacre Fox* (n.p.: Angela McPherson and Susan McPherson, 2011).

Maguire, Moira J., 'Foreign adoptions and the evolution of Irish Adoption Policy, 1945–52', in *Journal of Social History*, 36:2, Winter 2002, pp 387–404.

Martin, Peter, 'Irish censorship in context', in *Studies: An Irish Quarterly Review*, 95:379, Autumn 2006, pp 261–8.

Maume, Patrick, 'Elam (Dacre Fox), Norah', in *Dictionary of Irish Biography* (www.dib.ie).

Maume, Patrick, 'Guerin, Veronica', in *Dictionary of Irish Biography* (www.dib.ie).

Maume, Patrick, 'O'Faolain, Nuala', in *Dictionary of Irish Biography* (www.dib.ie).

Milotte, Mike, *Banished Babies: The Secret History of Ireland's Baby Export Business* (Dublin: New Island Books, 2012).

Mitchell, Angus, 'Historical revisit: Mythistory and the making of Ireland: Alice Stopford Green's undoing', in *Irish Historical Studies*, 44:166, 2020, pp 349–73.

Mitchell, Angus, 'Woman of the fifth province: Remembering Alice Stopford Green', in *Ríocht na Midhe*, 32, 2021, pp 121–52.

Montague, John, Nuala Ní Dhomhnaill and Paul Durcan, *The Poet's Chair: The First Nine Years of the Ireland Chair of Poetry* (Dublin: Lilliput Press, 2008).

Morgan, Hiram, 'In search of Owen Roe O'Neill', in *History Ireland*, 4:3, Autumn 1996, p. 5.

Murphy, William, 'Green, Alice Sophia Amelia Stopford', in *Dictionary of Irish Biography* (www.dib.ie).

Murphy, William, 'Martyn, Edward', in *Dictionary of Irish Biography* (www.dib.ie).

New Ireland Forum Report (Dublin: The Stationery Press, 1984).

Ní Dhomhnaill, Nuala, *Writings from the Ireland Chair of Poetry: Cead Isteach / Entry Permitted* (Dublin: UCD Press, 2017).

O'Brien, Edna, *The Lonely Girl* (New York: Random House, 1962).

O'Brien, Edna, *Girls in Their Married Bliss* (London: J. Cape, 1964).

O'Brien, Edna, *August Is a Wicked Month* (London: Jonathan Cape, 1965).

O'Brien, Edna, *Casualties of Peace* (London: Jonathan Cape, 1966).

O'Brien, Edna, *Mother Ireland: A Memoir* (London: Weidenfeld and Nicolson, 1976).

O'Brien, Edna, *Country Girl* (London: Faber, 2012).

O'Brien, Edna, *The Country Girls Trilogy* (London: Faber, 2017).

O'Brien, Edna, *Girl* (London: Faber, 2019).

O'Callaghan, Margaret and Caoimhe Nic Dháibhéid, 'MacBride, (Edith) Maud Gonne', in *Dictionary of Irish Biography* (www.dib.ie).

O'Carroll, Brendan, *The Mammy* (Dublin: O'Brien Press, 1994).

Ó Drisceoil, Donal, '"The best banned in the land": Censorship and Irish writing since 1950', in *The Yearbook of English Studies*, 35, 2005, pp 146–60.

O'Faolain, Nuala, *Almost There: The Onward Journey of a Dublin Woman* (London: Michael Joseph, 2003).

O'Faolain, Nuala, *The Story of Chicago May* (London: Michael Joseph, 2005).

O'Faolain, Nuala, *A More Complex Truth* (Dublin: New Island Books, 2010).

O'Faolain, Nuala, *A Radiant Life* (New York: Abrams Image, 2011).

O'Faolain, Nuala, *Are You Somebody?* (Dublin: New Island Books, 2021).

O'Grady, John N., 'Purser, Sarah Henrietta', in *Dictionary of Irish Biography* (www. dib.ie).

O'Hara, Maureen with John Nicoletti, *'Tis Herself: An Autobiography* (New York: Simon & Schuster, 2004).

O'Reilly, Emily, *Veronica Guerin: The Life and Death of a Crime Reporter* (London: Vintage, 1998).

O'Sullivan, T. F., *The Young Irelanders* (Tralee: Kerryman, 1944).

Pašeta, Senia, '1798 in 1898: The politics of commemoration', in *Irish Review*, 22, 1998, pp 46–53.

Rouse, Paul, 'O'Sullivan, Terry', in *Dictionary of Irish Biography* (www.dib.ie).

Steele, Karen, 'Raising her voice for justice: Maud Gonne and the "United Irishman"', in *New Hibernia Review/Iris Éireannach Nua*, 3:2, 1999, pp 84–105.

Steele, Karen, *Women, Press, and Politics During the Irish Revival* (New York: Syracuse University Press, 2007).

Stoker, Charlotte, *On Female Emigration from Workhouses* (Dublin: Alexander Thom, 1864).

Stoker, Charlotte, 'Experience of the cholera in Ireland 1832', in *The Green Book: Writings on Irish Gothic, Supernatural and Fantastic Literature*, 9, 2017, pp 11–18.

Stopford Green, Alice, *Henry II* (London: Macmillan, 1888).

Stopford Green, Alice, *The Making of Ireland and Its Undoing, 1200–1600* (London: Macmillan, 1908).

Stopford Green, Alice, *Irish Nationality* (London: Williams & Nordgate, 1911).

Stopford Green, Alice, *The Old Irish World* (Dublin: M. H. Gill & Son, 1912).

Stopford Green, Alice, *Ourselves Alone in Ulster* (Dublin: Maunsel, 1918).

Stopford Green, Alice, *The Government of Ireland* (London: Labour, 1921).

Stopford Green, Alice, *History of the Irish State to 1014* (London: Macmillan, 1925).

Tiernan, Sonja, *Eva Gore-Booth: An Image of Such Politics* (Manchester: Manchester University Press, 2012).

Tiernan, Sonja, '"Challenging the headship of man": Militant suffragism and the *Irish Citizen*', in Mark O'Brien and Felix Larkin, eds, *Periodicals & Journalism in Twentieth-Century Ireland* (Dublin: Four Courts Press, 2014), pp 61–74.

Tiernan, Sonja, 'Levine, June', in *Dictionary of Irish Biography* (www.dib.ie).

Tiernan, Sonja, *Irish Women's Speeches: Voices That Rocked the System* (Dublin: University College Dublin Press, 2021).

Twenty-Fifth Anniversary Celebration: An Túr Gloine Stained Glass and Mosaic Works, 24 Upper Pembroke Street Dublin (Dublin: Printed at the Sign of the Three Candles, 1928).

Wainwright, Michael, 'Female suffrage in Ireland: James Joyce's realization of unrealized potential', in *Criticism*, 51:4, 2009, pp 651–82.

Ward, Margaret, *Maud Gonne: Ireland's Joan of Arc* (London: Pandora, 1990).

Ward, Margaret, *Unmanageable Revolutionaries: Women and Irish Nationalism* (London: Pluto Press, 1995).

Ward, Margaret, 'Irish suffrage: Remembrance, commemoration, and memorialization', in Oona Frawley, ed., *Women and the Decade of Commemorations* (Bloomington: Indiana University Press, 2021), pp 171–88.

Wiley, Christopher and Lucy Ella Rose, eds, *Women's Suffrage in Word, Image, Music, Stage and Screen: The Making of a Movement* (London: Routledge, 2021).

Williams, Paul, *Evil Empire: John Gilligan, His Gang and the Execution of Journalist Veronica Guerin* (Dublin: Merlin Publishing, 2001).

WSPU, *Tortured Women: What Forcible Feeding Means: A Prisoner's Testimony* (London: G. Oliver & Co., 1914).

Index

Page references for illustrations are italicised.